Won from the Heart

Written and published for the good people of
Shepherd Wellness Community.

S H E P H E R D

*Wellness
Community*

*in the service of those
affected by AIDS*

Won from the Heart

*Won from the Heart is published with the authority of the
Board of Directors of Shepherd Wellness Community.*

Board of Directors

**Editor: J. Michael Bell
Author: Robert Alan Le Bras
Cover Design and Lettering: Cheryl Brugette
Assistants: Aliette, Faye Allen Bell and Cathy Herman**

**Cover Art: <u>Luncheon of the Boating Party,</u>
oil on canvas, 1881,
by Pierre-Auguste Renoir (1841-1919)
used with permission of
The Phillips Collection, Washington, D.C.**

*For information address:
Won from the Heart/SWC, PO Box 5619, Pittsburgh, PA 15207*

ISBN 0-9660802-1-1

*This First Edition printed and published in the United States of America by
Venture Graphics, 119 Federal Street, Suite 200, Pittsburgh, PA 15212.*

Contents

Mission ....Page 4

Introduction ....Page 5

Foreward ....Page 6

Wellness...Page 7

Invocation ....Page 8

Appetizers & Snacks...................................... Section 1

Pasta, Rice, Eggs & Cheese .... Section 2

Seafood .... Section 3

Beef.. Section 4

Poultry .... Section 5

Pork .... Section 6

Lamb, Veal & Other Meats .... Section 7

Potatoes & Vegetables.................................. Section 8

Soups, Salads, Sandwiches & Sauces.......... Section 9

Bread & Breakfast .... Section 10

Pies, Cakes & Frostings .... Section 11

Cookies & Candies....................................... Section 12

Cooking Helps .... Section 13

Sponsors... Section 14

Shepherd Wellness Community

Programs and Services

The services of the Shepherd Wellness Community are unique -- provided by no other agency in our area but supported by all AIDS-related agencies. Because there is no charge for these services, our devoted volunteers are crucial to our AIDS/HIV young people, parents, loved ones and friends. Over the past ten years, requested programs and services have been added to the Shepherd Wellness Community. Wellness provides:

- Biweekly community dinners, where our members socialize, share pleasures and pain with "family," receive AIDS/HIV information, join in groups that support people living with HIV and loved ones affected by the disease and enjoy a hot meal in a safe, caring environment;
- A Drop-In Center, which is open six days a week, where those living with HIV get together, enjoy programs, light meals and snacks, use laundry facilities, learn about the latest AIDS treatment and research in our library and on the Internet and select gently used linens from our resource "store";
- Temporary emergency food assistance for anyone with AIDS/HIV;
- Our Wellness van to take SWC members in need of a ride to Wellness events and activities; and
- 2,000 copies of our expanded newsletter are printed each month and mailed to members, detailing information in the HIV-affected community, calendar events and personal sharing.

Children and Families HIV Network

Beginning its work in late 1991, the Children and Families HIV Network began holding events and activities for children (both infected and affected) and as an opportunity for parents to talk, network and gather strength from one another. Today the organization also conducts monthly meetings to educate local organizations and agencies and acts as an advocate for the emerging population of HIV-diagnosed mothers. The Network's affiliation with Shepherd Wellness should ensure that the complex needs of infected/affected women, children and families will continue to be addressed.

The Pittsburgh NAMES Project

As a graphic illustration of the AIDS epidemic, the Pittsburgh NAMES Project displays the AIDS Memorial Quilt throughout Allegheny and surrounding counties. Its goals are to provide a creative means for remembrance and healing, assist with HIV prevention education and increase public awareness of AIDS. When the local chapter of the NAMES Project joined with Wellness, it added a second panelmaking workshop that regularly meets at the Drop-In Center the last Saturday of each month.

Newest SWC Member Organizations

Over the past two years, two organizations have become affiliated with Wellness under our umbrella of services. In 1995 the Pittsburgh chapter of the NAMES Project joined SWC, and in 1997 the Children and Families HIV Network became our newest affiliate.

Introduction

How do I begin to introduce the book you now hold in your hands? Do you really need to be told that more than "just another cookbook," Won from the Heart is, rather, a testament to the the love and the loss, the hopes and the dreams of all the people in the world whose lives have been affected by HIV?

Should I explain how this diverse listing of recipes and names came to be? Is it important to know the recipes on the pages which follow came from wonderful people from places as distant and different as Africa and Australia? England and France? Hollywood and Washington? Will knowing that some of the caring people who are opening their kitchens and their hearts, are for the first time showing support for AIDS causes make this book any better or any worse? I doubt it because although we are unique there is a common thread which sadly binds us all. That thread is HIV/AIDS.

It is my desire for you to have a quality, easy to use cookbook which in a subtle and profound way allows you the opportunity to symbolically roll up your sleeves and join in the fight against this insidious enemy. By doing this you show that the battle against AIDS is a battle best won from the heart.

Won from the Heart is presented to you as a loving and living testament to all the brave individuals who have suffered to this dreadful killer, the loss of sons and daughters mothers and fathers, partners and friends. This work is also presented to all those loved ones who no longer have a living place at the table but who are always with us spiritualy whenever we break bread.

Do any of the reasons or efforts which went into the making of Won from the Heart matter? What really matters is that you have a living testement and cookbook in your hands now and byy buying it, you add yourself to this list of people who care.

J. Michael Bell, Editor
Won from the Heart

Foreward

The mission of the Shepherd Wellness Community is stated clearly and the volunteers engaged in this program have committed themselves to providing the support for those whose lives have been affected by AIDS. Those of us who are privileged to be "recipe-givers" for this cookbook Won From the Heart represent only a fraction of the number of people who need to be involved in helping relieve the heartbreak caused by this disease.

We all tend to live in our own little "cocoons" believing that we are safe and secure, assured that bad things that happen to other people will never happen to us! The truth is that bad things do happen to good people everyday, and it has never been more clearly demonstrated than through this vicious disease called AIDS.

There is much talk today in medical circles about remedies for remission and even possible cures. Funds for research seem to be available and encouraging reports make headlines.

While all of this is good news, there continues to be a world of people in all of our communities who are living with the physical, mental and morale crushing ravages of this disease. They have faced or are facing not only their own mortality but also the loss of loved ones.

We have always felt that cooperation and compassion are very special Pittsburgh/Western Pennsylvania qualities. The Shepherd Wellness Community proves this again as it provides comfort and love to those most in need.

So, as good food and fellowship go together, we hope that the funds generated by Won From the Heart will help continue both the physical and spiritual mission of the Shepherd Wellness Community.

Elsie Hillman

Wellness

Since the founding of the Shepherd Wellness Community in 1987, food has played a very important role in our existence. Our bi-weekly dinners have always provided a safe haven for persons living with HIV, their family, friends and significant others. As all of you are aware, there is a calming and reassuring feeling around family, food and friends. In the atmosphere provided at these dinners persons, both infected and affected by HIV, have been able to share information, fears and hopes about living with this potentially life-threatening disease.

From these beginnings, it follows logically, that *Won from the Heart* has evolved.

I would like to take this opportunity to thank all the individuals who have contributed to this publication. It is because of you that this project has come to fruition. Many of your recipes have already been served at our Drop-In Center as well as our larger community dinners. And the food is delicious!

I would also like to thank our underwriters who have made publication of this cookbook possible.

Proceeds from the sale of this entirely volunteer effort will help to keep the Shepherd Wellness Community alive and enable us to continue providing services to persons affected by this epidemic until there is a cure.

Edward H. Shultz, President
Board of Directors, Shepherd Wellness Community

Invocation

"Oh that today, you would hear God's voice", says the Psalmist (95:7a).

"Oh that today" a cure and a vaccine will be found for HIV. Someday modern science will hear that voice and lay hold of that vaccine and cure; but for now, we live in hope of that day.

"Oh that today" we will come to see that the difference that so often divide us, really are meant by a loving Creator to enrich us, ethnic, racial, nationality, gender, age, religion, sexual orientation and so on. Someday, this priest prays that all humanity will hear God's voice saying, "I pronounce them good." But for now we live in hope for that day.

On a "today", only a decade ago, this priest did hear that voice; and brought forth the Shepherd Wellness Community. The message of God on that day was then, as now, hope for a new day when HIV would only be a memory.

Won from the Heart, today, is a sign and symbol of that yearning.

Father Lynn Edwards, Episcopal Priest
Vicar of the Historic Landmark Church of the Good Shepherd
Founder of the Shepherd Wellness Community

Won from the Heart

Recipe   **Page**

Sausage Balls 1-1
Ted's Favorite Pizza 1-2
Pissaladière 1-3
Artichoke Dip.. 1-4
Elaine's Fruit Dip.. 1-5
Cheese Log... 1-6
Cheese Puffs 1-7
M. Rosa Cruz, v. de Parra's Salsa 1-8
Spiced Nutty Bananas 1-9
Annenberg Cheese Puffs... 1-10
Grapes with Sour Cream 1-11
Pizza Dip... 1-12
Mom's Caramel Popcorn 1-13
Marty's Nutty Cheese Roll 1-14
Boiled Shrimp in Beer 1-15
Stuffed Mushrooms... 1-16
Crunch Mix.. 1-17
San Francisco Seasoned Shrimp 1-18
Bread Pudding with Whiskey Sauce 1-19
Fruits in Orange Vanilla Sauce 1-20
Coconut Mandazi... 1-21
Aquarium Jello 1-22
Bill Elliot's Sweet and Tangy Meatballs................................. 1-23
Spinach Dip... 1-24
Hot Cherry Apple Cider... 1-25
Black Olive Dip.. 1-26
Mother's Jell-O Mold 1-27
Clam Dip 1-28
Shrimp Dip 1-29
Quick Crabtree Cocktail 1-30
Medallion Onion Dip.. 1-31
Triopitas 1-32
Hot Cheese Dip... 1-33

Appetizers & Snacks

Sausage Balls
Submitted by: Judy Waldner in memory of Timmy.

Meal: Appetizer   Servings: 8
Prep Time: 1 hour   Cost: Inexpensive

Ingredients

1 pound each bulk hot sausage and
   sweet sausage
1 egg
1/2 teaspoon ground sage
1/3 cup bread crumbs

1/2 cup catsup
1/2 cup bottled chili sauce
4 tablespoons brown sugar
2 tablespoons cider vinegar
2 tablespoons soy sauce

Preparation

Mix together the sausages, egg, sage and bread crumbs. Form into small balls (about walnut size) and fry until cooked all the way through. In a separate pot mix together catsup, chili sauce, brown sugar, vinegar and soy sauce. Heat this mixture over medium to low heat until hot, do not boil or it will scorch. Drain sausage balls onto a paper towel. Place sausage balls in an oven safe dish and pour hot glaze over. Serve warm. May be made a day or two ahead and kept in the refrigerator.

Appetizers & Snacks

Ted's Favorite Pizza

Submitted by: Jane Fonda

Meal: Appetizer	Servings: 4
Prep Time: 1 hour	Cost: Moderate

Ingredients

1 onion, chopped
2 garlic cloves, peeled and minced
8 ounces (250 g) ground bison or lean (10%) ground beef
1 tablespoon herbes de Provence
8 ounces (250 g) fresh mushrooms, sliced
2 pounds Roma plum tomatoes, peeled, seeded and diced

1 teaspoon salt
1/2 teaspoon ground black pepper
1/4 cup (1oz/30 g) grated Parmesan cheese
1 pound (500 g) pizza dough
1 cup (4 oz/125 g) shredded lowfat Mozzarella cheese

Preparation

Preheat oven to 425 degrees (220 degrees C). Coat a large baking sheet with nonstick cooking spray. Coat a large nonstick frying pan with nonstick cooking spray. Place over medium heat, add the onion and garlic and sauté for 2 minutes. Add the bison or beef and herbs and sauté until the meat is no longer pink, about 5 minutes for bison and 7 minutes for beef. Add the mushrooms, tomatoes, salt and pepper and simmer until the liquid evaporates, about 10 minutes. Remove from the heat and stir in the Parmesan cheese. On a lightly floured work surface, roll out the pizza dough into a 12-inch (30-cm) round. Place on the prepared sheet and form a 1/2-inch (12mm) raised lip around the edge. Top with the meat mixture and the Mozzarella, leaving a 1/2-inch (12-mm) border around the edge. Bake until the crust is golden and the cheese is bubbly, about 15 minutes. To serve, slice into quarters and place on 4 individual plates.

Suggestions

Herbes de Provence are a blend of dried herbs typical of Provence, France. To make your own, combine 1/2 teaspoon each of thyme, rosemary, sage, marjoram, basil, fennel seed and mint.

Appetizers & Snacks

Pissaladière
(Provençal Onion Pizza)
Submitted by: Cheryl Brugette

Meal: Appetizer   Servings: 6
Prep Time: 2 hours   Cost: Inexpensive

Pizza Dough Ingredients

2-1/4 teaspoon active dry yeast   1/2 teaspoon salt
1 teaspoon brown sugar   1-1/2 cups all purpose flour (1/4 cup extra
1/2 cup lukewarm water (105 degrees to   as needed)
  115 degrees)

Preparation

Combine yeast, sugar and water in a bowl. Let stand until foamy, about 5 minutes. Stir in salt and flour to form a stiff dough. Turn dough out onto a lightly floured surface and knead for about 10 minutes, adding additional flour as needed to make dough smooth and elastic. Shape dough into a ball and place in a lightly oiled bowl, turning to coat. Cover with a slightly damp dishtowel and let rise about an hour.

Onion Topping Ingredients

2 tablespoons olive oil   1/2 teaspoon salt
4 large onions, sliced

Preparation

Heat oil over medium heat for 1 minute. Add onions and sprinkle with salt. Cover, reduce heat and simmer for 20 minutes. Uncover, stir and increase heat to medium. Cook until onions turn golden brown, about 25 minutes. Set aside.

Assembly Ingredients

3 tablespoons corn meal   6 black olives, sliced
1/4 cup grated Parmesan cheese

Preparation

Preheat oven to 450 degrees. Lightly oil a baking sheet and sprinkle with corn meal. Punch dough down and turn onto a lightly floured surface. Roll dough into a 10x12 rectangle and transfer to a baking sheet. Spread onions evenly over the surface of the dough. Sprinkle with the cheese and olives. Bake on center rack of oven until crust is golden and crispy, about 12 minutes. Cut and serve.

Artichoke Dip

Submitted by: Faith Prince

Meal: Appetizer
Prep Time: 1 hour

Servings: 8
Cost: Inexpensive

Ingredients

2 cans artichokes, washed, drained, and
   chopped
3/4 cup Parmesan cheese
1 teaspoon onion powder

1 cup mayonnaise
1 tablespoon sherry
Bread crumbs

Preparation

Mix all ingredients together. Bake in a preheated 350 degree oven for 30 minutes, or until bubbly.

Appetizers & Snacks

Elaine's Fruit Dip

Submitted by: Elaine Lynch

Meal: Appetizer
Prep Time: 15 minutes

Servings: 8
Cost: Inexpensive

Ingredients

1 (16-ounce) cream cheese, room
temperature
1 (7-ounce) jar marshmallow cream

Food coloring, optional

Preparation

Place cream cheese into a mixing bowl. Open marshmallow fluff and microwave for 30 seconds. Spatula marshmallow fluff into the cream cheese bowl. Mix with electric mixer until fully blended, add food coloring, if using it. Can be used immediately or refrigerated for up to 2 weeks. May need microwaved if it's right out of the refrigerator to make it a "dipping" consistency. After you make it a few times you may decide to use less marshmallow for a cheesier taste.

Cheese Log

Submitted by: Paul Gerhardt

Meal: Appetizer   Servings: 8
Prep Time: 2 hours   Cost: Inexpensive

Ingredients

1 (8-ounce) package cream cheese
1 (5-ounce) can chicken
1 tablespoon mayonnaise

1 teaspoon soy sauce
1 cup walnuts, finely chopped

Preparation

Mix all ingredients, except walnuts, thoroughly. Spoon onto wax paper and gently roll to form a log 1-1/2 inches by 10 inches. Chill. Spread walnuts on wax paper and gently unroll log onto the walnuts. Serve with any crackers.

Vegetarian?: Yes

Appetizers & Snacks

Cheese Balls
Submitted by: Paul Gerhardt

Meal: Appetizer   Servings: 8
Prep Time: 1 hour   Cost: Inexpensive

Ingredients

16 ounces cream cheese   6 tablespoons mayonnaise
1 cup Parmesan cheese   8 slices white bread
6 green onions, finely chopped

Preparation

Mix all the ingredients thoroughly, except for the bread. Cut bread into rounds, toasting on one side. Spread cheese on other side. Press cheese side into additional Parmesan cheese. Broil for a few minutes.

Appetizers & Snacks

M. Rosa Cruz, v. de Parra's Salsa

Submitted by: Tim & Xavier Evans

Meal: Appetizer   Yields: 12 ounces
Prep Time: 5 minutes   Cost: Inexpensive

Ingredients

2 large ripe tomatoes
1 small white onion or Spanish onion,
   diced
1 heaping tablespoon of chopped, fresh
   cilantro or coriander

3 meduim cloves of garlic, diced
2 or 3 hot chilis, diced
Salt to taste

Preparation

Immerse tomatoes in boiling water for 30 seconds. Immediately place into very cold water. Remove skins, stem, and quarter them. Combine all ingredients in blender. Blend on low for just a few seconds until all ingredients are chopped and mixed, but not enough to take away all of the consistency. Taste. Adjust chilis, salt, garlic and cilantro, if necessary.

Suggestions

Better to start with a small number of chilis so it doesn't come out too hot. This is good served with Frijoles a La Mexicana In Section 8.

Appetizers & Snacks

Spiced Nutty Bananas
Submitted by: Barb Kiura

Meal: Appetizer or Dessert   Servings: 6
Prep Time: 45 minutes   Cost: Moderate

Ingredients

6 ripe but firm bananas, sliced
2 tablespoons chopped, unsalted
  cashews
2 tablespoons chopped, unsalted
  peanuts
2 tablespoons dried coconut
1 tablespoon raw sugar

1-1/4 teaspoon cinnamon
1/2 teaspoon freshly grated nutmeg
2/3 cup orange juice
3 tablespoons rum
1 tablespoon butter
Heavy cream to serve

Preparation

Preheat oven to 400 degrees. Place bananas in a greased, shallow ovenproof dish. Mix together the cashews, peanuts, coconut, sugar, cinnamon and nutmeg in a small bowl, set aside. Pour the orange juice and rum over the bananas, then sprinkle with the nut and sugar mixture. Dot the top with butter, then bake in the oven for 15 to 20 minutes or until the bananas are golden and the sauce is bubbly. Serve with the cream. Freshly grated nutmeg makes all the difference in this recipe. More rum can be added, if preferred. Chopped, mixed nuts can be used instead of the peanuts.

Annenberg Cheese Puffs
Submitted by: Senator Arlen Specter

Meal: Appetizer   Servings: 20
Prep Time: 2 hours, 15 minutes   Cost: Inexpensive

Ingredients

1 (8-ounce) package cream cheese,
   softened
1 cup grated Cheddar cheese
1 medium onion, chopped

1 egg yolk
Salt and pepper to taste
20 slices thin bread rounds
Paprika for garnish

Preparation

Combine cream cheese, cheddar cheese, onion and egg yolk. Season with salt and pepper. Chill for at least 2 hours then prepare puffs. Toast bread slices. Spread cheese mixture on toasted rounds. Sprinkle with paprika and broil for a few minutes, until lightly browned.

Grapes with Sour Cream

Submitted by: David Doorley in memory of Jim Hanneken.

Meal: Appetizer or Dessert   Servings: 4
Prep Time:2 hours   Cost: Inexpensive

Ingredients

1 (8-ounce) container sour cream   1 pound seedless, green grapes
Brown sugar to taste

Preparation

Sweeten sour cream to taste with brown sugar. Wash grapes, remove stems, dry with paper towels. Put grapes in bowl with sour cream. Stir gently until grapes are covered with sour cream. Cover and refrigerate for about 2 hours, can be prepared the day before. Serve in sherbets, delicious and refreshing. Peaches, strawberries, or blueberries can be substituted for the grapes.

Appetizers & Snacks

Pizza Dip
Submitted by: Dana Magnone

Meal: Appetizer   Servings: 8
Prep Time: 30 minutes   Cost: Inexpensive

Ingredients

4 ounces cream cheese   Green pepper, diced
4 ounces sour cream   Pizza sauce to top
Dash of each, oregano, garlic powder   Mozzarella cheese to top
1/2 cup onions, diced   French bread baguettes

Preparation

Mix all ingredients thoroughly, except for the pizza sauce, cheese and bread. Place in a small ovenproof dish and top with the sauce and cheese. Bake in a preheated 350 degree oven for 15 minutes. Cut up French bread baguette to serve with the dip.

Vegetarian?: Yes

Mom's Caramel Popcorn

Submitted by: Jeff Carson

Meal: Snack   Servings: 2 pans
Prep Time: 1 hour, 30 minutes   Cost: Inexpensive

Ingredients

2 cups brown sugar
2 sticks butter
1/2 cup white corn syrup
1 teaspoon salt

1 teaspoon butter flavoring
1/2 teaspoon baking soda
16 cups popped corn, unpopped kernals
  removed

Preparation

Combine brown sugar, butter, corn syrup and salt. Boil 5 minutes, stir in butter flavoring and baking soda. Pour immediately over popped corn. Place in 1 or 2 large flat pans. Bake in a preheated 250 degree oven for 1 hour, stirring every 15 minutes. Peanuts may be added just before placing in the oven. Store after cooling in tightly covered container.

Marty's Nutty Cheese Roll
Submitted by: Marty Ingles

Meal: Appetizer   Servings: 10
Prep Time: 2 hours, 15 minutes   Cost: Inexpensive

Ingredients

1 (8-ounce) package cream cheese
2 ounces bleu cheese
4 ounces sharp cheddar cheese,
   shredded
1/4 teaspoon garlic powder

Dash Worcestershire sauce
1 tablespoon brandy
1 tablespoon sherry wine
Dash white pepper
1 cup chopped walnuts

Preparation

Blend all ingredients, except walnuts. Make into a ball and roll in walnuts. Cover with plastic wrap and refrigerate for 2 hours.

Boiled Shrimp in Beer

Submitted by: June Le Bras

Meal: Appetizer   Servings: 6
Prep Time: 1 hour   Cost: Moderate

Ingredients

1 pound headless, shell-on shrimp
1 quart water
1 (12-ounce) beer
1 lemon, cut up

2 stalks celery, diced
1 onion, cut up
2 bay leaves
Red pepper sauce to taste

Preparation

Combine all ingredients, except shrimp, in a medium pot. Bring to a boil, add shrimp and cover. Return to a boil and simmer for 3 to 4 minutes. Remove from heat and stir. Let stand 3 to 4 more minutes. Remove shrimp from liquid, cool promptly with cold running water. Drain and chill. Serve with cocktail sauce.

Stuffed Mushrooms

Submitted by: Krista Mechling

Meal: Appetizer
Prep Time: 30 minutes

Servings: 6
Cost: Inexpensive

Ingredients

1 tablespoon butter
1/2 green pepper, chopped
2 onions, chopped
1/2 cup pepperoni
6 tablespoons Parmesan cheese

1 teaspoon oregano
1 cup crushed Ritz crackers
1 cup chicken bouillon
2 packages mushroom caps

Preparation

Sauté green pepper and onion in the butter. Mix with the remaining ingredients thoroughly. Place a teaspoon of the mixture on each mushroom cap. Place on a cookie sheet and bake in a preheated 350 degree oven for 15 to 20 minutes.

Crunch Mix
Submitted by: Pat Zerega

Meal: Snack
Prep Time: 5 minutes

Servings: As many as you make
Cost: Inexpensive

Ingredients

Raisins
Peanuts
M & M's

Butterscotch or chocolate morsels
Cranraisins
Dried apple pieces or other dried fruit

Preparation

Mix equal parts of all ingredients, store in airtight bags. You can adjust amounts of the different ingredients to suit yor tastes.

Appetizers & Snacks

San Francisco Seasoned Shrimp

Submitted by: Senator Dianne Feinstein

Meal: Appetizer   Servings: 4
Prep Time: Overnight   Cost: Moderate

Ingredients

2 tablespoons lemon juice   1 large onion, sliced into rings
Salt and pepper to taste   3 tablespoons pimento, in a jar
3 tablespoons olive oil   1/4 cup olives, sliced
1pound shrimp   1 lemon, cut into wedges

Preparation

Mix the lemon juice, salt, pepper, and olive oil for a marinade. Cook and shell the shrimp. Set the shrimp inside the marinade and let sit for 2 to 3 hours or overnight in the refrigerator. Place the onion rings in with the shrimp and mix well. Add the pimento and olive slices before serving. Place lemon wedges around the shrimp.

Bread Pudding with Whiskey Sauce

Submitted by: Michael Schultz

Meal: Dessert or Snack   Servings: 8
Prep Time: 1 hour, 15 minutes   Cost: Inexpensive

Ingredients

1 quart milk, warmed
1/2 loaf Italian bread or 10 slices white
   bread, cut up
4 eggs
1 cup sugar

1 teaspoon vanilla
1/2 teaspoon nutmeg
1 teaspoon cinnamon
1/4 cup butter, melted
1/2 cup raisins

Preparation

In large bowl, combine milk and bread, set aside. In medium bowl beat eggs slightly then add sugar. Add to bread mixture. Stir in vanilla, nutmeg, cinnamon, butter and raisins. Pour into a buttered 2-quart dish. Set dish in larger shallow pan, pour hot water to the depth of 1-inch into the larger pan. Bake in a preheated 350 degree oven for 1 hour or until knife inserted in center comes out clean. Top with Whiskey Sauce (recipe follows).

Whiskey Sauce Ingredients

1/4 cup water
1/2 teaspoon cornstarch
1 cup heavy cream
1 cup sugar

Pinch of cinnamon
1 tablespoon butter
1 tablespoon bourbon or other liquor

Preparation

In small bowl, dissolve cornstarch in the water. In medium saucepan, combine remaining ingredients, except bourbon, and bring to a boil over high heat. Cook, stirring frequently, until sugar is dissolved (about 3 minutes). Stir in cornstarch mixture. Cook until sauce thickens (about 3 minutes). Remove from heat and stir in bourbon.

Fruits in Orange Vanilla Sauce

Submitted by: Barbara Kiura and Victor Wahome

Meal: Dessert
Prep Time: 2 hours

Servings: 6
Cost: Inexpensive

Ingredients

1 teaspoon grated orange rind
2 cups orange juice
1/2 teaspoon vanilla extract
3 bananas, cut into bite size pieces

1/2 to 1 honey dew melon, cut into bite
  size pieces
1 teaspoon lemon juice
1 teaspoon sugar, if needed

Preparation

In a saucepan, bring orange juice, orange rind and sugar to a gentle boil. Reduce heat and let mixture simmer until syrupy, about 15 minutes. Remove from heat and let cool. Once cool add vanilla extract. Place fruit in large bowl and mix with lemon juice. Pour sauce over fruit. For best results chill before serving. Be creative and use the fruits of your choice.

Appetizers & Snacks

Coconut Mandazi

Submitted by: Barbara Kiura and Victor Wahome

Meal: Breakfast or Snack   Servings: 8
Prep Time: 30 minutes   Cost: Inexpensive

Ingredients

1 egg
1/3 cup coconut milk
1/3 cup milk
1/2 teaspoon vanilla extract
1/3 teaspoon crushed cardamom seeds

2-1/3 cups self-rising flour
1 teaspoon baking powder
2 teaspoons sugar, as needed
Vegetable oil, enough for deep frying

Preparation

Place the egg, coconut milk, milk, vanilla extract, cardamom seeds, flour, baking powder and sugar in a food processor. Process to make a smooth, pourable consistency. Use more milk if to thick. Set the smooth, creamy batter aside for about 15 minutes. Heat vegetable oil in deep fryer. When hot, place a spoonful of the batter in the oil carefully. Let fry for 3 to 5 minutes, until both sides are golden brown. Use a slotted spoon to remove. Cover the cooked mandazi to keep warm and continue to cook the remaining batter. Serve at once. Best served for breakfast with chai or milk, or as a midday snack.

Aquarium Jell-O

Submitted by: Traci Sanders

Meal: Dessert   Servings: 10
Prep Time: 3 hours   Cost: Inexpensive

Ingredients

2 boxes blue Jell-O   Lots of gummy fish
2 boxes unflavored gelatin   Parsley

Preparation

Make first box of Jell-O and add unflavored gelatin to it, put in freezer to cool quickly. Prepare second box of Jell-O and add unflavored gelatin to it, set on counter to cool. Take freezer Jell-O out when almost set. Make small slits in the top and set fish in upside down. Pour cooled but not set counter Jell-O on top. Put back in refrigerator to chill. Repeat for as many layers as you like but always use equal boxes of blue Jell-O with unflavored gelatin. This takes a few times to get just right but don't be afraid to experiment. The parsley makes good sea plants. Tip the bowl side ways while setting. When set and ready to serve fill a larger pan with warm water and set Jell-O pan in the water up to the rim for a few minutes. Turn upside down on a plate and refrigerate until ready to serve.

Appetizers & Snacks

Bill Elliot's
Sweet and Tangy Meatballs
Submitted by: Bill Elliot

Meal: Appetizer

Servings: 10

Prep Time: 1 hour

Cost: Inexpensive

Ingredients

2 pounds ground beef
1 egg
1 large onion, minced
1-1/2 teaspoons salt

1 (12-ounce) bottle chili sauce
1 (10-ounce) jar grape jelly
3 tablespoons lemon juice

Preparation

Mix meat, egg, onion and salt. Shape into 1-inch balls and cook at 350 degrees until brown. Remove from pan and drain. Combine chili sauce, jelly, and lemon juice. Cook over medium heat, stirring constantly until jelly melts. Add meatballs and simmer for 10 to 15 minutes.

Appetizers & Snacks

Spinach Dip

Submitted by: Pamela Brock-Allen

Meal: Appetizer   Servings: 12
Prep Time: 2 hours, 30 minutes   Cost: Inexpensive

Ingredients

1 (10-ounce) package chopped spinach,
   fresh or frozen
1-1/2 cups sour cream
1 cup mayonnaise
1 package vegetable soup mix
1 (8-ounce) can water chestnuts,
   chopped

3 green onions, chopped
1 large, round loaf pumpernickle bread
Celery sticks
Carrot sticks
Heads of cauliflower
Broccoli floret

Preparation

Thaw and squeeze dry frozen spinach or clean and chop fresh spinach, remove the large stem. Stir together spinach, sour cream, mayonnaise, soup mix, water chestnuts and onions. Blend well. Cover and refrigerate for 2 hours before serving. Cut out center of the bread, creating a bowl. Pour chilled vegetable dip in center of the bread. Break up the remainder of the bread into bite size pieces. Place bread bowl on center of a platter and surround with bread chunks and vegetables.

Appetizers & Snacks

Hot Cherry Apple Cider

Submitted by: Pamela Brock-Allen

Meal:　　　Any　　　　　　　Servings: 12
Prep Time: 30 minutes　　　　Cost:　　Inexpensive

Ingredients

11 cups apple cider or apple juice
1 (16-ounce) package frozen,
　unsweetened, pitted, tart red cherries
1/4 cup honey or packed brown sugar
6 sticks cinnamon

1 teaspoon whole cloves
Extra cinnamon sticks, optional
2 medium apples, cut into 12 wedges total,
　optional

Preparation

Combine apple cider, cherries, honey, 6 sticks cinnamon and cloves in a dutch oven. Bring to a boil. Reduce heat, cover and simmer for 10 minutes. Strain through a sieve lined with cheesecloth. To serve: Pour into cups. Garnish each cup with cinnamon sticks and apples.

Black Olive Dip

Submitted by: Halle Berry

Meal: Appetizer   Servings: 6
Prep Time: 30 minutes   Cost: Inexpensive

Ingredients

4 cups low-fat sour cream
8 to 12 tablespoons black olive puree or
  tapenade (available in specialty
  shops)

2 to 4 tablespoons lemon juice
2 tablespoons extra virgin or cold pressed
  olive oil

Preparation

In a medium bowl, mix all ingredients thoroughly. Taste for seasoning and adjust black olive puree and lemon juice according to your tastes. Serve with pita bread triangles and an assortment of raw vegetables or lightly steamed vegetables.

Appetizers & Snacks

Mother's Jell-O Mold

Submitted by: Evelyn Brock

Meal: Appetizer or Dessert
Prep Time: 30 minutes

Servings: 8 to 10
Cost: Inexpensive

Ingredients

2 (4-ounce) boxes lime Jell-O
2 cups boiling water

2 cups cold water
4 ounces cream cheese

Preparation

Add boiling water toJell-O. Stir until dissolved, about 2 minutes. Add cold water, chill. Once Jell-O starts to set, whip in cream cheese. Pour Jell-O into mold and chill in refrigerator.

Clam Dip

Submitted by: Chrissy Lyons in memory of Love Chunks.

Meal: Appetizer   Servings: 8
Prep Time: 1 hour   Cost: Inexpensive

Ingredients

1 (8 ounce) package cream cheese,   1 small clove garlic, minced
softened   1/2 teaspoon lemon juice
1 (6-ounce) can minced clams, save   1/4 teaspoon Worcestershire sauce
juice   Salt to taste

Preparation

Combine cream cheese and clams, add just enough clam juice to make a nice dipping consistency. Add garlic, lemon juice, Worcestershire sauce and salt. Mix thoroughly, cover and chill. Serve with crackers, chips or raw vegetables.

Appetizers & Snacks

Shrimp Dip

Submitted by: Chrissy Lyons in memory of Drew.

Meal: Appetizer
Prep Time: 15 minutes

Servings: 6 to 8
Cost: Inexpensive

Ingredients

1 can cream of shrimp soup
1 (8-ounce) package cream cheese

1 tablespoon lemon juice
1 tablespoon sherry

Preparation

Put soup and cream cheese in microwave safe bowl and microwave for 3 to 4 minutes. Remove and stir with fork. Add lemon juice and sherry and blend. Microwave another 1 to 2 minutes. Serve hot with crackers, chips or vegetables.

Quick Crabtree Cocktail
Submitted by: Dorothy Langer

Meal: Appetizer   Servings: 4
Prep Time: 10 minutes   Cost: Inexpensive

Ingredients

Small chunks crabmeat   1 head lettuce, shredded
1 bottle cocktail sauce

Preparation

Combine crabmeat and cocktail sauce. Place shredded lettuce in the bottom of cocktail cups and top with crabmeat mixture. May substitute shrimp for the crabmeat.

Medallion Onion Dip

Submitted by: Cathy Patterson

Meal:	Appetizer or Snack	Servings:	4 to 6
Prep Time:	30 minutes	Cost:	Inexpensive

Ingredients

1 medallion onion, chopped fine

1 cup mayonnaise

1 cup shredded Swiss cheese

Preparation

Mix all ingredients thoroughly. Place in a greased casserole dish. Bake in a preheated 350 degree oven for about 15 minutes or until cheese is bubbly. Serve with crackers.

Triopitas

Submitted by: Jill Kornberg

Meal: Appetizer   Servings: 6
Prep Time: 1 hour   Cost: Inexpensive

Ingredients

6 eggs
1/2 pound Feta cheese, crushed
1/4 pound Romano cheese, shredded or
  grated

1/2 teaspoon pepper
1 package phyllo (Filo) dough, available in
  freezer section

Preparation

Mix together the eggs, Feta cheese, Romano cheese and pepper, set aside. Follow thawing directions on the dough. When thawed, lay out 1 sheet of the phyllo and cut into 3-inch strips. On each of the pieces, place a heaping teaspoon of the mixture at the bottom end of the strip. Fold the dough over the mixture in a triangle fashion tucking in the last fold. Deep fry in hot oil until golden brown, about 30 to 60 seconds.

Hot Cheese Dip

Submitted by: Floyd Patterson

Meal: Appetizer or Snack   Servings: 6 to 8
Prep Time: 30 minutes   Cost: Inexpensive

Ingredients

1 cup mayonnaise   1 (4- to 6-ounce) can chilies or Jalapeños
1 cup Parmesan cheese

Preparation

Stir everything together in an oven-proof baking dish. Place in a preheated 350 degree oven and bake until bubbly hot. Allow to cool slightly before serving.

Pasta, Rice, Eggs & Cheese

Recipe   **Page**

Quiche American 2-1
Wild Rice with Mushrooms... 2-2
Lasagna 2-3
Macaroni and Coleslaw Salad 2-4
Cold Sesame Noodles 2-5
Eggs Fette.. 2-6
Chicken Lasagna 2-7
Naughty Noodles 2-8
Lunchtime Gloop.. 2-9
Colorful Cajun Rice Dish.. 2-10
Spaghetti Alla Puttanesca.. 2-11
Low Cholesterol Egg Custard 2-12
Dave's Favorite Pasta.. 2-13
Baked Linguini 2-14
Italian Rice 2-15
Pasta Salad.. 2-16
Heather's Spicy Rice and Beans.. 2-17
Anthony Michael Hall's Cheezy Meat Lasagna...................... 2-18
Penne Danielle... 2-19
Linguini with Chicken, Broccoli and Dijon Cream Sauce 2-20

Pasta, Rice, Eggs & Cheese

Quiche American

Submitted by: The Author

Meal: Any
Prep Time: 1 hour

Servings: 6
Cost: Inexpensive

Ingredients

1 refrigerated or frozen pie crust shell
1 pint whipping cream or half-and-half
3 eggs
1/8 teaspoon white pepper
1 tablespoon dried parsley
1/2 pound Swiss or Monterey Jack
    cheese, grated

1 pint mushrooms, sliced
1/4 cup green onions, diced
1/4 pound cooked ham or bacon, cubed
1 tablespoon grated Parmesan or Romano
    cheese

Preparation

Step 1:   Preheat oven to 375 degrees. Using a fork, poke the base of the pastry
          shell several times. Place on a cookie sheet, heat for approximately 5
          minutes, then remove from oven.

Step 2:   In a medium-size bowl, thoroughly mix whipping cream or half-and-half,
          eggs, white pepper and parsley.

Step 3:   Evenly distribute cheese, mushrooms, green onions and meat in pastry
          shell. Pour mixture over solid ingredients carefully filling pastry shell to the
          top. Sprinkle with grated cheese and bake for 40 to 45 minutes until you
          can cleanly insert and remove a wooden pick from the center.

Suggestions

Quiche may be served as a main course or a side dish with your meal. Feel free to
experiment with other cheeses, meats and vegetables. Dry white wine, such as
Bordeaux, Reisling, or Chablis, is an excellent compliment to this French haute-
cuisine.

Pasta, Rice, Eggs & Cheese

Wild Rice with Mushrooms
Submitted by: Nancy Squibb

Meal: Dinner   Servings: 6 to 8
Prep Time: 2 hours   Cost: Inexpensive

Ingredients

1 cup uncooked wild rice
1/4 cup butter
1/2 cup slivered almonds (optional)
2 tablespoons snipped chives or green
  onions

1 (8-ounce) can mushroom stems and
  pieces
3 cups chicken broth

Preparation

Wash and drain rice. Melt butter in large skillet, add rice, almonds, chives and
mushrooms. Cook and stir until almonds are golden, about 15 minutes. Heat oven to
325 degrees. Pour rice mixture into an ungreased 1-1/2 quart casserole dish. Heat
chicken broth to boiling, stir into casserole dish. Cover tightly and bake about 1-1/2
hours or until all liquid is absorbed and rice is tender and fluffy.

Pasta, Rice, Eggs & Cheese

Lasagna

Submitted by: John Jarrett

Meal: Dinner
Prep Time: 2 hours

Servings: 10 to 12
Cost: Moderate

Ingredients

1 package lasagna noodles
3 quarts water
1-1/2 pounds ground beef
3/4 cups chopped onion
1 green pepper
2 cans tomato paste [1 (12-ounce) can and 1 (6-ounce) can]
2-1/4 cups hot water
1 cup plus 2 tablespoons red burgundy wine
1-1/2 tablespoons minced parsley

1 tablespoon plus 1 teaspoon minced garlic
1 tablespoon salt
1 teaspoon oregano
3/4 teaspoon basil
3/4 teaspoon rosemary
1/2 teaspoon ground black pepper
3 bay leaves, crumbled
3 eggs, slightly beaten
1 quart cottage cheese, drained
3 (6-ounce) packages Mozzarella cheese
1/2 cup grated Parmesan cheese

Preparation

Cook noodles in 3 quarts boiling salt water until tender, drain. Brown meat, onion and green pepper over low heat until soft, drain. Blend tomato paste, water, wine and all seasonings together in saucepan. Bring to a boil, add meat mixture and simmer for 15 minutes, and set aside. Blend eggs with cottage cheese in a bowl, and set aside. In a 9x13 baking pan, alternately layer meat sauce, noodles, and Mozzarella cheese ending with the sauce mixture. Place all of the cottage cheese-egg mixture in center. Sprinkle liberally with the Parmesan cheese. Bake in a preheated 350 degree oven 45 to 50 minutes. Let stand for at least 15 minutes before cutting.

Pasta, Rice, Eggs & Cheese

Macaroni and Coleslaw Salad
Submitted by: Mardi Isler

Meal: Lunch or Dinner   Servings: 6
Prep Time: 3 hours   Cost: Inexpensive

Salad Ingredients

2 cups cooked elbow macaroni
1 small head cabbage, finely shredded
1 small green pepper, minced

1 small red pepper, minced
1/2 cup celery, minced
1 cucumber, peeled, quartered, seeded,
  and sliced

Dressing Ingredients

1 cup mayonnaise
1/4 cup cider vinegar
1 teaspoon salt

3 tablespoons sugar
1/4 teaspoon white pepper

Preparation

Whisk all dressing ingredients until smooth. Mix dressing and salad ingredients thoroughly. Chill for at least 2 hours before serving.

Cold Sesame Noodles

Submitted by: Daniel Gamble
for all the mothers of Wellness who do so much.

Meal: Lunch or Dinner   Servings: 4
Prep Time: 1 hour   Cost: Inexpensive

Ingredients

1/2 pound whole wheat noodles or
   lomein noodles
1/4 cup peanut butter
1/4 cup warm water
3 tablespoons soy sauce

2 tablespoons rice wine vinegar
1 tablespoon sesame oil
1 teaspoon hot chili oil
Chopped scallions
Toasted sesame seeds

Preparation

Cook pasta al dente. Drain and rinse with cold water, set aside. Mix the peanut butter, warm water, soy sauce, vinegar, sesame oil and chili oil. Toss with noodles. Top with chopped scallions and sesame seeds. Chill lightly.

Eggs Fette

*Submitted by: William Fette "in memory of everyone
I've known that has passed from this plague."*

Meal: Dinner   Servings: 1
Prep Time: 45 minutes   Cost: Expensive

Ingredients

1 egg, hard boiled   Lettuce, shredded
Caviar   Boiled lobster, cold
Tomato, sliced

Preparation

Cut a small section from the pointed end of a hard cooked egg. Remove yolk, fill with caviar and replace the cap. Place on a slice of tomato, shredded lettuce and surround with pieces of cold boiled lobster. Serve with the following dressing.

Dressing Ingredients

1-1/2 tablespoons fresh squeezed lemon   1 tablespoon Worcestershire
   juice   1/2 cup mayonnaise
2 tablespoons thick chili sauce

Preparation

Mix lemon juice, chili sauce and Worcestershire sauce thoroughly. Add the mayonnaise.

Pasta, Rice, Eggs & Cheese

Chicken Lasagna
Submitted by: Bob Newhart

Meal: Dinner   Servings: 10
Prep Time: 1 hour, 15 minutes   Cost: Inexpensive

Ingredients

4 spicy turkey Italian sausage links
1 pound ground chicken
2 tablespoons olive oil
3-1/2 cups spaghetti sauce
1 package Lasagna noodles
1 (8-ounce) package low fat Mozzarella
  cheese

1 (8-ounce) pakcagelow fat cheddar
  cheese, shredded
4 cups Ricotta cheese or low fat cottage
  cheese
Grated Parmesan cheese

Preparation

Remove casings from sausage. Brown chicken and sausage in olive oil. Add
spaghetti sauce. Cook lasagna according to directions. Lay on flat surface. Spread
1/2 cup meat sauce on the bottom of a 9x13 pan. Cover with some noodles, some of
the 4 cheeses and some sauce. Repeat all layers ending with meat sauce. Sprinkle
with remaining cheeses and cover with tin foil. Bake in a preheated 375 degree oven
for 30 minutes. Remove foil and bake another 5 minutes. Let stand at least 10
minutes before cutting.

Pasta, Rice, Eggs & Cheese

Naughty Noodles
Submitted by: Carina de Wit-Lord

Meal: Lunch or Dinner   Servings: 4
Prep Time: 1 hour, 30 minutes   Cost: Moderate

Ingredients

1 (16-ounce) box Penne, Ziti, or
 Rigatoni
1/2 tablespoon olive oil
4 large red bell peppers or a
 combination of red, orange, and
 yellow bell peppers, halved and
 deseeded

3 large, firm tomatoes
1 cup pitted calamata olives, chopped
3 to 4 large cloves garlic, minced
1-1/2 tablespoons extra virgin olive oil
1/2 teaspoon hot pepper flakes
Salt and pepper to taste
Grated Parmesan, optional

Preparation

Prepare pasta according to directions, keep warm. Preheat broiler to 500 degrees.
Cover broiler rack with aluminum foil and lightly grease with olive oil. Place peppers
on rack and brush with 1/2 tablespoon olive oil. Place rack under broiler on lowest
shelf and roast peppers until completely blackened on the outside, about 15 minutes.
Place peppers in a paper bag, fold and let sit for at least 15 minutes. Remove
peppers and peel off blackened skin and discard. Cut peppers into 1 inch cubes, set
aside. In a pan, boil water for tomatoes. Make a shallow cut, like an x, in the
tomatoes. When water comes to a boil, drop tomatoes in the water for 30 seconds.
Remove tomatoes with a slotted spoon and immediately place them in a bowl of ice
water. Peel tomatoes starting at the cut. Remove the stems. Cut tomatoes in chunks
and squeeze or scoop out the seeds, set aside. Chop pitted olives, set aside. Heat
olive oil in a non-stick fry pan over medium heat. Add garlic and toast until golden
brown, about 1 minute. Add peppers and tomatoes. Sauté until heated through, about
5 minutes. Add mixture to pasta and carefully stir to mix. Add olives, pepper flakes,
salt and pepper to taste. Heat through 3 to 5 minutes over low heat, stirring
occasionally to prevent scorching. Serve immediately, garnishing with Parmesan
cheese.

Suggestions

Good with green salad and/or garlic bread. Kalamata olives can be found in most
grocery stores and Middle Eastern grocery stores.

Pasta, Rice, Eggs & Cheese

Lunchtime Gloop
Submitted by: Stephen King

Meal: Lunch   Servings: 4
Prep Time: 30 minutes   Cost: Inexpensive

Ingredients

1 pound, cheap, greasy hamburger   2 cans Franco-American spaghetti (without meatballs)

Preparation

Brown hamburg in large skillet. Add Franco-American spaghetti and cook till heated through. Do not drain hamburg, or it won't be properly greasy. Burn on pan if you want - that will only improve the flavor. Serve with buttered Wonder Bread.

Suggestions

"My kids love this. I only make it when my wife, Tabby, isn't home. She won't eat it, in fact doesn't even like to look at it."

Colorful Cajun Rice Dish

Submitted by: Mary Helen Hough in memory of Michael Norris.

Meal:　　　Lunch or Dinner　　　Servings: 4
Prep Time: 30 minutes　　　　　Cost:　　Inexpensive

Ingredients

1 cup cooked ground beef, chicken or
　shrimp
1 package Cajun rice mix
1/2 cup whole kernel corn, drained

1/2 cup black beans
1 small jar salsa
1 cup grated sharp Cheddar cheese
Sour cream

Preparation

Brown meat in a skillet, drain and set aside. Cook rice as directed on package.
Remove from heat. Add drained corn, black beans, salsa and choice of meat. Top
with Cheddar cheese and sour cream.

Pasta, Rice, Eggs & Cheese

Spaghetti Alla Puttanesca

Submitted by: Joseph Lesnick
in memory of George W. Goss (1953 - 1995).

Meal: Dinner   Servings: 4 to 6
Prep Time: 1 hour   Cost: Inexpensive

Ingredients

3 tablespoons olive oil
2 garlic cloves, minced
1 (1-pound, 12-ounce) can Italian-style
  peeled tomatoes, do not drain
1/4 cup chopped, pitted, salt-cured black
  olives
2 teaspoons small capers, rinsed
1 teaspoon crushed dried red pepper

1/2 teaspoon dried oregano
Pinch of coarsley ground black pepper
1 (2-ounce) can flat anchovies, drained,
  blotted dry, cut into small pieces
2 tablespoons chopped Italian flat-leaf
  parsley
Salt
1 pound spaghetti

Preparation

Heat oil in large skillet, add garlic. Sauté over low heat about 1 minute, do not brown.
Stir in tomatoes with their juice, olives, capers, red pepper, oregano and black
pepper. Cook over medium heat, stirring to break up tomatoes, until sauce thickens,
about 15 minutes. Stir in anchovies and parsley, simmer another 2 minutes. Add salt
to taste. While sauce is simmering prepare noodles according to package directions.
Toss with sauce and serve immediately.

Low Cholesterol Egg Custard

Submitted by: Nancy Phillips in memory of those who believed in the power of hope, believed in the strength of love, and believed all things are possible.

Meal: Dessert   Servings: 4
Prep Time: 1 hour   Cost: Inexpensive

Ingredients

3-2/3 cup skim milk   1/2 cup sugar
1 cup egg substitute, cholesterol free 1 teaspoon vanilla extract

Preparation

Heat milk to below boiling then set aside. In a separate bowl, combine the egg substitute, sugar and vanilla. Gradually add the milk and mix thoroughly. Pour into cups. Bake in a preheated 325 degree oven for 45 minutes or until a crust forms on top.

Pasta, Rice, Eggs & Cheese

Dave's Favorite Pasta

Submitted by: R. David Thomas

Meal: Dinner
Prep Time: 3 hours

Servings: 4 to 6
Cost: Inexpensive

Ingredients

14 Roma tomatoes, chopped
4 cloves garlic, chopped
2 tablespoons fresh basil, chopped
2 tablespoons olive oil
2 tablespoons wine vinegar
1 pound angel hair pasta

1 tablespoon chicken broth
Fresh mushrooms
Pepper
Parmesan cheese
Red pepper and onions, optional

Preparation

Combine tomatoes, garlic, basil, olive oil and vinegar in a wooden bowl. Let sit at room temperature for at least 2 hours. Tomato mixture should be warm, room temperature. If not warm, microwave for 1 minute, but do not cook! Boil pasta in water with the chicken broth until done. Slice fresh mushrooms and place on a cookie sheet and spray lightly with Pam olive oil spray. Broil for a few minutes. Turn, and lightly spray with olive oil again and broil again for a few minutes. Drain pasta. Return to a bowl and toss with tomato mixture. Spoon sliced mushrooms on top and sprinkle with pepper and cheese. Sliced red peppers and onions may also be added to tomato mixture.

Pasta, Rice, Eggs & Cheese

Baked Linguini

Submitted by: Eric Stalnaker in memory of Phil. May your garden continue to flourish and grow. You're missed!

Meal: Dinner   Servings: 6
Prep Time: 1 hour   Cost: Inexpensive

Ingredients

3 lengths Italian sausage, hot or mild,
  chopped
2 bunches green onions with greens,
  chopped
1 large can mushrooms sliced or
  8 ounces fresh

1-1/2 sticks butter
1 pound linguini, cooked al dente and
  rinsed in cold water
Salt and pepper to taste
1-1/2 cups Mozzarella cheese
3/4 cup Parmesan cheese

Preparation

Sauté sausage, set aside. In a pan, sauté onions, mushrooms and butter for 20 minutes on medium heat. Mix together sausage, onion mixture and linguini. Place in a baking dish and add salt and pepper to taste. Mix the cheeses and place on top. Cover and bake in a preheated 350 degree oven for 30 minutes.

Pasta, Rice, Eggs & Cheese

Italian Rice

Submitted by: Larry and Peggy Logue for Stephen Thompson.

Meal: Dinner

Prep Time: 45 minutes

Servings: 4

Cost: Inexpensive

Ingredients

1 teaspoon butter
1 teaspoon olive oil
1/4 cup chopped onions
1 clove garlic, minced

1 cup white rice
2 to 3 cups chicken stock
2 to 3 teaspoons Parmesan cheese
1 (8-ounce) can tomato sauce

Preparation

Brown onions and garlic in butter and olive oil until tender. Add raw white rice and stir. Cook the rice until all moisture is gone then add chicken stock, 3/4 cup at a time. Keep adding stock until rice is tender, add tomato sauce in-between. When rice is tender, about 1/2 hour, add Parmesan cheese to top and mix in.

Pasta Salad
Submitted by: Pamela Brock-Allen

Meal: Lunch or Dinner   Servings: 12
Prep Time: Overnight   Cost: Inexpensive

Ingredients

1 package linguini noodles, spaghetti
   noodles, or angel hair pasta
1 small bunch fresh broccoli, chopped
1 small head cauliflower, chopped
2 carrots, shredded
2 stalks celery, chopped

1 green pepper, thinly sliced
1 small red onion, thinly sliced
6 to 9 mushrooms, sliced
Chunks of cheese, any style
1 bottle Salad Supreme
1 bottle Italian dressing

Preparation

Boil pasta noodles until tender, rinse with cool water. Add all vegetables and the cheese then toss. Sprinkle entire bottle of Salad Supreme and salad dressing over noodles. Toss well and cover. Refrigerate over night. Serve with hot rolls as a main dish or use as a side dish.

Heather's Spicy Rice and Beans

Submitted by: Heather Hummel

Meal: Lunch or Dinner   Servings: 2 to 4
Prep Time: 30 minutes   Cost: Inexpensive

Ingredients

1/2 cup salsa, the hotter the better but
   mild or medium will work
2 cups cooked rice, minute rice works
   well

Red pepper flakes, optional
1 (8-ounce) can baked beans

Preparation

Mix the salsa and rice for a moist consistency, add more salsa if rice seems dry.
Sprinkle red pepper flakes into baked beans to taste. Combine bean mixture with rice
mixture and mix well. Serve warm. Serve with grilled chicken.

Pasta, Rice, Eggs & Cheese

Anthony Michael Hall's Cheezy Meat Lasagna

Submitted by: Anthony Michael Hall

Meal: Lunch or Dinner   Servings: 10
Prep Time: 2 hours   Cost: Inexpensive

Ingredients

1 pound ground beef
Box of lasagna noodles
Large container Ricotta cheese
Chopped parsley

3 cups Mozzarella cheese, or more
   according to tastes
Large jar spaghetti sauce

Preparation

Brown meat until cooked through, drain and set aside. Cook noodles according to directions and rinse in cold water. In a large bowl, mix the Ricotta cheese, parsley and 1 cup Mozzarella cheese, set aside. Mix the cooked meat with the spaghetti sauce. In a 9x13-inch pan layer the noodles until the bottom is covered. Spoon a thin layer of the sauce mixture on top of the noodles then put a layer of the cheese mixture. Keep repeating layers until all mixtures are used, ending with the meat sauce. Sprinkle the top with the last 2 cups of Mozzarella cheese. Bake in a preheated 350 degree oven for about 1 hour. When the cheese is melted in the center and the top cheese is slightly browned then it's done. Timing will depend on the thickness of the layers.

Pasta, Rice, Eggs & Cheese

Penne Danielle
Submitted by: Danielle and Steve Barczykowski

Meal: Dinner   Servings: 4
Prep Time: 1 hour   Cost: Inexpensive

Ingredients

8 ounce dried penne
1/4 cup olive oil
1/2 cup diced onion
1/2 cup diced green pepper
2 cloves garlic, finely chopped

1 Roma tomato, peeled, seeded and
   chopped
1/2 cup stuffed green olives
1/2 cup pitted black olives
1/3 cup grated Parmesan cheese
Salt and cracked black pepper to taste

Preparation

Cook pasta according to directions. Rinse in cold water and set aside. In the empty pot, heat oil on high until hot. Add onions and green peppers to oil and sauté until tender, about 3 to 4 minutes. Add garlic to oil and sauté another minute or two, do not burn. Add the tomato and olives to the onion mixture and turn off the heat. Rinse cooked pasta in hot water and shake off excess water. Add vegetable mixture to pasta and mix. Toss with the Parmesan cheese and season with the salt and pepper.

Linguini with Chicken, Broccoli and Dijon Cream Sauce

Submitted by: Patti Curry

Meal: Dinner   Servings: 4
Prep Time: 1 hour   Cost: Inexpensive

Ingredients

2-1/2 quarts water   1 (8-ounce) box linguini noodles
1 clove garlic, minced   4 cups broccoli florets (1/2-pound)
1/3 cup Dijon mustard   2 teaspoons extra virgin olive oil
1/4 cup half-and-half   2 boneless, cooked chicken breasts, diced

Preparation

Bring the water to a boil in 6 quart or larger pot. Meanwhile, place garlic and mustard in a 3 quart bowl and whisk in half-and-half. When water boils add noodles, cover and bring back to a boil. Crack pot lid. Add broccoli and cook 7 more minutes or until noodles are barely tender. Drain noodles and broccoli into a colander. Pour noodles into bowl containing Dijon sauce. Drizzle oil over noodles, add chicken and Parmesan cheese. Toss gently to coat noodles.

Recipe   **Page**

"Let's" Scampi 3-1
Guillaume Crab Cakes 3-2
Linguine with White Clam Sauce 3-3
Seafood Thermidor 3-4
Shrimp in Garlic Wine Sauce 3-5
Shrimp Squash Casserole 3-6
Imperial Crab 3-7
Pan Roasted Oysters 3-8
Fried Snapper 3-9
Crabs Chesapeake 3-10
Lobster with Mustard Sauce 3-11
De Luxe Crabmeat 3-12
Lobster Pili Pili 3-13
Crab Cakes with Lemon Dill Sauce 3-14
Tommy Smothers' Favorite Grilled Avocado Swordfish 3-15
Lobster Oriental 3-16
Sweet-and-Sour Sauce Baked Fish 3-17
Succulent Fried Fish 3-18
Maryland Crab Cakes 3-19

Seafood

"Let's" Scampi

Submitted by: Nancy Squibb

Meal: Dinner   Servings: 4
Prep Time: 10 minutes   Cost: Moderate

Ingredients

4 cloves garlic
1 teaspoon salt
1 teaspoon oregano
1/4 teaspoon basil
1/2 cup butter
4 tablespoons olive oil

1 pound medium shrimp, cleaned
1 cup chopped, fresh parsley
1 (8-ounce) package spaghetti
Grated Parmesan cheese
Freshly ground black pepper

Preparation

Mince garlic, mix with salt, oregano and basil. Heat butter, oil and spices in skillet. Add shrimp and cook until pink and done. Add parsley and mix well. Serve over cooked, drained spaghetti. Sprinkle with Parmesan cheese and black pepper.

Seafood

Guillaume Crab Cakes

Submitted by: Robert Guillaume

Meal: Dinner   Servings: 6 to 8
Prep Time: 30 minutes   Cost: Moderate

Ingredients

3 cups white crab meat
1/2 cup finely chopped carrots
1/2 cup finely chopped celery
1/2 cup finely chopped green bell
   pepper
1/2 cup finely chopped yellow bell
   pepper
1/2 cup finely chopped red bell pepper

1/2 teaspoon crushed red cayenne pepper
2 tablespoons chopped fresh parsley
1/2 teaspoon fresh basil
1 to 2 eggs, enough to make cakes stick
Bread crumbs, flour or cracker meal
2 to 3 tablespoons vegetable oil
Salt and pepper to taste

Preparation

Mix all ingredients. Form cakes 1/2 inch thick by 4 inches round. Roll in bread crumbs, flour, or cracker meal. Using 2 to 3 tablespoons vegetable oil, fry in hot skillet, low to medium heat, until golden brown on both sides.

Seafood

Linguine with White Clam Sauce

Submitted by: Rebecca Bold in memory of Bob Hawthorn.

Meal: Dinner   Servings: 4
Prep Time: 15 minutes   Cost: Inexpensive

Ingredients

1 (8-ounce) can minced clams
1 (8-ounce) can chopped clams
1 small onion, chopped
3 cloves garlic, minced

1/3 cup olive oil
2 tablespoons butter
1 teaspoon leaf oregano, crumbled
1/2 teaspoon salt

1/8 teaspoon fresh ground pepper
Linguine, cooked
1 (6-ounce) jar marinated artichoke hearts
1/2 jar roasted red peppers
2 tablespoons fresh parsley, chopped
1 teaspoon grated lemon rind
2 tablespoons lemon juice
Parmesan cheese, grated
1 can whole baby clams

Preparation

Drain clam juice from minced and chopped clams, reserve. Sauté onions and garlic in oil and butter until tender, but not brown, about 5 minutes. Add reserved clam juice, oregano, salt and pepper. Bring to a boil over high heat. Cook until reduced to 1 cup, about 5 minutes. Cook linguine according to directions. Lower heat under clam juice mixture, add reserved clams, artichoke hearts, roasted red peppers, parsley, lemon rind and lemon juice, heat thoroughly. Toss with hot linguine. Serve with grated Parmesan cheese and whole baby clams.

Seafood Thermidor

Submitted by: The Author

Meal: Dinner   Servings: 4
Prep Time: 20 minutes   Cost: Expensive

Ingredients

1 pound fresh or frozen fish fillets
1/2 pound crabmeat, clams, shrimp,
    and/or scallops (any combination)
1 lemon slice
1 small onion, quartered
1 can cream of shrimp soup
3 tablespoons flour
1/4 cup milk
1/2 teaspoon fresh lemon juice
1/4 cup white wine

1/2 teaspoon Dijon mustard
1/4 cup shredded Mozzarella cheese
3 tablespoons snipped fresh parsley
1/2 cup soft bread crumbs
2 tablespoons Parmesan cheese
3 tablespoons butter
1/2 teaspoon paprika
Lemon slices, thin slices of green onion,
    and parsley for garnish

Preparation

Thaw fish, if frozen. Cut into 1/2 inch cubes. Place all seafood in a pan or skillet, add lemon slice and onion. Add water, just to cover. Bring to a boil then reduce heat and simmer for 4 minutes. Meanwhile, in a small saucepan, blend soup and flour. Gradually stir in milk, lemon juice and wine. Cook, stirring constantly, until thick. Stir in mustard, Mozzarella cheese and parsley. Carefully, drain seafood thoroughly and gently fold in sauce. Spoon mixture into a lightly greased, medium-sized casserole dish. Combine bread crumbs, Parmesan cheese, butter and paprika. Sprinkle over casserole and broil for 1 to 2 minutes. Serve over rice.

Seafood

Shrimp in Garlic Wine Sauce

Submitted by: June Le Bras

Meal: Dinner   Servings: 4 to 6
Prep Time: 15 minutes   Cost: Moderate

Ingredients

1/4 cup olive oil
5 cloves garlic, finely chopped
1/2 cup freshly chopped parsley,
   packed

2 pounds fresh shrimp, cleaned and
   deveined
1/2 cup dry white wine
Salt and pepper to taste

Preparation

Heat oil and garlic over medium heat for 3 minutes. Add parsley and shrimp and cook for 2 minutes over medium to high heat. Add the wine and cook until the shrimp are done, about 3 to 5 minutes (do not over cook). Add salt and pepper to taste.

Shrimp Squash Casserole

Submitted by: Mrs. Lyndon B. Johnson

Meal: Dinner	Servings: 8
Prep Time: 1 hour	Cost: Moderate

Ingredients

3 cups yellow squash, sliced 1/4-inch
   thick
3/4 cups raw shrimp
2 tablespoons butter
2 tablespoons flour

1/2 teaspoon salt
1/8 teaspoon pepper
1 cup chicken broth
1/2 cup whipping cream
1 tablespoon finely minced onion

Preparation

Thoroughly rinse squash and shrimp, set aside. Heat butter in saucepan. Gradually, blend in flour, salt, and pepper. Cook until it gets bubbly. Remove from heat and add chicken broth, stirring constantly. Bring to a boil for 1 or 2 minutes. Blend in cream and onions. Mix in raw shrimp. Layer squash in a 1-1/2 quart casserole dish. Spoon 1/2 of the shrimp mixture over squash. Repeat with remaining squash and shrimp mixture. Cover tightly and bake in a preheated 400 degree oven for 30 minutes.

Topping Ingredients

1/2 cup coarse ground bread crumbs
1/4 cup grated Parmesan cheese

1 tablespoon butter

Preparation

Toss crumbs, Parmesan cheese and butter. After baking squash for 30 minutes, top with bread crumb mixture. Reduce oven heat to 350 degrees and return casserole to oven for another 15 minutes or until crumbs are golden brown.

Seafood

Imperial Crab

Submitted by: Senator Barbara Mikulski

Meal: Dinner
Prep Time: 45 minutes

Servings: 6
Cost: Moderate

Ingredients

1 pound backfin crab meat
Salt and red pepper to taste
1 green pepper, diced
2 eggs, well beaten (save 2
    tablespoons)

5 tablespoons mayonnaise
1 tablespoon onion, chopped
6 cleaned crab shell
Red pepper to garnish

Preparation

Pick over crab meat. Combine with salt, red pepper, green pepper, eggs, 4 tablespoons mayonnaise and onion. Fill shells. Add 1 tablespoon mayonnaise to remaining egg and put over each filled shell. Dot with red pepper. Bake in a preheated 350 degree oven for about 30 minutes.

Pan Roasted Oysters

Submitted by: Senator Barbara Mikulski

Meal: Dinner   Servings: 4
Prep Time: 20 minutes   Cost: Moderate

Ingredients

1 pint oysters   1/8 teaspoon pepper
2 tablespoons butter   1/2 teaspoon salt
Pinch of paprika   Buttered toast

Preparation

Drain oysters, and place in shallow buttered baking dish. Melt butter, add seasonings, and pour over the oysters. Bake in a preheated 400 degree oven about 10 minutes or until edges begin to curl. Serve immediately over buttered toast.

Seafood

Fried Snapper
Submitted by: Lyndy Kelley

Meal: Dinner
Prep Time: 2 hours

Servings: 6
Cost: Moderate

Ingredients

4 cups water
1/2 cup white vinegar
6 medium red snapper, cleaned
1 tablespoon salt
2 teaspoons finely chopped habanero
  pepper
Juice of 2 limes
1/2 cup flour

1/2 cup canola oil
1/2 teaspoon thyme
Salt and pepper to taste
1 medium onion, finely chopped
1 whole habanero pepper
2 medium tomatoes, peeled, seeded, and
  chopped coarsely
1 lime to squeeze over finished dish

Preparation

Mix a pinch of salt with 1 cup water, and 1 tablespoon vinegar. Wash the fish in the mixture and pat dry with a paper towel, discard mixture. From head to tail slice each fish diagonally, about 1/4 inch deep. Mix the salt with the chopped habanero until it forms a paste. Place some of it into the slit of each fish. Pour the lime juice over the fish and let sit for 45 minutes to 1 hour. Remove the fish from the lime juice and pat dry with a paper towel. Roll each one in flour, shake off excess. Heat the oil in a large skillet and fry the fish over medium heat until golden brown. Remove and set aside. Add the thyme, salt, pepper, onion and whole habanero to the oil and cook until onion is lightly browned, stirring occasionally. Add the tomatoes and cook until a thick sauce forms. Add the remaining water and bring to a boil. Lower the heat and simmer for 5 minutes. Add the fish to the sauce and continue simmering an additional 5 minutes. Remove fish and sqeeze lime juice over it and serve with white rice.

Crabs Chesapeake
Submitted by: Johnny Mathis

Meal: Dinner   Servings: 6
Prep Time: 1 hour   Cost: Moderate

Ingredients

6 strips bacon
2 tablespoons chopped onion
2 tablespoons chopped parsely, add
   string beans, corn, or cabbage to
   taste as a variation
2 cups flaked fresh crabmeat

1/2 cup tomato purée
1/2 cup water
1/2 teaspoon salt
Few dashes black pepper
2 cups uncooked rice

Preparation

Cook and crumble bacon, set aside. Save half of the bacon drippings and sauté the onion, parsley and crabmeat. Add tomato purée, water, salt and pepper. Cook over low heat until blended and heated. Prepare rice according to directions and add the bacon. Serve crabmeat mixture over the rice and bacon.

Seafood

Lobster with Mustard Sauce

Submitted by: Johnny Mathis

Meal: Dinner   Servings: 2
Prep Time: 1 hour, 15 minutes   Cost: Expensive

Ingredients

1 (2-pound) live lobster
Salt and pepper
3 tablespoons butter
1-1/2 cups heavy cream

3 tablespoons mustard
1 tablespoons capers, drained
1 tablespoon cornstarch

Preparation

Place lobster in boiling salted water for 5 minutes, drain. Dot fleshy underside with salt and pepper. Butter a large sheet of foil and place lobster in center and wrap completely. Place in a dish and bake in a preheated 400 degree oven for 45 minutes. Mix cream, mustard, capers, cornstarch, salt and pepper. Heat over moderate heat, stirring constantly until boiling. Remove from heat. Cut lobster in half and pour sauce over. Good served with rice.

Seafood

De Luxe Crabmeat

Submitted by: Dr. and Mrs. Herbert C. Brown, Nobel Laureate

Meal: Dinner
Prep Time: 1 hour

Servings: 2 to 3
Cost: Moderate

Ingredients

2 tablespoons butter
2 buds fresh, squeezed garlic
Pepper to taste

2 tablespoons fresh squeezed lemon juice
8 ounces frozen crabmeat

Preparation

In a double boiler place the butter, garlic, and pepper. After the butter is melted, add the lemon juice and mix well. Allow to cook until just before serving. Just before serving add the crabmeat and heat through, stirring carefully. Serve over steamed rice.

Suggestions

A 4-ounce can of drained button mushrooms may be added to the butter-lemon mixture before adding the crabmeat. Cooked shrimp or lobster meat may be substituted for the crabmeat.

Seafood

Lobster Pili Pili
Submitted by: Barbara Kiura

Meal: Dinner   Servings: 2 to 4
Prep Time: 45 minutes   Cost: Expensive

Ingredients

4 tablespoons vegetable oil
2 onions, chopped
1 teaspoon fresh, chopped ginger
1 pound fresh or canned tomatoes,
   chopped
1 tablespoon tomato paste
8 ounces peeled, cooked shrimp
2 teaspoons ground coriander

1 green chili, seeded and chopped
1 tablespoon ground, dried shrimp or
   crayfish
2-1/2 cups water
1 green bell pepper, seeded and sliced
Salt and fresh ground black pepper
2 cooked lobsters, halved
Fresh cilantro sprigs for garnish

Preparation

Heat the oil in a large skillet. Fry the onion, ginger, tomatoes, and tomato paste for 5 minutes or until the onions are soft. Add the shrimp, ground coriander, chili, and ground shrimp and stir to mix well. Stir in the water, green pepper, salt, and pepper. Bring to a boil and simmer, uncovered, over moderate heat for 20 to 30 minutes or until the sauce is reduced. Add the lobsters to the sauce for a few minutes, until heated through. Arrange the lobster halves on a warm plate and pour sauce over them. Garnish with cilantro sprigs and serve with white rice.

Seafood

Crab Cakes with Lemon Dill Sauce

Submitted by: Cheryl Whitney

Meal: Lunch or Dinner   Servings: 4
Prep Time: 15 minutes   Cost: Moderate

Ingredients

1 package Old Bay Seasoning
1/2 cup mayonnaise

1 pound lump crab meat
Lemon dill sauce (see below)

Preparation

Mix all ingredients, except lemon dill sauce, thoroughly. Form into patties and cover with sauce.

Lemon Dill Sauce Ingredients

2/3 cup mayonnaise
1/3 cup plain yogurt
2 tablespoons chopped fresh or
   1 tablespoon crumbled dried dill

1 teaspoon Dijon mustard
1/8 teaspoon fresh ground pepper
1 tablespoon plus 1 teaspoon fresh lemon
   juice

Preparation

Make sauce by combining all ingredients in a bowl and whisking well. Serve over the crab cakes.

Seafood

Tommy Smothers' Favorite Grilled Avocado Swordfish

Submitted by: Tom Smothers

Meal: Dinner   Servings: 4
Prep Time: 3 hours   Cost: Moderate

Ingredients

4 fresh Swordfish steaks, 1- to 1-1/2-
  inch thick
1 avocado, cut in small chunks
1 red onion, minced
1 teaspoon chopped cilantro
1/2 teaspoon lemon juice

2 cloves garlic, minced
4 tablespoons soy sauce
1 teaspoon Worcestershire sauce
1/2 tablespoon lemon juice

Preparation

Carefully cut a large pocket in the center of the swordfish and set aside. Mix the avocado, onion, cilantro, lemon juice and 1 clove garlic in a large bowl. Stuff the mixture into the fish and secure with a toothpick if need be. Mix together the soy sauce, Worcestershire sauce, lemon juice and last clove garlic. Pour over the fish and let marinate for a few hours in the refrigerator. Grill over hot coals for 2 to 4 minutes per side, until done or burnt, whichever comes first. Seasonings can be adjusted to your personal tastes.

Seafood

Lobster Oriental
Submitted by: Carroll Baker

Meal: Dinner   Servings: 6
Prep Time: 20 minutes   Cost: Expensive

Ingredients

1 small clove garlic, minced
2 tablespoons olive oil
2 pounds uncooked lobster meat, diced
2 tablespoons rum
1/2 cup chicken broth

1 cup snow peas
1 cup bean sprouts
1 cup sliced water chestnuts
2 cups coarsely cut Chinese cabbage
2 cups cooked white rice

Preparation

Sauté garlic with olive oil in a large skillet over medium heat until transparent; do not brown. Add lobster to garlic and cook, turning pieces. Stir in rum, broth, snow peas, bean sprouts, water chestnuts and cabbage into lobster mixture. Simmer uncovered for 5 minutes. Serve over rice.

Seafood

Sweet-and-Sour Baked Fish

Submitted by: Buddy Hackett

Meal:　　　　Dinner　　　　　　　Servings: 4 to 6
Prep Time:　45 minutes　　　　　Cost:　　Moderate

Ingredients

1 whole fish 2- to 3-pounds, or a size
　which will fit into your skillet or wok
　(choices: carp, sea bass, red
　snapper, cod)
1 slice (1/8 inch thick) ginger root

1 clove garlic
1 tablespoon peanut, corn, or other oil
2 tablespoons cornstarch
1/3 cup oil

Preparation

Wash the fish inside and out, then pat it dry with paper towels. Rub the fish inside and out with the ginger root and garlic. Rub oil on the outside. This will help keep it from sticking when fried. Pat the cornstarch on the outside of the fish. Set aside while you prepare the sauce.

Sauce Ingredients

5 tablespoons sugar
1 tablespoon lemon juice
3 tablespoons rice vinegar or red wine
　vinegar

2 tablespoons catsup
1 tablespoon soy sauce
1 tablespoon cornstarch
1/2 cup cold water

Preparation

In a one-quart pot combine sugar, lemon juice, vinegar, catsup and soy sauce. Bring to a boil, reduce heat and simmer uncovered for 2 to 3 minutes. Stir the cornstarch and water together until it is smooth. Blend the cornstarch-water mixture into the sauce, stirring until it boils and thickens. Keep the sauce warm over a very low heat. Put the 1/3 cup oil into a wok or 12 inch skillet and heat to medium. If the oil is too hot the fish will stick. If you use a wok, swish the oil around so the sides are coated to also prevent sticking. Carefully place the fish into the pan or wok and cook for 3 minutes, all the while spooning oil over the top of the fish. Cover and continue to cook for another 5 to 10 minutes, depending on the size. Uncover and carefully turn the fish over. Brown the other side for about 2 minutes. Very carefully transfer the fish to a large platter. Pour the sauce over the fish and serve immediately.

Seafood

Succulent Fried Fish

Submitted by: Bill Cosby

Meal: Lunch or Dinner
Prep Time: 30 minutes

Servings: 1 to 4
Cost: Inexpensive

Ingredients

1/2 stick butter
2 cloves garlic, peeled
Piece of ginger, peeled
1/2 cup corn oil

4 rinsed fillets of fish
Salt, pepper, paprika to taste
1/2 cup flour or corn meal

Preparation

Place butter, corn oil, garlic and ginger in unheated frying pan. Turn heat on under the pan and let it get very hot while taking care not to burn the ginger and garlic. Season the fish with the salt, pepper and paprika. Put the flour or corn meal in a plastic bag and season with more salt, pepper and paprika. Remove garlic and ginger from the pan. Lightly flour the fish and place in the hot oil. Cook for about 15 minutes.

Suggestions

Have more fish on hand. the hungry <u>person</u> who ate all of the four fillets will want more.

Seafood

Maryland Crab Cakes

Submitted by: Dr. Robert Forsythe

Meal: Dinner
Prep Time: 30 minutes

Servings: 6
Cost: Inexpensive

Ingredients

1 pound crab meat
4 slices white bread, crust removed
1 tablespoon mayonnaise
1 tablespoon Worcestershire sauce
1/4 teaspoon dry mustard

1/4 teaspoon salt
1 egg, beaten
1 tablespoon chopped fresh parsley
1 tablespoon baking powder
1 tablespoon Old Bay Seasoning

Preparation

Clean crab meat by squeezing through fingers to remove all shell and cartilage (low priced crab meat is fine for crab cakes if you clean it properly). Break bread into small pieces and moisten with a little milk. Mix the crab meat and bread then add the other ingredients and mix together. Shape into cakes and fry in skillet with 1/2 inch of hot oil until brown on both sides. Watch closely or they will burn. Do not place many cakes in skillet at one time. The same mixture can also be shaped into small balls and deep fried for hot appetizers. Serve these with cocktail sauce or with catsup seasoned with horseradish and Old Bay Seasoning.

Beef

Recipe   Page

Burgundy Beef 4-1
Survival Chili 4-2
Sloppy Joes 4-3
Stuffed Green Peppers 4-4
Sauer Braten.. 4-5
Barbeque Meatloaf... 4-6
Swedish Meatballs 4-7
Mel's Meatloaf Surprise 4-8
Easy Burritos... 4-9
Kathy Mattea's Goulash.. 4-10
Beef Bourguignon 4-11
Grilled Steak with Shitake Mushrooms and Garlic.................. 4-12
Stuffed Shells.. 4-13
Tzimmis... 4-14
Stuffed Green Peppers 4-15
Turkish Stuffed Grape Leaves 4-16
Big Phil's Steak Stir Fry.. 4-17
Leutonian Cabbage Rolls.. 4-18
Homemade Meatballs and Sauce 4-19
Steakburgers... 4-20
Keftedes.. 4-21
Company Roast Beef.. 4-22
Stone Harbor Hamburgers.......... 4-23
Stuffed Cabbage 4-24
Archangel's Meatballs 4-25

Beef

Burgundy Beef

Submitted by: Nancy Squibb

Meal: Dinner   Servings: 4
Prep Time: 7 hours   Cost: Moderate

Ingredients

2 pounds round steak, cut into 1/2 inch
   cubes
1 cup burgundy wine

Cooking oil
2 cans cream of mushroom soup
1 package onion soup mix

Preparation

Put beef and wine in casserole dish and let stand for 1 hour. Remove meat and brown in hot cooking oil. Meanwhile, add soups to wine in casserole dish, mix well. Add meat and juices from pan to casserole dish, mix well. Cover tightly and bake at 250 degrees for 6 hours. Serve over rice or noodles. May be prepared a day ahead of time and put in the refrigerator until ready to bake.

Beef

Survival Chili

Submitted by: Randy Milne

Meal: Dinner   Servings: 6
Prep Time: 4 hours   Cost: Moderate

Ingredients

2 tablespoons oil
1/2 cup minced onion
1 teaspoon minced garlic
2-1/2 pounds lean boneless beef chuck,
    cut into 1/2 inch cubes
1 (12-ounce) can of beer
1/2 teaspoon black pepper
1 (8-ounce) can whole tomatoes,
    crushed
1 (8-ounce) can tomato sauce

1/2 cup chopped green pepper
1/16 teaspoon ground red pepper
1-1/2 teaspoons ground cumin
1 teaspoon salt
1/2 teaspoon crushed oregano leaves
1/2 teaspoon paprika
1-1/2 cups water
1 (4-ounce) can green chilies, undrained
    and chopped
4 teaspoons chili powder

Preparation

In large saucepot heat oil until hot. Sauté onion and garlic. Add 1/2 of the meat and
brown well on both sides. Remove meat with a slotted spoon and then finish browning
other 1/2 of the meat. Return all meat to the saucepot after browning and add the
remaining ingredients. Bring to a boil, reduce heat and cover. Simmer for 3 hours and
stir occasionally. Add more water if needed.

Beef

Sloppy Joes
Submitted by: Peggy Hager
in memory of Chuck Johnston (8/20/65 - 6/11/92).

Meal: Lunch or Dinner   Servings: 4
Prep Time: 45 minutes   Cost: Inexpensive

Ingredients

2 tablespoons olive oil
1 pound ground meat
1/2 cup onion, chopped
1/2 cup celery, diced
1/4 large green pepper, chopped
1/2 teaspoon garlic powder or 2 fresh
  cloves, chopped very fine
2 tablespoons vinegar
1 tablespoon brown sugar

1 (12-ounce) jar chili sauce
1/4 cup catsup
1/2 teaspoon chili powder
1/4 cup water
1 teaspoon salt
1/8 teaspoon pepper
1 tablespoon Worcestershire sauce
1/2 teaspoon paprika
1 tablespoon parsley, chopped

Preparation

Brown meat in oil, drain off excess fat. Add all remaining ingredients. Simmer, uncovered, for 30 minutes. Spoon onto buns to serve.

Stuffed Green Peppers

Submitted by: Richard & Lynda Petty, Car #43
in memory of Tim Richmond.

Meal: Dinner   Servings: 6
Prep Time: 1 hour   Cost: Inexpensive

Ingredients

6 bell peppers, cut in half and cleaned   2 eggs
1-1/2 pounds ground meat   1 cup catsup
1 medium onion, chopped fine   1 cup cornflakes
1 tablespoon chili powder   Salt and pepper to taste

Preparation

Boil peppers in water for 5 minutes. Mix all other ingredients together. Stuff peppers and place in a large glass dish. Pour sauce that follows over peppers and bake in a preheated 375 degree oven for 30 to 40 minutes.

Sauce Ingredients

2-1/2 cups catsup and tomato paste,   2 tablespoons ground mustard
    use more catsup than paste   1 tablespoon vinegar
2 tablespoons brown sugar

Preparation

Combine all ingredients thoroughly before pouring over peppers.

Beef

Sauer Braten

Submitted by: Robert Sankey

Meal: Dinner
Prep Time: 1 to 3 days

Servings: 6
Cost: Moderate

Ingredients

1-1/2 cups apple cider
1/2 cup cider vinegar
1 tablespoon ground ginger
1 tablespoon ground allspice
1 tablespoon cinnamon
1 onion, chopped
1 carrot, chopped

2 stalks celery, chopped
2 tablespoons sugar
2 pounds round steak, trim fat
2 tablespoons oil
10 to 12 ginger snap cookies, ground to
   powder

Preparation

Combine all ingredients, except for the steak, oil and cookies, to make marinade. Place steak in a large glass dish and add marinade ingredients. Marinate for 24 hours (up to 72 hours for best flavor) in the refrigerator. When ready, remove meat from marinade, pat dry. Brown meat in skillet using the oil, set aside. Strain the marinade through a colander (some recipes call for the marinate to be processed to a liquid, it's your choice) into the skillet. Stir in the ginger snaps, bring to a simmer. Add the steak and continue to simmer for 20 minutes. If sauce is to thin, add more ginger snaps. If too thick, more apple cider. Ladle over Poor Man's Dumplings on Page 10-8. Serve with brown bread and a stout beer.

Beef

Barbeque Meatloaf

Submitted by: Thelma Ferrell
in memory of Hubert Osborne.

Meal: Dinner   Servings: 6
Prep Time: 1 hour, 30 minutes   Cost: Inexpensive

Ingredients

1-1/2 pounds lean ground beef
1 cup bread crumbs
1 egg

1 medium onion, cut up
Salt and pepper to taste
1 (8-ounce) can tomato sauce

Preparation

Mix all ingredients together and shape into a loaf. Place in a bread pan and pour the following sauce over the loaf before baking.

Sauce Ingredients

2 tablespoons vinegar
3 tablespoons brown sugar
2 tablespoons mustard

2 tablespoons Worcestershire sauce
1 (8-ounce) tomato sauce
1/2 can water

Preparation

Mix all ingredients together. Pour over loaf and bake in a preheated 375 degree oven for 1 hour and 15 minutes.

Beef

Swedish Meatballs

Submitted by: Dana Magnone

Meal: Dinner   Servings: 6
Prep Time: 1 hour   Cost: Moderate

Ingredients

6 slices toasted bread   2-1/2 teaspoons salt
2/3 cup milk   1/2 teaspoon pepper
1/2 pound ground pork   1/2 teaspoon nutmeg
3-1/2 pounds ground beef   1/3 cup butter
4 eggs   1-1/2 cups water
2 onions, diced   4 ounces mushrooms

Preparation

Soak toast in milk until soft. Thoroughly mix milk, ground pork, ground beef, eggs, onions, salt, pepper and nutmeg in a large bowl. Form mixture into walnut-size meatballs. Brown meatballs in butter. Add water and simmer for 30 minutes. Finish by adding mushrooms and heating through.

Beef

Mel's Meatloaf Surprise
Submitted by: Melvin and Beverly Pollock
for Larry and Robert Pollock, victims of AIDS.

Meal: Dinner   Servings: 4 to 5
Prep Time: 1 hour, 30 minutes   Cost: Inexpensive

Ingredients

1/2 teaspoon olive oil
1 medium onion (preferably Vidalia),
  chopped
3 mushrooms, chopped
1 pound ground chuck
1 pound ground turkey

1 slice of bread (preferably whole wheat)
1/4 cup apple sauce
1/2 teaspoon crushed garlic
1 raw egg
1/2 teaspoon salt free seasoning
1/4 cup soy sauce

Preparation

Place olive oil, onion and mushrooms in a microwave-safe bowl and simmer in microwave for 2-1/2 minutes. Combine mixture with the remaining ingredients by hand and mold into a loaf. Set loaf in a draining pan and place in a preheated 375 degree oven for 1 hour and 15 minutes.

Beef

Easy Burritos
Submitted by: Faye Allen Bell

Meal: Lunch or Dinner   Servings: 6
Prep Time: 30 minutes   Cost: Inexpensive

Ingredients

1 pound ground beef
1 package burrito seasoning mix
1-1/3 cup water
6 (10-inch round) tortillas

1 (16-ounce) can refried beans
1 (8-ounce) package shredded cheese
1 (8-ounce) jar thick and chunky salsa

Preparation

Cook meat over medium to high heat for 3 to 4 minutes or until no longer pink, drain. Add water and seasoning and cook another 3 to 4 minutes or until thickened. Warm tortillas according to directions. On each tortilla spread refried beans, 1/3 cup meat, 2 tablespoons cheese, and 2 tablespoons salsa. Fold and serve.

Beef

Kathy Mattea's Goulash
Submitted by: Kathy Mattea

Meal: Dinner   Servings: 8
Prep Time: 2 hours   Cost: Inexpensive

Ingredients

1 pound ground beef or turkey (can be omitted for vegetarians)
1 green bell pepper, sliced
1 red bell pepper, sliced
1 medium yellow onion, sliced
1 can mild, green chilis, optional
1 (8-ounce) can tomato sauce
1 teaspoon cumin powder

1 teaspoon chili powder
Cayenne pepper, optional
1/2 small can jalepenos, optional
1 can kidney beans
1 can white cannellini beans. optional (these are hard to find, another white bean can be used)
1/2 pound cooked macaroni

Preparation

Brown ground meat, add peppers, onion and chilis, if using them. Cook until peppers and onion are turning soft. If you are not using meat, cook peppers and onion in a little olive oil and add a little water to finish. Add tomato sauce and the spices. If need be add a little more spices, according to your tastes. The cayenne and jalepenos do add a lot of heat to this recipe. Add the beans and heat through and the juicey parts start to thicken up. Add macaroni last until it is heated through. Note: This freezes well and is great the next day after all the flavors have gotten into everything. Do not be afraid to experiment with the spices and come up with your own ideas.

Beef

Beef Bourguignon

Submitted by: Candace O'Keefe

Meal: Dinner

Prep Time: 3 hours, 30 minutes

Servings: 6

Cost: Moderate

Ingredients

1/2 pound mushrooms, sliced
1/4 cup butter
3 slices bacon, cut up
2 pounds boneless beef, cut into 2-inch cubes
2 tablespoons flour
2 cloves garlic, crushed
1 tablespoon tomato paste

1-1/4 cups red cooking wine
2 beef bouillon cubes
2 tablespoons sugar
1/4 teaspoon salt
1/4 teaspoon thyme
1 small bay leaf
1 peppercorn
1/2 pound small, white onions

Preparation

In large pot, sauté mushrooms in butter, remove and set aside. Fry bacon until crisp, remove and set aside. Add meat to drippings and brown well. Blend in flour. Add garlic, tomato paste, wine and seasonings. Cover and simmer for 2 hours, stirring occasionally. Add onions, mushrooms and bacon, simmer another hour longer. Add additional wine if liquid has evaporated. Serve over rice, noodles, or mashed potatoes.

Beef

Grilled Steak with Shitake Mushrooms and Garlic

Submitted by: Laurie Johnson for Sid.

Meal: Dinner   Servings: 4
Prep Time: 1 hour   Cost: Moderate

Ingredients

3-1/2 tablespoons soy sauce
3-1/2 tablespoons Chinese rice wine
1 tablespoon sugar
2 pounds shell steak
2 tablespoons vegetable oil

1 pound shitake mushroom caps, thinly
  sliced
12 cloves garlic, thinly sliced
1/2 cup chicken broth

Preparation

Mix together 2-1/2 tablespoons soy sauce, 1-1/2 tablespoons Chinese rice wine and 1 tablespoon sugar. Marinate steak in the mixture for 30 minutes at room temperature. Heat vegetable oil in a wok or skillet, add mushrooms and garlic and stir fry for 1 minute. Add broth and remaining rice wine, continue to stir fry until mushrooms are soft and liquid is evaporated. Add remaining soy sauce, reduce heat and keep warm. Grill steak on an oiled rack, 5 to 6 inches from heat, approximately 10 to 12 minutes on each side. After grilling, let meat stand for 10 minutes then slice across the grain. Transfer the steak to a platter and serve topped with the mushrooms.

Stuffed Shells

Submitted by: Traci Sanders

Meal: Lunch or Dinner   Servings: 10
Prep Time: 45 minutes   Cost: Inexpensive

Ingredients

1 large box shells
1 pound ground beef or turkey
4 large cloves garlic
Large jar spaghetti sauce
Large package Mozzarella cheese
Large handfull of Parmesan or Romano
  cheese

2 tablespoons parsley
2 tablespoons basil
2 tablespoons oregano
Dash of sage, thyme, rosemary, marjoram,
  and savory

Preparation

Cook noodles according to directions, set aside. In a large skillet, brown meat with the garlic and drain well. While still warm, add spices and cheeses except for a handful of Mozzarella. Mix all well, it will be messy. Spread a thin layer of spaghetti sauce in the bottom of a 9x13-inch pan. Fill shells with meat mixture and line up in the pan, open end up. Cover with remaining sauce and cheese. Bake in a preheated 375 degree oven for 20 to 30 minutes or until cheese is melted and a little crispy. Spices may be adjusted to your tastes.

Beef

Tzimmis

Submitted by: Terry G. Gouchnour

Meal: Dinner   Servings: 6
Prep Time: 4 hours   Cost: Inexpensive

Ingredients

3 pound beef brisket   1/2 pound prunes
2 bunches carrots   Salt and pepper to taste
3 to 4 sweet potatoes   4 cups boiling water
2 to 3 white potatoes

Preparation

Sear meat in fat. Mix all vegetables together. Set in a roasting pan and arrange vegetable mixture in circle around meat. Sprinkle with salt and pepper. Add the boiling water and cover. Bake in a 350 degree oven for 3 hours, 30 minutes. Uncover and add sweet paste (recipe follows). Bake an additional 30 minutes.

Sweet Paste Ingredients

1/3 cup brown sugar   1/4 cup cold water
2 tablespoons flour

Preparation

Mix ingredients well.

Stuffed Green Peppers

Submitted by: Christine Salera Seiler

Meal: Dinner   Servings: 2
Prep Time: 1 hour   Cost: Inexpensive

Ingredients

2 large green peppers
1 pound ground beef
3 cloves minced garlic or 1-1/2
    tablespoon garlic powder
1/4 of large onion, grated fine or
    1 tablespoon onion powder

1 (15-ounce) can tomato sauce
1/3 cup long grain white rice
1/2 cup water
Salt and pepper to taste
3/4 cup Cheddar cheese

Preparation

Cut peppers in half, lengthwise, and remove stems and seeds. Immerse peppers in boiling water for 3 minutes. Sprinkle insides with salt and invert to drain. Brown ground beef and drain grease. Stir in garlic, onion, 1/2 can tomato sauce, uncooked rice, water, salt and pepper. Let simmer for 15 minutes. Stir in 1/2 cup cheese and mix through. Fill pepper halves with the meat mixture. Coat the bottom of a 13x9-inch pan with tomato sauce. Place stuffed peppers in the pan and cover with remaining tomato sauce. Bake in a preheated 375 degree oven for 12 minutes. Cover the peppers with the rest of the cheese and bake another 2 minutes.

Turkish Stuffed Grape Leaves

Submitted by: Scout Thomas

Meal: Dinner	Servings: 8 to 10
Prep Time: 2 hours	Cost: Inexpensive

Ingredients

3 pounds ground beef or lamb
1 cup dry rice
1/4 cup lemon juice
1/4 cup tomato juice

1/2 onion, finely chopped
1 clove crushed garlic
1 large jar grape leaves
1 (48-ounce) can tomato juice

Preparation

Mix together ground beef, rice, lemon juice, 1/4 cup tomato juice, onion and garlic. Make into meatball shapes, depending on the size of the grape leaves. Be sure to cut off any excess stems from the leaves. Start filling the leaves with meat mixture at stem base. While rolling the leaves be sure to tuck sides in. In the bottom of a pot, pour some tomato juice to cover the bottom so the leaves don't stick. Place the leaves in the pot, stacking them on top of each other. When all leaves have been wrapped pour remaining tomato juice over them until it is level with the leaves. Bring to a boil. Cover and simmer for 1-1/2 hours, depending on amount of leaves. The sauce that follows compliments the taste of the grape leaves well.

Sauce Ingredients

1 quart plain yogurt

1-1/2 teaspoons garlic salt

Preparation

Mix ingredients well and let sit for an hour.

Beef

Big Phil's Steak Stir Fry

Submitted by: Phillip Thompson

Meal: Lunch or Dinner
Prep Time: 1 hour

Servings: 4
Cost: Moderate

Ingredients

Steamed rice
1 medium Vidalia onion, peeled and
sliced
1/2 green pepper, sliced medium
thickness

2 large steaks, cut into strips
2 teaspoons soy sauce, may need more
Lawrey's "red hot" seasoned salt, to taste
8 large frozen broccoli spears

Preparation

Start cooking rice according to directions, it should be done about the same time as the stir fry. Combine the onions and green peppers, set aside. Take the steaks and add the soy sauce and seasoned salt to taste. Combine with the vegetables in a large skillet and set aside. Boil some water for the broccoli and cook them for about 3 to 4 minutes. The key is to get and keep them hot without them getting mushy. Start stir frying the meat and vegetables on medium-high heat, constantly stirring. Add more soy sauce and/or seasoned salt according to your tastes. Cook until meat has reached a desired doneness for you. Remove immediately and serve over rice, placing 2 broccoli spears on each side of the plates.

Beef

Leutonian Cabbage Rolls

Submitted by: Sons and Daughters of Leutonia,
Lawrence Pius Shmenge Memorial Chapter

Meal: Dinner
Prep Time: 3 hours

Servings: 6
Cost: Inexpensive

Ingredients

1 large head cabbage
1-1/2 pounds ground beef
1 egg
1/2 cup cooked rice
2 stalks celery, diced and sautéed
2 small onions, diced and sautéed

Salt and pepper to taste
1/4 pound bacon, sautéed, reserve
  drippings
2 cans tomato sauce
2 cans water
Flour to thicken to consistency of gravy

Preparation

Parboil cabbage in large pot of salted water. Mix meat with egg, rice, celery, 1 small onion, salt and pepper. Take small balls of meat mixture and wrap in cabbage leaves. Place in roast pan. Mix on stove top bacon, drippings, tomato sauce, remaining onion, water and flour. When a gravy consistency is reached pour over cabbage rolls. Bake in a preheated 350 degree oven for 1hour, 30 minutes.

Beef

Homemade Meatballs and Sauce
Submitted by: Judith Di Perna

Meal: Dinner
Prep Time: All Day

Servings: 8 to 10
Cost: Inexpensive

Meatball Ingredients

3 pounds ground beef or a mixture of
   ground pork, beef and veal
5 large eggs
1/3 cup crushed or fresh parsley
   chopped very fine

1/4 cup crushed basil or 10 fresh basil
   leaves chopped very fine
Seasoned salt and pepper
3 cups grated bread crumbs
3/4 cup Romano cheese

Preparation

Mix together the meat, eggs, parsley, basil, salt and pepper. Use a fork to do most of the mixing to ensure meat stays tender. Add the bread crumbs and thoroughly mix well with your hands. Shape into balls a little larger than golf balls. On medium heat, sauté meatballs on all sides forming a protective barrier.

Sauce Ingredients

2 cloves garlic, optional
Light olive oil
1 large can tomato sauce
1 large can tomato puree
1 large can crushed tomatoes

1 large can tomato paste
2 beef bouillon cubes
1 whole large onion
2 to 3 cans water
1 to 2 cups wine, optional

Preparation

In large pot, sauté garlic in olive oil. Add sauce, puree, tomatoes, paste, bouillon and onion. Add the water until the sauce is about 2 inches from the top. Add meatballs to sauce and simmer on low heat all day. Serve topped with the cheese.

Steakburgers

Submitted by: Barbara Shearer

Meal: Lunch or Dinner
Prep Time: 45 minutes

Servings: 4
Cost: Inexpensive

Ingredients

1 cup bread crumbs
1/2 cup milk
1 pound ground chuck, steak or round
  steak
1 onion, minced
1/2 teaspoon salt

1/8 teaspoon pepper
4 tablespoons Worcestershire sauce
2 tablespoons vinegar
1/4 cup sugar
1 cup catsup

Preparation

Mix together the bread crumbs, milk and meat. Form into patties and brown on both sides, set aside. Mix together remaining ingredients and pour over patties. Cover and simmer for 20 minutes.

Beef

Keftedes

Submitted by: Jill Kornberg

Meal: Dinner
Prep Time: Overnight

Servings: 6
Cost: Inexpensive

Ingredients

1 pound ground beef
2 slices wet bread, squeeze out excess
  water
1 medium onion, chopped
1/2 teaspoon garlic powder or minced
  garlic
1/3 cup vinegar

1/3 cup oil
1 egg
1/2 handful mint leaves, crumbled
1/2 handful grated Romano cheese
4 tablespoons hot water
Salt and pepper to taste
Flour, enough to coat patties

Preparation

Mix all above ingredients, except flour, and let sit overnight in refrigerator. Form into patties and coat with flour. Fry in a pan until well done and crispy. To make Keftedes Sauce reserve drippings and add to the Pasta Sauce on Page 9-34.

Beef

Company Roast Beef

Submitted by: Reverend David and Kathy Keller

Meal: Dinner   Servings: 6 to 8
Prep Time: Overnight   Cost: Moderate

Ingredients

4 to 5 pounds chuck or rump roast
2 large onions, thinly sliced
1 green pepper, thinly sliced
1/2 cup dry red wine
1/4 cup water

1/2 pound fresh mushrooms, sliced
1 teaspoon Worcestershire sauce
1 teaspoon seasoned salt
1 teaspoon garlic salt

Preparation

Place the meat in a Dutch oven. Combine everything else and pour over the roast. Bake at 325 degrees for at least 4 hours adding more wine or water as needed. Cool to room temperature on serving dish. Put dish in refrigerator and leave overnight. The next day slice meat, put it back into the sauce and reheat for dinner.

Beef

Stone Harbor Hamburgers
Submitted by: Bill Hackney

Meal: Lunch or Dinner
Prep Time: 45 minutes

Servings: 4 to 6
Cost: Inexpensive

Hamburger Ingredients

1 pound ground round
3 tablespoons chopped onion
1/2 teaspoon salt
1/2 teaspoon seasoned pepper

1/2 teaspoon Italian herbs
1 tablespoon chopped parsley
1 crushed clove garlic
1/4 cup coffee cream

Preparation

Mix all ingredients lightly. Grill 12 minutes for medium. 7 minutes for rare. Top with mushroom sauce.

Mushroom Sauce Ingredients

1 stick butter
1-1/2 tablespoons catsup
1-1/2 teaspoons Worcestershire sauce

1 teaspoon dry mustard
1 tablespoon lemon juice
12 ounces sliced mushrooms

Preparation

Melt the butter. Mix in the other ingredients then add the mushrooms and cook for 5 minutes.

Stuffed Cabbage

Submitted by: Senator Carl Levin

Meal: Lunch or Dinner   Servings: 4 to 6
Prep Time: 1 hour, 30 minutes   Cost: Inexpensive

Ingredients

1 pound ground beef
1/4 cup uncooked rice
1 egg

Grated onion or onion powder to taste
1/4 teaspoon salt
Steamed cabbage leaves

Preparation

Mix the beef, rice, egg, onion (or onion powder) and salt. Place a big spoonful of the mixture on a cabbage leaf and roll making sure all ends are folded in. Cook the stuffed leaves in the following sauce.

Sauce Ingredients

1/4 cup lemon juice or vinegar
1/4-1/2 cup brown sugar

1 cup tomato sauce, water or tomato juice
   to cover

Preparation

Simmer at least one hour, but longer if possible.

Beef

Archangel's Meatballs

Submitted by: John Martine

Meal: Dinner
Prep Time: 1 hour

Yields: 24 to 26 meatballs
Cost: Inexpensive

Ingredients

3 to 4 slices stale Italian bread soaked
  in water
1 pound freshly ground round steak or
  chuck roast
1/2 cup chopped parsley (flat leaf Italian
  preferably)

1/3 cup freshly grated Romano cheese
1 large egg
Salt and pepper to taste
1/3 cup vegetable oil for frying

Preparation

While the bread is soaking, Place beef, parsley and cheese in a large mixing bowl. Thoroughly squeeze-dry the bread. Tear off chunks of the bread and add it to the bowl. Add the egg, salt and pepper and mix until everything is evenly distributed. Start making the meatballs by using the palm of one hand (left if your are right-handed) and three fingers of the other hand. Use enough of the mixture to make a ball slightly smaller than a golf ball. Heat the oil in a non-stick frying pan. Once the bottoms have browned, turn the meatballs until browned all over.

Suggestions

I make enough meatballs to fill the frying and while they are browning, I am making up the next batch. These can be placed in your favorite sauce and served with pasta. Smaller versions of these meatballs can also be used in the traditional Italian wedding soup.

This recipe was never written down, but learned Sunday after Sunday by watching my mother, Archangel Traficante Martine, prepare these meatballs to be served with pasta as a part of our traditional Sunday repast. Although these were cooked barely an hour or two before being placed on the table, most of us were able to have at least one or two or three prior to their being placed in the simmering tomato sauce. Every time I make these meatballs for friends or family, I am brought back to those happy memories of my youth. Please enjoy!

Poultry

Recipe	Page
Spicy Chicken	5-1
Coq au Vin Blanc	5-2
Arroz con Pollo	5-3
Parmesan Chicken Breasts	5-4
Texas White Chili	5-5
Fajitas Xavier	5-6
Senator Richard Lugar's Famous Lime and Cilantro Grilled Turkey Breast in Pita Pockets	5-7
Chicken and Rice Pilaf	5-8
Mrs. Helms' Recipe for Chicken Pot Pie	5-9
Mel Tillis' Chicken and Rice Supreme	5-10
Dove on the Grill	5-11
Marty's Garlic Chicken with Potatoes	5-12
Chicken Can Can	5-13
Chicken and Lima Beans	5-14
Honey-Pecan Fried Chicken	5-15
Turkey Shepherd's Pie	5-16
Duck and Wild Rice	5-17
Honey Mustard Chicken	5-18
Dick Smothers' Refrigerator Stir Fry	5-19
Chicken Tettrazini	5-20
Chicken in Foil	5-21
Greek Chicken	5-22
Chicken Casserole with Stuffing	5-23
Chinese Barbecued Chicken	5-24
Chicken Breast Supreme	5-25
Rich and Famous Chicken	5-26
Chicken Romano	5-27
Chicken Divan	5-28
Spiced Roast Chicken	5-29
Chicken with Spinach and Feta	5-30
Spicy Habanero Legs	5-31
Chicken and Grapes in Sauterne	5-32
Pollo a la Pasquale	5-33
Paprikash Chicken	5-34
Chicken Tarragon/Lemon	5-35
Pheasant Stuffed Cabbage	5-36

Poultry

Spicy Chicken

Submitted by: Elizabeth Taylor

Meal: Dinner   Servings: 4
Prep Time: 3 hours or more   Cost: Inexpensive

Ingredients

2 teaspoons curry powder
1 teaspoon cumin
1/2 teaspoon ground ginger
1/2 teaspoon tumeric

1/2 clove garlic, crushed
1 onion chopped
1 teaspoon fresh ginger, grated
1 medium chicken, cut into serving pieces
   and skinned

Preparation

Combine dry ingredients with garlic, onion and fresh grated ginger. Coat chicken with mixture and refrigerate for 2 hours, preferably longer. Place on moderately hot barbecue grill or broil in oven approximately 30 minutes or until done, turning once.

Poultry

Coq au Vin Blanc

Submitted by: The Author in memory of Freddie Mercury.

Meal: Dinner   Servings: 4
Prep Time: 3 hours   Cost: Expensive

Ingredients

1 large chicken, cut into serving pieces
1/4 cup vegetable oil
3 tablespoons flour
1/4 cup Cognac
3 onions, quartered
2 cloves garlic, diced
3 cups dry white wine
1 tablespoon sugar
1 teaspoon salt
1/4 teaspoon onion powder
1 teaspoon chopped parsley
1/4 teaspoon tarragon

1/8 teaspoon thyme
1/8 teaspoon black pepper
1 pint mushrooms
1 cup green peppers
2 tablespoons butter
1 teaspoon sugar
3 tablespoons Cognac
1 tablespoon Madeira
3 tablespoons flour
1/4 cup water
1 tablespoon chopped parsley

Preparation

Step 1:   Brown chicken pieces in hot oil. Drain when brown. Sprinkle chicken with
          flour. Stir pieces until absorbed. Pour 1/4 cup Cognac over chicken and set
          aflame with match. Allow flame to burn out.

Step 2:   Add quartered onions, garlic, wine, sugar, salt, onion powder, parsley,
          tarragon, thyme and black pepper. Stir until mixture starts to boil. Reduce
          heat and simmer for 1 hour.

Step 3:   Sauté mushrooms and green peppers in butter for 2 minutes. Drain and set
          aside.

Step 4:   When chicken is done, add mushrooms, green peppers, Cognac and
          Madeira. Heat 5 minutes. Mix flour with water until a paste forms. Finish the
          sauce by slowly adding the paste while stirring constantly. Sprinkle with
          chopped parsley.

Suggestions

Serve the same wine used during preparation with the meal.

Poultry

Arroz con Pollo
Submitted by: George Romero

Meal: Dinner   Servings: 6 to 8
Prep Time: 3 hours   Cost: Expensive

Ingredients

4-5 pounds of chicken - 2 whole fryers cut into pieces, or separately packaged breasts, legs, wings...whichever you prefer. (The taste is improved by using parts that contain bones.)
3 teaspoons salt
Freshly ground black pepper to taste
Juice of 2 limes
3/4 cup olive oil - my father liked the strong taste of a hearty Spanish olive oil, but many (like myself) prefer the gentler quality of *extra-virgin*.
8 tablespoons (1 stick) unsalted butter
2 medium-sized onions, finely chopped
2 medium-sized green bell peppers, seeded and finely chopped
10 garlic cloves, minced - here again it's a matter of your taste...or the tastes of your guests. My father used 24 cloves. I use 12 to 18 depending on their size. I've found the fresh chopped garlic in jars, available in most supermarkets, is fine for this recipe. I use 12 teaspoons.
1-1/2 cups canned crushed tomatoes - if you prefer some extra zest, use a flavored tomato sauce...preferably one that you've made yourself, though *Newman's Own* will do.

1-1/2 pounds chorizos (optional) - spicy Spanish sausage available in specialty markets. I have used hot Italian sausage, but I cook it separately and press slices of it into the rice when the casserole is nearly ready. Many people prefer not to add any sausage at all. The recipe tastes terrific without it. It's a Spanish tradition, however, to include this added surprise of taste and texture.
1 teaspoon ground cumin
1 teaspoon oregano
2 bay leaves
3/4 cup dry white wine
5 cups chicken stock - canned stock will serve, but I doctor it with bullion cubes or *Bovril* for extra taste. I much prefer to make my own stock (recipe follows) which can be prepared in advance and kept frozen.
2 cups rice - *Valencia* (Spanish rice) if possible, though *Uncle Ben's* is fine.
1 teaspoon powdered saffron (or 1 vial of saffron threads) - some supermarkets and most gourmet shops carry saffron, but I must admit that it's difficult to find. Saffron is essential to many Spanish recipes, especially those which contain rice. It provides a "special" flavor that really, really makes a difference. If you're going to go to the effort of cooking *Arroz con Pollo*, I strongly urge you to go to the *extra* effort of locating saffron.
2 cups early sweet peas
1 jar whole pimientos, sliced into thin strips for garnish
Black olives, for garnish

Arroz con Pollo (continued)
Submitted by: George Romero

Preparation

Step 1: Wash the chicken and dry it with paper towels. If you are using whole chickens, chop them into small pieces (or have the butcher do it for you). Drumsticks and wings can be left whole, but breasts, even pre-packaged, should be cut into 1-1/2 inch cubes. Sprinkle all the pieces with the salt, pepper and lime juice (at least one hour ahead).

Step 2: If you are using *Valencia* rice, soak it for one hour in cold water to cover with 1/4 teaspoon of powdered saffron. (If you are using saffron threads, turn 3 or 4 of them to powder in your fingers. After soaking, drain and set aside. If you are using *Uncle Ben's* or the equivalent, eliminate this step and see step 5.

Step 3: If you are using chorizos, cook the links in a saucepan full of water for 30 minutes to eliminate fat. Let cool, then cut into thin slices. If you are using hot Italian sausage, slice it first with a sharp knife. Boil the slices for 20 minutes, drain, and let stand.

Step 4: In a large, heavy casserole over medium heat, heat 1/2 cup of the olive oil and 3 tablespoons butter until it is fragrant, then brown the chicken 6 to 8 minutes on each side. Remove the chicken and set it aside. Add the remaining oil and cook the onions, bell peppers and garlic until the onion is transparent (8 to 10 minutes). Add the tomatoes (or tomato sauce), cumin, oregano and bay leaves Cook for 5 minutes, stirring constantly. Add the browned chicken, the chorizos (if you are using real chorizos, not other sausage) and the wine, combining the mixture well. Cook for another 5 minutes.

Step 5: Add 2 cups of the stock. Check the seasoning for taste. Add salt, pepper and more oregano if needed (The mixture should be well seasoned since the rice will absorb much of the flavor).

Step 6: If you are using *Uncle Ben's* rice, or the equivalent, sauté the dry rice in a skillet with the remaining 5 tablespoons of butter, making sure all grains are covered and golden

Step 7: Remove the bay leaves. Add the rice and the saffron to the casserole (if using saffron threads, powder them in your fingers). Bring to a boil over high heat. Cook uncovered, until most of the liquid has been absorbed. Stir all ingredients vigorously so that the rice is laced throughout with the chicken parts. Add additional stock, 1/2 cup at a time, until rice is cooked to a fluffy consistency (25 to 30 minutes). You will not need all 5 cups of the stock. Remove from heat.

Poultry

Arroz con Pollo (continued)
Submitted by: George Romero

Step 8:   Preheat oven to 350 degrees.

Step 9:   If you are using hot Italian sausage, at this point press the slices into the rice with your fingers, so they are buried.

Step 10:   Spread peas over the entire surface of the casserole. Decorate with pimiento slices and black olives (be creative).

Step 11:   Place casserole in oven for 20 minutes. (If rice has absorbed all the liquids, carefully pour more stock over the casserole so it will not bake dry.)

Stock Ingredients

4 quarts canned chicken broth
1 whole chicken, chopped into 8 parts
3 or 4 veal bones (if available)
1 large onion, peeled and quartered
4 ripe plum tomatoes, quartered
3 large carrots, peeled and cut into
   1 inch pieces
3 celery stalks, cleaned and cut into
   1 inch pieces (use leaves)

1 bunch of parsley, cleaned
10 garlic cloves, crushed
1-1/2 teaspoons salt (or to taste)
12 black peppercorns (or to taste)
3 bay leaves
1/2 teaspoon powdered saffron (or 8
   threads, crushed)
Any other vegetable or meat seasoning
   you desire

Preparation

Step 1:   Place all solid ingredients in a large stock pot. Cover with canned chicken broth. (If it does not cover add water.) Bring to a boil over medium-high heat and cook for 20 minutes, skimming the surface occasionally to remove fat and other floating residue. Reduce heat and simmer, partially covered, for 2 hours, adding water, if necessary, to keep ingredients covered.

Step 2:   Remove from heat and cool to room temperature. Strain through a colander to remove all solids. Then pour through a strainer lined with cheesecloth into a large bowl.

Step 3:   Refrigerate, allowing fats to rise to the surface. Skim off fats and pour clarified stock into storage containers. (A friend taught me to use large *Ziplok* bags which can be stored flat, saving space.) Stock will keep for several days in a refrigerator, or it can be frozen.

Poultry

Arroz con Pollo (continued)

Submitted by: George Romero

Suggestions

This is a family recipe, handed down to me by my father, for a traditional chicken and rice casserole. *Arroz con Pollo* appears on the menu in most Hispanic restaurants but I, having grown up with my father's Cuban variation, have never found one that tasted better. The preparation is somewhat time consuming, but not at all complicated. It's the sort of dish that can be cooked on a Sunday afternoon while watching the *Steelers* and sipping a *cervesa*.

Serve at a table so guests can appreciate the look of your decorated casserole. I use a clay pot handed down from generations who believed that it not only enhanced appearance, but brought decades of *"seasoning"* to the flavor.

Accompany with a salad and good bread.

Poultry

Parmesan Chicken Breasts
Submitted by: Barbara F. Rodebaugh

Meal: Dinner   Servings: 2
Prep Time: 1 hour   Cost: Inexpensive

Ingredients

2 chicken breasts, deboned and
   skinless
1 cup bread crumbs
1/2 cup grated Parmesan cheese

2 teaspoons garlic flakes
2 teaspoons onion salt
1 cup buttermilk

Preparation

Cut chicken breasts in half, and using a mallet, pound until 1/4 inch thick. Combine bread crumbs, Parmesan cheese, garlic flakes and onion salt. Dip chicken breasts in buttermilk then into bread crumb mixture. Let set for 30 minutes. Quick fry 3 to 5 minutes on each side.

Poultry

Texas White Chili

Submitted by: J. Michael Bell
in memory of all who have passed in the race for the cure.

Meal: Dinner   Servings: 10
Prep Time: 2 hours   Cost: Moderate

Ingredients

1 pound dry white beans
1 quart chicken stock, 1/2 quart extra
  may be needed
2 medium onions, chopped
2 teaspoons garlic
1 teaspoon salt
1 tablespoon corn oil
1 (4-ounce) can green chilies, chopped
2 teaspoons ground cumin

2 teaspoons crushed, dried oregano
2 teaspoons ground coriander
1/8 teaspoon cloves
1/8 teaspoon cayenne pepper
4 cooked boneless, skinless, chicken
  breasts, diced
1/2 cup grated Monterey Jack cheese
4 green onions, thinly sliced

Preparation

Combine beans, one quart of stock, half of the onion, garlic and salt in large kettle.
Bring to a boil. Reduce heat, cover, and simmer 1-1/2 hours or until beans are very
tender. Add remaining chicken stock as needed. Heat oil in skillet, add remaining
onion and cook until tender and clear, about 5 minutes. Add chilies, cumin, oregano,
coriander, cloves and cayenne pepper, mix thoroughly and cook another 20 minutes.
Add bean and skillet mixture together. Place chicken in the bottom of a bowl, spoon
chili over the top and sprinkle with the cheese and green onions.

Poultry

Fajitas Xavier

Submitted by: Tim & Xavier Evans

Meal: Dinner
Prep Time: 1 hour

Servings: 8
Cost: Inexpensive

Tortilla Ingredients

8 tortillas

Butter

Preparation

Preheat oven to 350 degrees. Spread butter in a very, very thin layer on top of each tortilla, stack them, and wrap them in foil. Place tortillas in center of oven rack and cook for 15 minutes. A short cut would be to use the microwave oven. If using the microwave, skip the butter and wrap the tortillas in a damp towel and heat them a few minutes before serving.

Filling Ingredients

1 pound skinless, boneless, chicken
   breasts, cut into strips
1 teaspoon vegetable oil
4 large cloves garlic, diced
1 small red pepper, cut in strips
1 small green pepper, cut in strips

1 small onion, diced
1 small tomato, cut in quarters, then
   halved again
1 teaspoon "epazote de comer", available
   in Mexican food stores
Salt to taste

Preparation

Put oil in large frying pan. Add chicken and fry until no longer pink. Add garlic and stir until garlic is translucent. Add peppers and onions. Cook 3 to 4 minutes, until vegetables are no longer raw. Add tomatoes, salt and epazote de comer. Stir, cover, and heat about 5 minutes more until tomatoes are no longer firm. Taste and adjust garlic, salt and epazotede comer, if necessary. Spoon mixture into the heated tortillas. Toppings to taste such as guacamole, sour cream and salsa (see Page 1-8). Fold tortillas over starting with the left side as it faces you, then the bottom, then the right side.

Poultry

Senator Richard Lugar's Famous Lime and Cilantro Grilled Turkey Breast in Pita Pockets

Submitted by: Senator Richard Lugar

Meal: Dinner   Servings: 10 to 20
Prep Time: 1 hour, 45 minutes   Cost: Moderate

Ingredients

1-1/2 pounds turkey breast tenderloins
2 limes, juiced
1 tablespoon paprika
1/2 teaspoon onion salt
1/2 teaspoon garlic salt
1/2 teaspoon cayenne pepper
1/4 teaspoon white pepper

1/2 teaspoon fennel seeds
1/2 teaspoon thyme
10 pitas, cut in half
1-1/2 cups lettuce, shredded
1-1/2 cups avocado salsa (recipe follows)
1-1/2 cups sour cream salsa (recipe
    follows - optional)

Preparation

Rub turkey with the lime juice. In small bowl, combine paprika, onion salt, garlic salt, cayenne pepper, white pepper, fennel seeds and thyme. Sprinkle mixture over fillets. Cover and refrigerate for at least an hour. Preheat charcoal grill for direct heat cooking. Grill turkey 15 to 20 minutes or until meat thermometer reaches 170 degrees or turkey is no longer pink in the middle. Turn tenderloins over halfway through the grilling time. Allow turkey to stand 10 minutes. Cut into 1/4 inch strips. Fill each pita half with turkey, lettuce, avocado salsa, and, if desired, the sour cream sauce.

Poultry

Senator Richard Lugar's Famous Lime and Cilantro Grilled Turkey Breast in Pita Pockets (continued)

Submitted by: Senator Richard Lugar

Avocado Salsa Ingredients

1 avacodo, diced
1 lime, juiced
2 tomatoes, seeded and diced

1/2 cup green onion, minced
1/2 cup green pepper, minced
1/2 cup fresh cilantro

Preparation

In small bowl, combine avacodo and lime juice. Stir in tomatoes, green onion, green pepper and cilantro. Cover and refrigerate until ready to use.

Sour Cream Sauce Ingredients

1 cup sour cream
1 teaspoon salt
1/4 cup green onion, minced

1/4 cup green chili peppers, minced
1/4 teaspoon cayenne pepper
1/2 teaspoon black pepper

Preparation

In a small bowl, mix all above ingredients thoroughly. Cover and refrigerate until ready to use.

Chicken and Rice Pilaf

Submitted by: Jazmine Brockington
in memory of Giovanni, Craig Allen, Ricki and William.

Meal: Dinner   Servings: 4 to 5
Prep Time: 1 hour, 30 minutes   Cost: Moderate

Ingredients

1-1/3 cups pre-cooked rice
1/2 envelope dry onion soup
1 can condensed cream of mushroom
  soup
1/4 cup sherry (optional)
1-1/4 cups boiling water

Salt and pepper to taste
4 to 5 chicken breasts, boneless
4 to 5 tablespoons butter, depends on
  amount of chicken used
Paprika

Preparation

In casserole dish, combine rice, onion soup, mushroom soup, optional sherry, boiling water, salt and pepper. Place chicken on top, brush with the butter, then sprinkle paprika on top for coloring. Cover, bake in a preheated 375 degree oven for 1-1/4 hours or until chicken is done.

Mrs. Helms' Recipe for Chicken Pot Pie

Submitted by: Senator and Mrs. Jesse Helms

Meal: Lunch or Dinner   Servings: 8
Prep Time: 2 hours, 30 minutes   Cost: Inexpensive

Crust Ingredients

1 cup self-rising flour
1 cup milk

1 stick melted butter
1 teaspoon baking powder

Preparation

Mix all above ingredients thoroughly.

Filling Ingredients

1 chicken, cooked and deboned
1 cup chicken broth
1 can cream of mushroom soup

1 can cream of chicken soup
1 large can mixed vegetables, drained

Preparation

Cube chicken. Put the filling into a 9x11-inch glass dish. Pour the dough mixture over the top of the chicken. Bake in a preheated 325 degree oven for 45 minutes.

Mel Tillis'
Chicken and Rice Supreme

Submitted by: Mel Tillis

Meal: Dinner   Servings: 6
Prep Time: 2 hours   Cost: Moderate

Ingredients

1 (4-pound) whole chicken, cut into
    serving pieces
1/4 red bell pepper, chopped
1/4 yellow bell pepper, chopped
1/4 green pepper, chopped
1 stalk celery, chopped
1 carrot, chopped

1 large onion, chopped
3 cloves garlic, minced
3 cups Jasmine Rice (found in oriental
    food stores)
1 teaspoon black pepper
1 teaspoon salt
5 cups water or chicken broth

Preparation

Remove excess skin and fat from chicken, leaving some for flavoring. Place into a medium pot. Put all vegetables, garlic, rice, salt and pepper into the pot. Mix all ingredients thoroughly by hand. Add the water or chicken broth, if using the broth do not add salt or it will be to salty. Put the pot on the stove and bring to a boil. After it comes to a boil put a lid on and turn heat to low. Let cook at low heat for approximately 1 hour.

Poultry

Dove on the Grill

Submitted by: Senator Richard Shelby

Meal: Dinner   Servings: 1
Prep Time: 45 minutes   Cost: Moderate

Ingredients

Dove (allow at least 2 per person)   Bacon (1/2 slice per bird)
Salt, pepper, Worcestershire to taste

Preparation

Sprinkle dove with seasonings. Wrap each dove with bacon. Secure with toothpick if necessary. Cook over medium fire until done, about 20 to 30 minutes. Turn occasionally.

Suggestions

Variation: Wrap 1/2 strip of bacon around a water chestnut and a boneless dove breast. Season lemon butter with Worcestershire sauce and baste frequently. Cook on grill or broil until bacon is done.

Marty's Garlic Chicken with Potatoes

Submitted by: Joanna Kerns in memory of Robert Watts.

Meal: Dinner   Servings: 1
Prep Time: 1 hour, 45 minutes Cost: Moderate

Ingredients

Chicken breasts with skin (allow 1 or 2 per person)
Potatoes with or without skins, cut in pieces (allow 1 or 2 potatoes per person)

Lots of garlic, peeled, cleaned, and minced
Salt
Paprika
Olive oil

Preparation

In a large baking dish, lay chicken fat side up with potatoes. Sprinkle garlic (lots of it), salt, paprika and olive oil on chicken and potatoes. Bake in a preheated 350 degree oven for 1 hour and 20 minutes. Half way through cooking time, turn chicken breasts.

Vegetarian?: No

Poultry

Chicken Can Can

Submitted by: Barb Loesch

Meal: Lunch or Dinner   Servings: 6
Prep Time: 1 hour   Cost: Inexpensive

Ingredients

1 can cream of celery soup
1 can cream of mushroom soup
1 can cream of chicken soup
1 can chicken with rice soup

1 can of water
1 can of evaporated milk
3 cups cooked chicken
1 can of chow mein noodles

Preparation

Add only the 1 can of water to this recipe. Mix all ingredients together and bake in a preheated 350 degree oven for 45 minutes.

Chicken and Lima Beans

Submitted by: Demetra Patukas in memory of George Patukas.

Meal: Dinner   Servings: 6
Prep Time: 1 hour, 45 minutes   Cost: Moderate

Ingredients

1 large onion, chopped
1/2 cup olive oil
1 chicken, cut up
Salt and pepper to taste

2 tablespoons tomato paste or 4 ounces
   tomato sauce
1 cup water
4 to 5 tablespoons fresh or dried dill
2 packages frozen baby lima beans

Preparation

Sauté onion in oil until transparent. Add chicken and brown on all sides. Add salt and pepper. Dissolve tomato paste in water or add the tomato sauce to the water and add to the chicken. Add the dill and enough water to just about cover the chicken. Simmer for about 1/2 hour to 3/4 hour or until chicken can be pinched. Add lima beans. Cook rapidly for a few minutes then lower flame and cook until a good portion of the liquid has been cooked away.

Poultry

Honey-Pecan Fried Chicken

Submitted by: Alex and Jean Trebek

Meal: Dinner
Prep Time: 2 hours, 30 minutes

Servings: 8
Cost: Moderate

Ingredients

8 chicken breasts
4 cups buttermilk
1 cup flour
3/4 teaspoon salt
1/4 teaspoon garlic powder

1/4 teaspoon cayenne pepper
1 cup butter
1/2 cup honey
1/2 cup coarsely chopped pecans
Vegetable oil

Preparation

Wash chicken pieces and pat dry. Pour buttermilk into a large bowl. Add chicken, cover and refrigerate 1-1/2 hours. Drain chicken. Combine flour, salt, garlic powder and cayenne pepper. Dredge chicken in flour mixture, shaking off excess. Let chicken stand for 20 minutes at room temperature. Melt butter in heavy, small saucepan over low heat. Stir in honey and bring to a boil. Add pecans and simmer, glazing for 15 minutes. Meanwhile, heat 1/2-inch to 3/4-inch oil in heavy, large skillet. Add chicken (do not crowd) and fry until crisp, golden brown and cooked through, about 7 minutes per side. Drain on paper towels and arrange on platter. Pour glaze over top and serve immediately.

Suggestions

Chicken skins may be removed to decrease fat. Also, it is nice to lightly roast the pecans for a slighly different flavor.

Turkey Shepherd's Pie

Submitted by: Elsie Hillman for so many friends.

Meal: Dinner   Servings: 6
Prep Time: 1 hour   Cost: Inexpensive

Ingredients

1 pound ground turkey
1/2 pound ground veal or beef
Salt
Pepper
1 large yellow/orange pepper, cut into
   strips
1 medium onion, chopped
4 cloves garlic, crushed

1 (14 1/2-ounce) can tomatoes (boxed
   Pomi seedless tomato or 8 ounces
   tomato sauce and 7 ounces light cream)
1 cup chicken broth, divided
1 tablespoon Worchestershire sauce
1/4 teaspoon dried rosemary
1/2 teaspoon red pepper sauce (optional)
2 tablespoons flour
Mashed potatoes

Preparation

Spray skillet with non-stick cooking spray. Combine turkey and other meat and cook in skillet 4 to 5 minutes, breaking up lumps. Remove meat with slotted spoon, add salt and pepper. Wipe skillet clean and spray again with non-stick cooking spray over medium heat. Add pepper, onion and garlic. Cook until soft, but still slightly crispy. In a large saucepan, bring the tomatoes, 3/4 cup chicken broth, Worchestershire sauce, rosemary and optional pepper sauce to a boil. Add pepper mixture and reduce heat to low, simmering for 5 minutes. Season to taste. In a small bowl, stir 1/4 cup chicken broth into 2 tablespoons flour until smooth. Stir broth into tomato mixture until thickened and remove from heat. Stir meat mix into tomato mixture and turn into casserole dish. Cover with mashed potatoes and bake in a preheated 375 degree oven for 15 to 20 minutes until points are brown.

Vegetarian?: No

Poultry

Duck and Wild Rice
Submitted by: Johnny Mathis

Meal: Dinner
Prep Time: 2 hours

Servings: 8
Cost: Expensive

Ingredients

2 or 3 ducks
Salt and pepper
1/2 cup onion, chopped

1 green pepper, sliced
2 or 3 celery stalks, cut
3 cups water

Preparation

Clean ducks and rub with the salt and pepper. Place in baking pan, breast side up. Add onions, green pepper, celery and water to pan. Cover and bake in a preheated 325 degree oven for 2 hours or until ducks are tender. Baste occasionally. Serve on a bed of wild rice.

Honey Mustard Chicken

Submitted by: Senator Frank R. Lautenberg

Meal: Dinner   Servings: 6
Prep Time: 1 hour, 30 minutes   Cost: Inexpensive

Ingredients

1 stick butter, melted   Salt and pepper to taste
1/2 cup honey   1 (3- to 4-pound) chicken, cut up
1/4 cup dijon mustard

Preparation

Mix all ingredients, except chicken, thoroughly. Place chicken in a baking dish and pour honey mixture over it. Bake in a preheated 350 degree oven for 60 to 75 minutes or until nicely browned, basting often. Serve with rice.

Dick Smothers'
Refrigerator Stir Fry

Submitted by: Dick Smothers

Meal: Dinner	Servings: 4
Prep Time: 20 minutes	Cost: Inexpensive

Sauce Ingredients

1/3 cup canned chicken stock, defatted (set aside 1/4 cup)
1 tablespoon soy sauce
1 tablespoon teriyaki sauce

2 teaspoons fresh grated ginger root, optional
1 teaspoon corn starch

Preparation

Mix all ingredients thoroughly and set aside.

Stir Fry Ingredients

3 boneless chicken breasts, cut into 1 inch cubes
3 cloves garlic, chopped
Vegetable Oil

4 cups vegetables, use any combination you prefer (potatoes, peas, tomatoes, broccoli, corn, cauliflower, celery, just to name a few), cut into 1 inch cubes

Preparation

Sauté chicken and garlic until done. Coat wok or large skillet with vegetable oil and heat. Add 1/4 cup of chicken broth and vegetables. Stir fry vegetables for 2 to 3 minutes, stirring constantly. Add cooked chicken and sauce. Cook another 2 to 3 minutes, stirring constantly until liquid thickens.

Suggestions

Be creative with this recipe and use different vegetables each time.

Poultry

Chicken Tettrazini

Submitted by: Representative Sue Myrick

Meal: Dinner   Servings: 6
Prep Time: 1 hour, 30 minutes   Cost: Inexpensive

Ingredients

1 box rotini
12 teaspoons butter
Parmesan cheese
4 boneless chicken breasts, broken into
pieces

2/3 cup flour
2 cups chicken broth
4 cups half and half
1 teaspoon salt
4 tablespoons Sauterne

Preparation

Cook rotini according to directions. Toss with 4 teaspoons of butter and a bit of
Parmesan cheese. Cook chicken in the broth and save broth. Melt 8 teaspoons butter
and add the flour to thicken the sauce. Add chicken broth and the half and half and
cook until it thickens (i.e.-when it bubbles). Add the salt and Sauterne and let simmer.
Layer in a casserole dish the noodles, chicken and then sauce. Cover with Parmesan
cheese and bake in a preheated 350 degree oven for 25 to 30 minutes.

Poultry

Chicken in Foil

Submitted by: Brian Rohleder for Jim Hanneken.

Meal: Dinner
Prep Time: 1 hour

Servings: 4
Cost: Inexpensive

Ingredients

2 chicken breasts, halved
Vegetables, cut up (your choice)
Salt and pepper to taste

Herbs, Italian seasoning, garlic powder, oregano,
   rosemary, lemon pepper (your choice)
Butter
White Wine, 1/8 cup per chicken half

Preparation

Place 1/2 a chicken breast on a piece of heavy duty foil. Over the chicken pour
vegetables, salt, pepper, herbs, dots of butter and the wine. Fold foil completely to
enclose chicken. Place on a cookie sheet and bake in a preheated 350 degree oven
for about 40 minutes. Allow one pack per person.

Greek Chicken

Submitted by: Sandy Mervosh

Meal: Dinner   Servings: 3
Prep Time: 1 hour   Cost: Inexpensive

Ingredients

1 onion, chopped
1/2 teaspoon minced garlic
4 tablespoons olive oil

1 large bunch of fresh spinach
3 boneless, skinless chicken breasts
1 cup crumbled Feta cheese

Preparation

Sauté onion and garlic in 2 tablespoons olive oil. Add washed and trimmed spinach.
Cook until done, about 10 minutes. Beat chicken until flat. Place 2 tablespoons
spinach mixture in center of chicken and sprinkle with the cheese. Wrap chicken and
close with toothpicks. Brown in 2 tablespoons olive oil. Then bake in a preheated 350
degree oven for 1/2 an hour. Serve with roasted vegetables.

Poultry

Chicken Casserole with Stuffing

Submitted by: John Jarrett

Meal: Dinner   Servings: 8
Prep Time: 4 hours, 30 minutes   Cost: Inexpensive

Ingredients

1 whole chicken and 6 chicken breasts
1 large onion, chopped fine
1 stalk celery, chopped fine
2 sticks butter
Box of croutons or 1/2 bag onion and
   sage stuffing

1 large loaf Italian bread, broken into small
   pieces
2 eggs
1 can cream of chicken soup
1 can cream of celery soup
1-1/2 cans chicken broth

Preparation

Cook chicken in enough water to cover, may need to add more water during cooking, about 3 hours. Cool and debone, set aside. Save broth. Sauté onion and celery in the butter, set aside. Mix croutons and Italian bread then add sautéedd onion and eggs and just enough broth to make moist. Layer in a casserole dish, starting with the stuffing then the chicken. Repeat until all is used up. Mix together the cream of chicken soup, cream of celery soup and the cans of broth. Pour over chicken and cover. Bake in a preheated 350 degree oven for 25 minutes. Uncover and bake another 15 minutes.

Chinese Barbecued Chicken

Submitted by: Chevy and Jayni Chase

Meal:　　　Dinner　　　　　　Servings: 8
Prep Time:　2 hours, 30 minutes　　Cost:　　　Inexpensive

Ingredients

4 tablespoons peanut oil
2 tablespoons fresh ginger root,
　chopped
1/4 cup scallions, chopped
2 cloves garlic, chopped

1/3 cup soy sauce
1 tablespoon sugar
1 tablespoon sesame oil
17 chicken thighs or 3 pounds chicken
　parts

Preparation

In a small skillet or saucepan, heat peanut oil until hot. Add ginger, scallions and garlic, stir-frying for 1 minute. Add the soy sauce and sugar, bring to a boil. Turn off heat and add sesame oil. Marinate the chicken in this mixture for 1 to 2 hours. Remove chicken from marinade and barbecue or broil until golden brown. Baste with marinade. Turn pieces over and cook until done. Skin should be crispy.

Poultry

Chicken Breast Supreme

Submitted by: Joseph Lesnick
in memory of George W. Goss (1953 - 1995).

Meal: Dinner
Prep Time: 2 hours

Servings: 6
Cost: Inexpensive

Ingredients

3 medium whole chicken breasts,
   halved
3/4 teaspoon seasoned salt
Paprika
1 chicken bouillon cube
1 cup boiling water

1/4 cup Sauterne, optional
1/2 teaspoon instant minced onion
1/2 teaspoon curry powder
Dash of pepper
Mushroom sauce, recipe follows

Preparation

Sprinkle chicken with seasoned salt and paprika and place in a 11x7x1-1/2-inch baking pan. Dissolve bouillon cube in boiling water. Add wine, onion, curry powder and pepper. Pour over chicken and cover with foil. Bake in a preheated 350 degree oven for 30 minutes, then uncover and cook an additional 45 minutes, or until chicken is done. Remove chicken to warm platter, strain and reserve juces. Pour mushroom sauce over and serve.

Mushroom Sauce Ingredients

2 tablespoons flour
1/4 cup cold water

1 (3-ounce) can sliced mushrooms,
   drained

Preparation

In saucepan blend flour with water. Slowly add the reserved pan juices. Cook and stir over low heat until sauce thickens and bubbles, boil an additional 3 to 4 minutes. Add the mushrooms and heat through.

Poultry

Rich and Famous Chicken
Submitted by: Robin Leach

Meal: Dinner   Servings: 4 to 6
Prep Time: 4 hours   Cost: Expensive

Ingredients

8 tablespoons unsalted butter
3 tablespoons all-purpose flour
2 cups Essence of Silver and Gold (see Page 9-20)
Salt and fresh ground pepper to taste
2 large onions, sliced
1 whole chicken (3-1/2 to 5 pounds), cut into 8 pieces
1 cup Champagne
1/4 cup fresh basil leaves, finely chopped (2 tablespoons dried)
2 tablespoons fresh oregano, finely chopped (1 tablespoon dried)

1/2 teaspoon dried mustard
1 tablespoon fresh squeezed lemon juice
2 teaspoons steak sauce
1 pound carrots, peeled, halved, and cut into 1-inch pieces
1/2 pound white mushrooms, trimmed, wiped clean, and thinly sliced
1 cup green peas
4 medium potatoes, peeled and cut into 1/2-inch cubes
1 cup heavy cream

Preparation

In a medium, heavy saucepot melt 3 tablespoons of the butter over moderately high heat. Stir in the flour. Reduce heat to medium and cook slowly, whisking constantly, until well blended, about 3 to 5 minutes. Stir in Essence of Silver and Gold and bring to boil. Reduce heat and simmer until sauce is thickened and smooth, 7 to 10 minutes, stirring constantly. Season to taste with salt and pepper. Remove from heat and keep warm. Place the onions in the bottom of a baking dish. Cut 2-1/2 tablespoons of the butter into thin slices and place evenly over the onions. Rinse and pat the chicken dry. Season with salt and pepper. Place the chicken on top of the onions and sprinkle with 2 tablespoons of the Champagne. Add the basil, oregano, mustard, lemon juice and the steak sauce. Arrange the carrots, mushrooms and peas on top of the chicken. Top with thin slices of the remaining butter. Sprinkle with 2 more tablespoons of Champagne. Pour the sauce of Silver and Gold over the chicken and sprinkle with the remaining Champagne. Sink the potato cubes into the sauce, leaving them only slightly submerged. Cover tightly and bake in a preheated 425 degree oven until vegetables and chicken are done, about 45 to 50 minutes. Remove the cover and cook until the protruding potatoes are lightly browned, about 10 minutes. Arrange the chicken and vegetables on a serving platter, cover to keep warm. In a medium saucepan over high heat boil the cream until it is reduced by 1/2, 3 to 5 minutes. Add the reduced cream to the pan juices and boil for several minutes to reduce and thicken. Pour over the chicken and serve immediately. Note: This recipe can be done in a "romertopf" (a clay pot designed for kitchen use), in a covered baking dish, or in a dutch oven. If using a romertopf consult a clay pot cookbook for cooking times and temperatures.

Poultry

Chicken Romano

Submitted by: Laura Kunig in honor of Penn Staters' lost to AIDS.

Meal: Dinner
Prep Time: 30 minutes

Servings: 4
Cost: Inexpensive

Ingredients

2 chicken breasts, halved
1 cup Romano cheese
1/2 tablespoon garlic salt
1/2 cup flour
1/8 teaspoon pepper
1 teaspoon salt

3 eggs
1/2 cup water
1 tablespoon parsley flakes
Garlic powder
1 stick butter
Fresh lemon

Preparation

In a freezer bag, mix together the Romano cheese, garlic salt, flour, pepper and salt, set aside. Mix together the eggs, water, parsley flakes and garlic powder. Dip chicken into egg mixture then shake in freezer bag. Melt butter in a nonstick skillet. Cook the chicken for about 5 to 6 minutes on each side. Set cooked chicken on a paper towel to remove excess butter. Sprinkle with more Romano cheese and garnish with lemon before serving.

Chicken Divan

Submitted by: Evelyn Brock

Meal: Lunch or Dinner   Servings: 6
Prep Time: 1 hour   Cost: Inexpensive

Ingredients

6 chicken breasts
2 cans golden cream of mushroom soup
2 packages frozen or fresh broccoli,
   cooked

8 to 10 ounces sharp longhorn cheese,
   grated
1 cup bread crumbs
1 stick butter

Preparation

Place chicken in a 9x13-inch pan. Pour soup over chicken, cover with foil and bake in a preheated 375 degree oven for 45 minutes. Lay broccoli on top of chicken and cover with cheese. Cover and bake another 5 minutes. Melt butter and mix with bread crumbs. Sprinkle bread crumbs over chicken. Place chicken in oven and bake for 2 to 3 minutes, uncovered.

Poultry

Spiced Roast Chicken

Submitted by: Vice President Al Gore

Meal: Dinner   Servings: 4
Prep Time: 2 hours, 30 minutes   Cost: Moderate

Ingredients

2 tablespoons olive oil
1 onion, finely chopped
1 teaspoon garam masala
4 ounces button or brown mushrooms,
    chopped
1 cup coarsely grated parsnips
1 cup coarsely grated carrots
1/4 cup minced walnuts
2 teaspoons chopped fresh thyme

1 cup fresh white bread crumbs
1 egg, beaten
Salt and pepper to taste
1 (3-1/2-pound) chicken
1/4 cup water
1 tablespoon butter
2/3 cup marsala
Thyme and watercress sprigs for garnish

Preparation

In a large saucepan, heat olive oil. Add onion and sauté 2 minutes or until softened. Stir in 1 teaspoon garam masala and cook 1 minute. Add mushrooms, parsnips and carrots. Cook, stirring for 5 minutes. Remove from heat and add walnuts, thyme, bread crumbs, egg, salt and pepper. Stir to mix well. Stuff chicken with this mixture. Place breast side down in a roasting pan, add water. Roast 45 minutes, turn chicken breast side up and dot with butter. Roast about 45 minutes or until meat thermometer inserted in thickest part of thigh registers 185 degrees, do not touch bone. Transfer to platter and keep warm. Pour off and discard fat from roasting pan, add marsala to remaining cooking juices, stirring to scrape up any browned bits. Boil over high heat for 1 minute to reduce slightly, adjust seasonings. Garnish with thyme and watercress. Serve with seasonal vegetables.

Chicken with Spinach and Feta
Submitted by: LuAnn Johnson

Meal: Dinner
Prep Time: 1 hour, 30 minutes

Servings: 4
Cost: Moderate

Ingredients

4 tablespoons olive oil
1 medium onion, chopped
1 pound fresh spinach, stems removed
  and coarsely chopped
1/2 cup ricotta cheese
1/2 cup crumbled feta cheese

1 teaspoon dried basil
Freshly ground black pepper
4 boneless, split chicken breasts, with
  skins
1/2 teaspoon dried rosemary
1/4 teaspoon salt

Preparation

In a large skillet, heat 2 tablespoons olive oil and sauté onion until just soft. Add spinach, cook over medium heat about 10 minutes or until wilted. Place in bowl and let cool. Add the ricotta, feta, 1/2 teaspoon basil and season with pepper to taste. Loosen skin on chicken and stuff by putting 1/4 of spinach/cheese mixture between skin and meat of each breast. Place breasts in 9x13-inch pan, skin side up. Sprinkle remaining olive oil, basil, rosemary and salt on top. Bake in a preheated 375 degree oven for 45 minutes or until golden brown.

Spicy Habanero Legs

Submitted by: David and Deborah Patron

Meal: Dinner	Servings: 6
Prep Time: 3 hours	Cost: Inexpensive

Ingredients

6 chicken legs
2 eggs

4 to 5 tablespoons habanero sauce

Preparation

Remove skin and fat from chicken. In a separate bowl mix eggs and habanero sauce. Poke holes in chicken legs and pour habanero sauce over legs. Cover and refrigerate for at least 2 hours, turning occasionally. Cover a baking pan with aluminum foil, coat with cooking spray and place legs on top. Bake in a preheated 350 degree oven for 45 minutes, or until done.

Chicken and Grapes in Sauterne

Submitted by: Mary Ann Lyons

Meal: Dinner   Servings: 4
Prep Time: 45 minutes   Cost: Moderate

Ingredients

4 split chicken breasts
2 tablespoons butter
1/2 cup cooking sauterne
2 tablespoons orange marmalade
1-1/2 teaspoons basil

3/4 teaspoons salt
1/2 cup heavy cream
2 cups seedless grapes
Cooked rice

Preparation

Preheat an electric fry pan to 395 degrees. Brown the chicken breasts in the butter. In separate bowl, mix sauterne, orange marmalade, basil and salt. Pour over browned chicken and cook on 250 degrees for 20 minutes, keep covered. Remove chicken from pan and reduce heat. Add cream to the mixture in the pan. Bring to a boil and add grapes to desired consistency. Serve over rice.

Pollo a la Pasquale

Submitted by: Pat Macioce

Meal: Dinner   Servings: 6 to 8
Prep Time: 1 hour, 30 minutes   Cost: Moderate

Ingredients

4 boneless, skinless chicken breasts
1/2 cup dry white wine or white grape
  juice
8 ounces white or shittake mushrooms

1 can black olives
Salt and pepper to taste
1 clove garlic crushed

Preparation

Place all of the above in a casserole dish, cover and bake at 350 degrees for 45 minutes to an hour. This can also be made on top of the stove. Sauté on low for 25 minutes.

Paprikash Chicken

Submitted by: Floyd Patterson

Meal: Dinner   Servings: 4 to 6
Prep Time: 1 hour   Cost: Moderate

Ingredients

1 can cream of mushroom soup   1 tablespoon Hungarian paprika
8 ounces sour cream   Salt and pepper to taste
1 pint fresh mushrooms sliced   1 fryer chicken, cut up

Preparation

Preheat the oven to 350 degrees. Mix together everything except the chicken in a mixing bowl. Place the chicken in a baking dish and top with the mixture. Bake for 40 minutes or until done.

Suggestions

Serve over rice or egg noodles with steamed broccoli and carrots. Chicken is done when a fork is easily inserted and removed and the juices run clear.

Chicken Tarragon/Lemon
Submitted by: Diane Cilento

Meal: Dinner   Servings: 6
Prep Time: 2 hours   Cost: Inexpensive

Ingredients

1 whole chicken   3 fresh lemons
2/3 ounces butter   Salt and pepper to taste
Dried tarragon   Oil

Preparation

Take the chicken, whatever size, and trim the fat from the inside of the body cavity. Place butter inside the cavity. Put dried tarragon on top of the butter. Cut lemons in half and cover the tarragon (cut end first) with lemon. Repeat so that the bird is filled then sprinkle a small amount of tarragon on the outside skin. Salt and pepper to taste. Oil the skin and place in a hot oven to roast. When the bird is cooked and the outside skin is a delicate crisp light brown, take out of the oven and remove the lemons from inside the bird. Squeeze the lemon over the chicken and reserve the sauce which can be used to flavour the noodles you may serve with the dish.

Poultry

Pheasant Stuffed Cabbage

Submitted by: Mathieu Wahrung

Meal:	Dinner	Servings: 4
Prep Time:	2 hours	Cost: Expensive

Ingredients

1 pheasant, cut in pieces
Oil
1 leek, sliced
4 turnips, 2 sliced and 2 diced
4 carrots, 2 sliced and 2 diced
1 shallot, chopped
1/2 clove garlic, chopped
3 cups good white wine
2 cups chicken stock

Salt and pepper to taste
1 head cabbage
Fistful parsely, finely chopped
Fistful chervil
4 tomatoes, peeled, seeded and diced
4 mushrooms, diced
1 ounce butter
2 tablespoons flour
Nutmeg to taste

Preparation

In a skillet, fry pheasant until golden brown. Sauté in a little oil the leek, sliced turnips and sliced carrots. Add the wine and the chicken stock. Add the salt and pepper to taste then add the pheasant. Simmer for 1 hour. Carefully remove cabbage leaves and remove hard center. Blanche cabbage for 2 minutes, dry with absorbent paper towel and set aside. Blanche the diced turnips and carrots for 5 minutes in salted water. Use 1 teaspoon of salt per quart of water. Set aside the parsley and the chervil. Briefly sauté the mushrooms and set them aside. With butter and flour make a light roux. Once the pheasant is cooked, separate the flesh from the skin and chop it coarsely. Mix meat, vegetables, mushrooms and herbs. Adjust seasonings. Pass the sauce through a strainer and reduce it to a 1/4 of its original volume. Readjust seasonings. On a kitchen towel, place cabbage leaves to form a diameter of 20 inches. In the center, put a fistful of stuffing, cover with cabbage leaves. Alternate the layers of stuffing and cabbage while maintaining a spherical shape, close with the first leaves. Fold the towel and bind with strings. Cook in a pressure cooker for 15 minutes. Warm up the sauce, bind it with the roux.

Pork

Recipe	Page
Polish Casserole	6-1
Ham Loaf	6-2
Barbecued Pork Chops	6-3
Spicy Ham	6-4
Pork with Peppers	6-5
Sweet and Sour Pork	6-6
Kielbasa and Potato Casserole	6-7
Natrona Heights Ribs and Barbecue Sauce	6-8
Bourbon Kolbassi	6-9
Aunt Marion's Greens and Cabbage	6-10
Pork Fried Rice	6-11
Reuben Casserole	6-12
1-1/2 Pound Ham Loaf	6-13
Stuffed Pork Loin	6-14

Pork

Polish Casserole
Submitted by: Dr. Walter Szymanski

Meal: Dinner   Servings: 6
Prep Time: 2 hours   Cost: Inexpensive

Ingredients

1 can sauerkraut
1 head cabbage
1 pound pre-cooked/smoked sausage, sliced

4 potatoes, quartered
2 tablespoons butter
Garlic powder to taste
Parsely for garnish

Preparation

On the bottom of a casserole dish, place equal parts cabbage and sauerkraut. Make it a generous layer with some of the sauerkraut juices. If desired, skip the cabbage for more of a sauerkraut taste. Layer the sausage on top of the sauerkraut. Par boil the potatoes then layer them on top of the sausage. Then season with the butter, garlic powder and parsley. Cover dish and bake in a preheated 350 degree oven for about an hour, to allow the juices to flow up to the potatoes. Uncover dish and bake an additional 20 minutes so that the potatoes get a little brown.

Suggestions

This recipe is very flexible so adjustments can be made easily for larger crowds. Amounts of sausage and potatoes can be altered according to your tastes also.

Pork

Ham Loaf

Submitted by: Dr. Louis and June Le Bras

Meal: Dinner   Servings: 2 small loaves
Prep Time: 2 hours, 15 minutes   Cost: Inexpensive

Ingredients

1-1/2 pounds ham, ground
1 pound pork, ground
2 cups corn flakes
1/2 cup tomato sauce

1/2 cup milk
2 eggs
2 tablespoons catsup

Preparation

Mix all thoroughly and pack into 2 small loaf pans. Pour sauce on top of loaves.

Sauce Ingredients

1 cup brown sugar
2 teaspoons mustard
1/2 teaspoon ground cloves

1/4 cup vinegar
1/2 cup tomato sauce
2 tablespoons green pepper, chopped

Preparation

Mix all thoroughly. Pour over loaves and bake in a preheated 350 degree oven for 1-1/2 to 2 hours.

Pork

Barbecued Pork Chops

Submitted by: The Author

Meal:	Dinner	Servings: 6	
Prep Time:	30 minutes	Cost:	Inexpensive

Ingredients

2 pounds pork chops
Lemon pepper

Barbecue sauce

Preparation

Preheat grill. Cover pork chops with lemon pepper to taste. Place pork chops on grill cooking each side approximately 10 minutes. Coat top side of chops with barbecue sauce, grill and turn over. Coat other side of chops with barbecue sauce, grill for another 5 minutes.

Pork

Spicy Ham
Submitted by: Lyndy Kelley

Meal: Dinner
Prep Time: 4 hours

Servings: 6 to 8
Cost: Moderate

Ingredients

1 (6- to 7-pound) ham, with skin
1/4 cup vegetable oil
1 tablespoon Cajun seasoning

1 tablespoon salt
1 teaspoon ground black pepper

Preparation

Mix the oil, Cajun seasoning, salt, and pepper. Place the ham in a roasting pan, skin side up. Slice the skin in 1 Inch squares, 1/4 inch deep. Rub ham with the oil mixture and bake in a preheated 450 degree oven for 20 minutes. Lower heat to 350 degrees and continue baking for another 30 minutes per pound (3 to 3-1/2 hours).

Pork

Pork with Peppers

Submitted by: Bishop and Nara Duncan

Meal: Dinner   Servings: 6
Prep Time: 3 hours   Cost: Moderate

Ingredients

1 pound pork chops, pork loin, or
  tenderloin roast
1 tablespoon butter
1 onion, chopped
1 teaspoon ginger
1 red pepper, seeded and chopped

1 green pepper, seeded and chopped
3 tablespoons apple juice or cider
1 tablespoon Worcestershire sauce
1 tablespoon paprika
1 tablespoon tomato paste

Preparation

Fry the pork chops in pan, or cook the roast, whichever you choose to cook, and keep warm. Add butter to pan, cook onions until soft, add rest of the ingredients and gently cook until peppers are soft. Spoon over the pork you cooked.

Suggestions

For a truely festive look use 1 each red, green, yellow, and orange peppers and double all the other ingredients.

Pork

Sweet and Sour Pork

Submitted by: Nancy Phillips in memory of those who believed in the power of hope, belived in the strength of love, and believed that all things are possible.

Meal: Dinner   Servings: 6
Prep Time: 1 hour   Cost: Moderate

Ingredients

1-1/2 pounds boneless pork, cut into cubes
Oil
Salt and pepper to taste
1/2 cup barbecue sauce
1/4 cup vinegar

1 (1-pound, 4-1/2 ounce) can pineapple chunks, drained, reserve 1/2 cup syrup
1 tablespoon cornstarch
1 green pepper, cut in slices
Cooked rice
Soy sauce and water chestnuts, optional

Preparation

Brown pork in small amount of oil with the salt and pepper, set aside. Combine barbecue sauce, pineapple syrup, vinegar and cornstarch. Stir in with the pork, cover and simmer for 30 to 40 minutes. Add pineapple and green pepper. Simmer 10 minutes longer and serve with rice.

Suggestions

If desired, add 2 to 3 tablespoons soy sauce and more sugar if it needs more sweetness. Water chestnuts can be added as well.

Pork

Kielbasa and Potato Casserole

Submitted by: Bryan and Traci Sanders

Meal: Dinner   Servings: 10
Prep Time: 1 hour, 15 minutes   Cost: Inexpensive

Ingredients

10 to 12 medium potatoes, peeled and   2 medium onions, halved and sliced
    sliced   Salt, pepper, parsley and butter
1 package kielbasa, sliced at an angle
    (oblong shaped)

Preparation

Layer a 9x13-inch pan with the potatos, kielbasa, onions, salt, pepper and parsley.
Just put a few slices of butter inbetween the layers. Repeat the layers until everything
is used. Cover with foil. Bake in a preheated 375 degree oven for 45 minutes, uncover
and bake an additional 15 minutes or until potatoes are easily pierced.

Natrona Heights Ribs and Barbecue Sauce

Submitted by: Terry G. Gouchnour

Meal: Dinner   Servings: 4 to 6
Prep Time: 4 hours, 30 minutes   Cost: Moderate

Ingredients

1 chicken or beef bouillon cube
1/4 cup hot water
3 tablespoons butter
Small onion, minced
4 tablespoons brown sugar
2 tablespoons vinegar

2 tablespoons lemon juice
Salt and pepper to taste
Dash tabasco sauce
1 teaspoon prepared mustard
2 pounds ribs

Preparation

Combine bouillon cube with hot water, set aside. Melt butter in skillet and add onions until brown. Add brown sugar and stock until mixed then add remaining ingredients, except ribs. Simmer 20 minutes, covered. Add more brown sugar to suit your tastes. Bake ribs in a preheated 350 degree oven for 1/2 an hour. Baste with sauce every 15 minutes for next 3 hours. If ribs get too brown, cover for remaining time.

Pork

Bourbon Kolbassi

Submitted by: Carol Meador

Meal: Dinner   Servings: 6 to 8
Prep Time: 1 hour   Cost: Inexpensive

Ingredients

1-1/2 cups catsup   1/2 cup bourbon
1 cup light brown sugar   2 pounds sliced kolbassi, cut in chips like
                                     pickles

Preparation

Mix catsup, brown sugar and bourbon. Add kolbassi and simmer for 45 minutes. Skim off fat. Keep warm in a slow cooker (crock pot), but do not cook it in the slow cooker because the sauce will not thicken.

Pork

Aunt Marion's
Greens and Cabbage

Submitted by: Donna Brock

Meal: Dinner   Servings: 6
Prep Time: 1 hour, 30 minutes Cost: Inexpensive

Ingredients

2 or 3 ham hocks
2 or 3 pounds of greens (collards or
   kale)
2 to 3 onions

Seasoning salt to taste
Crushed hot peppers to taste
Head of cabbage
Pinch of sugar

Preparation

Boil ham hocks until tender. Chop greens and add to meat. Chop onions and add to greens. Add seasoning salt and crushed peppers. Cook for about 40 minutes. Then cut up cabbage and place in the greens. Add a pinch of sugar. Cook for about 20 more minutes. Serve with hot cornbread.

Pork

Pork Fried Rice
Submitted by: Nancy Hewitt

Meal: Dinner
Prep Time: 1 hour

Servings: 8
Cost: Inexpensive

Ingredients

1 (8-ounce) box white rice
2 eggs
Oil
Small bag frozen peas

Leftover pork or freshly cooked pork, cut in
   bite-size pieces
Green onions, diced
Soy sauce

Preparation

Prepare rice according to directions and let cool. Cool completely so the rice doesn't get lumpy. Whip the eggs and set aside. Heat oil in a wok and lightly brown the rice. Gradually mix in the eggs. Add the peas, pork, onions and soy sauce to taste.

Pork

Reuben Casserole
Submitted by: "The Shepherd Boys" Steel City Softball League

Meal: Dinner   Servings: 6
Prep Time: 1 hour, 15 minutes   Cost: Inexpensive

Ingredients

1 quart sauerkraut, drained
8 ounces noodles, cooked
2 cans cream of chicken soup
1 teaspoon dry mustard
1/2 cup mayonnaise

1/2 cup chopped onion
1 (12-ounce) can corned beef
8 ounces Swiss cheese, grated
1/2 cup dry bread crumbs, rye optional

Preparation

Grease a 9x13-inch pan and place sauerkraut on the bottom. Add noodles. Mix soup, mustard and mayonnaise. Spread over noodles. Spread onions, corned beef and Swiss cheese over the top. Sprinkle bread crumbs on top, cover with foil. Bake in a preheated 350 degree oven for 1 hour. Let sit for 5 minutes before removing from oven.

Pork

1-1/2 Pound Ham Loaf

Submitted by: Ed Shearer

Meal: Dinner   Servings: 6
Prep Time: 1 hour, 15 minutes   Cost: Moderate

Ingredients

1 egg
1/2 cup milk
1/2 cup bread crumbs
1/2 teaspoon salt and pepper to taste
1 pound ground ham

1/2 pound ground pork
1 cup brown sugar
1/2 teaspoon dry mustard
1/4 cup water
1/4 cup vinegar

Preparation

Mix together egg, milk, bread crumbs, salt, pepper, ham and pork. Make into a loaf and put into pan. Mix together remaining ingredients and pour over loaf. Bake in a preheated 325 degree oven for 1 hour, 15 minutes. For a bigger loaf, just double the recipe.

Stuffed Pork Loin

Submitted by: Wilma Eyman

Meal: Dinner   Servings: 8
Prep Time: 2 hours   Cost: Moderate

Ingredients

1/3 cup chopped onion
1 clove minced garlic
2 tablespoons oil
2 eggs slightly beaten
1 (6 ounce) package herb seasoned
  stuffing mix

2 to 4 pounds boneless pork loin, untied
  and flattened
2-6 ounce cans white crab meat
1 cup apple butter or apple sauce
1/2 cup water

Preparation

Sauté onions and garlic in oil until tender but not brown (about 2 minutes). Remove from heat and cool slightly. stir in eggs seasoning packet and stuffing crumbs. Spread this mixture evenly over the inside of the pork loin. Spread the crab meat on top of this. Roll up the meat and tie with twine. Place the meat in a roasting pan and roast at 400 degrees for 10 minutes. Remove from oven and coat meat with 1/4 cup of apple butter or sauce. Add water to bottom of pan. Cover and continue to roast at 350 degrees. Add more water as needed. Remove from the oven and spread remaining apple butter or sauce and continue to roast uncovered for another 25 minutes or until internal temperature of meat reaches 160 degrees. Let stand 15 minutes before slicing.

Lamb, Veal & Other Meats

Recipe   **Page**

Normandy Style Veal Chops 7-1
Roast Lamb with Saffron and Tomato 7-2
Three Alarm Lamb 7-3
Lamb in Barbecue Sauce 7-4
Lamb a la Breck 7-5
Shepherd's Pie 7-6
Veal Scallopini Allimore 7-7
Moussaka II 7-8
Broiled Venison Steak 7-9
Rabbit Sautéed with Cream 7-10
Fried Rabbit 7-11
Venison Steak with Chestnut Sauce 7-12
Marinated Leg of Venison 7-13
Shirley's Partridge Chicken 7-14

Lamb, Veal & Other Meats

Normandy Style Veal Chops
Submitted by: Cheryl Brugette

Meal: Dinner
Prep Time: 1 hour

Servings: 6
Cost: Moderate

Ingredients

2/3 cup butter
6 (6-ounce) veal loin chops, or pork loin
   chops
Salt and pepper to taste
1 cup heavy cream

6 tablespoons apple brandy (Calvados, if
   possible), or peach brandy
2 pounds golden delicious apples, peeled
   and quartered
1 tablespoon sugar

Preparation

Heat a 1/4 cup of the butter in a frying pan. Add the chops a few at a time. As they are browned, transfer them to an ovenproof dish. Season the chops with the salt and pepper and put them aside. Add the cream to the frying pan and stir to scrape up the residue from the bottom. Reduce by 1/3 then add the brandy. Pour the cream sauce over the chops and bake in a 350 degree oven for 15 to 20 minutes. Meanwhile, heat the rest of the butter in a frying pan, add the apple quarters and cook until golden. Halfway through cooking the apples sprinkle with the sugar. To serve, arrange the chops on a warmed serving dish and surround them with the apples. Pour the sauce over the chops.

Suggestions

My father, who cooked professionally for many years, would have considered it idiotic to ask what type of wine to serve with this dish. He would have insisted on white wine. I strongly recommend it. The white Burgundies or a good Chardonnay are particularly well suited to cream based cuisine. Also, the light, dry characteristics of these wines compliment the delicate flavor of veal while providing a counterpoint to the sweetness of the apples.

Lamb, Veal & Other Meats

Roast Lamb with Saffron and Tomato

Submitted by: Victor Wahome

Meal: Dinner   Servings: 6
Prep Time: Overnight   Cost: Expensive

Ingredients

3 cloves garlic
1 tablespoon fresh mint, finely chopped
2 teaspoons ground cumin
1 teaspoon dried thyme
3 tablespoons lemon juice

2 tablespoons olive oil
Salt and fresh ground pepper
3 pound leg of lamb or lean cut shoulder of
  lamb
Lamb stock for basting, optional

Preparation

Mix together the garlic, mint, cumin, thyme, lemon juice, olive oil, salt and pepper. Cut 3 fairly deep slits into the lamb and rub the mixture all over the meat, pressing well into the slits. Cover loosely with plastic and leave to marinate overnight in the refrigerator. Place lamb in a large baking dish, cover with foil and bake in a preheated 375 degree oven for 2 hours. Baste occasionally with pan juices, or stock, if preferred.

Saffron and Tomato Sauce Ingredients

2 tablespoons vegetable oil
1 red onion, sliced
3 cloves garlic, crushed
1 (12-ounce) can chopped tomatoes
2 teaspoons ground cinnamon
1 teaspoon dried tarragon

Generous pinch of saffron threads
4 slices fresh ginger
1 green chili, seeded and finely chopped
Salt and fresh ground pepper
2-1/2 cups lamb stock or water

Preparation

While lamb is roasting, make the above sauce. Heat oil in a large saucepan and fry the onion and garlic over a moderate heat for 4 to 5 minutes or until the onion is fairly soft. Add the tomatoes, cinnamon, tarragon, saffron, ginger, chili, salt and pepper. Stir well and cook, uncovered, for about 5 minutes. Add the stock or water, bring back to a boil and then simmer for about 30 minutes, until well reduced and fairly thick. Adjust the seasoning, if necessary, and then remove the pan from the heat. Transfer the cooked lamb to a serving plate, cover with foil and let stand in a warm place for 10 minutes. Pour off the excess fat from the roasting pan, then add the meat juices to the sauce and reheat. Carve the lamb into thin slices and serve with the sauce.

Lamb, Veal & Other Meats

Three Alarm Lamb

Submitted by: Lindy Kelley

Meal: Dinner   Servings: 4
Prep Time: 2 hours, 30 minutes   Cost: Moderate

Ingredients

2 pounds lamb, cut into 1 inch cubes
1 clove garlic, minced
2 large tomatoes, peeled, seeded,
   coarsely chopped
1 scallion, including green top, minced
1 shallot, minced
2 medium onions, chopped

1 habanero chili, seeded and minced
3 tablespoons curry powder
Salt and ground black pepper to taste
2 tablespoons butter
1/2 cup vegetable oil
2-1/2 cups water

Preparation

Place the meat in a large mixing bowl. Add garlic, tomatoes, scallions, shallot, onions, curry powder, chili, salt and pepper. Mix together and let marinate for 40 minutes. Heat the butter and oil in a large skillet. Remove lamb from marinade, reserve marinade, and brown on all sides. Add the marinade and water. Cover and cook for 1-1/2 hours or until meat is tender. Taste for seasoning and adjust if need be. Serve with tortilla chips or over white rice.

Lamb in Barbecue Sauce

Submitted by: Herb08 in memory of Michael Smith.

Meal: Dinner
Prep Time: 45 minutes

Servings: 6
Cost: Moderate

Ingredients

4 tablespoons butter
1/2 cup currant jelly
1/8 teaspoon cayenne pepper
2 tablespoons vinegar

1/2 teaspoon dry mustard
Salt to taste
6 slices cooked lamb

Preparation

Melt the butter in a large skillet, then add all the spices to the skillet. Stir and cook over medium heat until the sauce is smooth and hot. Add the lamb to the skillet. Turn it over in the sauce, coating the slices and heating them thoroughly.

Lamb, Veal & Other Meats

Lamb a la Breck

Submitted by: IDZI for Michael Smith

Meal: Dinner
Prep Time: 1 hour

Servings: 6
Cost: Moderate

Ingredients

2 cups finely chopped, cooked lamb
Salt and pepper
2 tablespoons minced onion

2 tablespoons minced celery with leaves
2 cups cooked macaroni
3 eggs, slightly beaten
2 cups milk

Preparation

Butter a 1-1/2 quart baking dish. Combine the lamb, salt, pepper, onion and celery in a bowl and mix well. Spread the macaroni on the bottom of the baking dish and put the lamb mixture over it. Mix the eggs and milk together and pour on top. Bake in a preheated 350 degree oven for 30 to 40 minutes or until the custard is firm. Serve very hot.

Lamb, Veal & Other Meats

Shepherd's Pie

Submitted by: Herb08 for Michael Smith.

Meal: Dinner
Prep Time: 2 hours

Servings: 6
Cost: Moderate

Ingredients

3 cups chopped, cooked lamb
1 large clove garlic
1 small onion
1 teaspoon rosemary, crumbled
4 tablespoons butter

2 tablespoons flour
1/4 cup beef or lamb broth
Salt and pepper to taste
4 medium potatoes, cooked and mashed,
   about 3 cups

Preparation

Combine the lamb, garlic, onion and rosemary. Put through a meat grinder twice or chop very fine in a food processor. Melt the butter in a large skillet and add the flour. Cook for a few minutes until smooth and blended. Slowly add the broth, stir and cook until the gravy is thickened, cooking at least 5 minutes to get rid of the raw flour taste. Add the lamb mixture, stir to blend, and add salt and pepper to taste. Spoon into a 1-1/2 quart casserole or deep pie dish. Spread the potatoes on top and cover evenly to the edge of the casserole. Make a crisscross design with a fork. Bake in a preheated 375 degree oven for 35 to 40 minutes or until the meat is bubbling hot and the potatoes are browned.

Lamb, Veal & Other Meats

Veal Scallopini Allimore

Submitted by: Pat Zerega

Meal: Dinner
Prep Time: 1 hour

Servings: 4
Cost: Moderate

Ingredients

1-1/2 pounds veal, pounded to 1/4-inch
   thick
Salt and pepper to taste
Flour
4 tablespoons butter

3 tablespoons olive oil
3/4 cup beef stock
6 lemon slices
1 tablespoons lemon juice

Preparation

Season meat with salt and pepper. Dip in flour. Melt 2 tablespoons butter then add oil, when foaming stops add meat. Sauté meat on each side for 2 minutes, until golden brown. Remove to a plate. Pour off most of the fat, leave a film. Add 1/2 cup beef stock, briskly boil for 2 minutes. Stir and scrape parts that are clinging to pan. Return meat to pan and place lemon slices on top. Cover and simmer 10 minutes, until tender. Transfer to a plate and surround with the lemon slices. Add remaining beef stock to pan, boil until glaze, add lemon juice. Cook and stir for 1 minute. Remove from heat, swirl remaining butter, pour over the meat.

Lamb, Veal & Other Meats

Moussaka II

Submitted by: Herb08 in memory of Michael Smith.

Meal: Dinner   Servings: 6
Prep Time: 2 hours   Cost: Moderate

Ingredients

4 medium egplants
2 tablespoons olive oil
1 cup finely chopped onion
1/2 pound mushrooms, chopped fine
2 cups ground, cooked lamb
3 cloves garlic, chopped fine

1 teaspoon thyme, crumbled
1 teaspoon rosemary, crumbled
1 teaspoon salt
1/2 teaspoon fresh, ground pepper
2-1/2 cups tomato sauce

Preparation

Oil a 2 quart mold that is about 7 inches in diameter and 4 inches deep, such as a charlotte mold or a deep cake pan. Rinse a cookie sheet with cold water and shake off excess. Slice the eggplants in half and make several deep gashes in their flesh, taking care not to cut into the skin. Rub the cut surfaces with olive oil and place, skin side down, on the cookie sheet. Bake in a preheated 375 degree oven for 30 minutes or until the flesh is tender. Set aside to cool. In a large bowl, mix onion, mushrooms, lamb, garlic, thyme, rosemary, salt and pepper. Carefully scoop out the eggplant flesh, chop it and then mix with the lamb mixture. Use the skins to line the mold, placing the purple, outer sides against the mold. If necessary, patch so that none of the mold is exposed. Let 3 to 4 inches hang over the side of the mold. Pack the lamb mixture into the mold and enclose it with the excess skin that is hanging over. Place in a pan of boiling water and bake for 1 hour, 30 minutes. Remove from the oven and let stand for 10 minutes. Heat the tomato sauce while the Moussaka is cooling. Turn the Moussaka onto a platter and spoon a little tomato sauce over the top. Serve the remaining tomato sauce at the table.

Lamb, Veal & Other Meats

Broiled Venison Steak

Submitted by: Herb08 in memory of Michael Smith

Meal: Dinner
Prep Time: 30 minutes

Servings: 2
Cost: Moderate

Ingredients

1 venison steak, 3/4 to 1-inch thick
4 tablespoons butter, softened
Salt
Freshly ground pepper

1 cup dry red wine
3/4 teaspoon allspice
1/2 cup currant jelly

Preparation

Preheat the broiler. Rub the steak with butter and sprinkle liberally with salt and pepper. Place the steak 4 inches below the broiling element on a rack in a shallow pan. Broil 4 minutes each side. Remove the steak to a warm platter. Set the pan over a burner and add the wine, allspice and jelly to the drippings. Bring to a boil and stir until smooth and blended. Spoon a little sauce over the steak then place the rest in a bowl to be used at the table.

Lamb, Veal & Other Meats

Rabbit Sautéed with Cream

Submitted by: Herb08 in memory of Michael Smith.

Meal: Dinner
Prep Time: 45 minutes

Servings: 4
Cost: Moderate

Ingredients

4 pound domestic rabbit, cut into serving
    pieces
6 tablespoons flour
Salt and pepper to taste

2 tablespoons butter
2 tablespoons oil
1-1/2 cups light cream

Preparation

Wipe the rabbit pieces with a damp towel and pat dry. Dust with 4 tablespoons of flour and the salt and pepper. Heat the butter and oil in a large skillet, brown the rabbit on each side, cover, and cook for 25 minutes, or until the juices run clear. Transfer the rabbit to a warm platter. Add the remaining flour to the pan drippings, stirring and scraping the bits from the bottom of the pan. Slowly stir in the cream and cook, stirring over medium heat until the sauce is thickened, at least 5 to 6 minutes. Spoon some of the sauce over the rabbit, serving the rest at the dinner table.

Lamb, Veal & Other Meats

Fried Rabbit

Submitted by: IDZI for Michael Smith.

Meal: Dinner
Prep Time: 45 minutes

Servings: 6
Cost: Moderate

Ingredients

4 pound domestic rabbit, in serving
   pieces
4 tablespoons flour

Salt and pepper to taste
3 tablespoons shortening

Preparation

Wipe the rabbit with a damp towel and pat dry. Lightly dust each piece with flour then sprinkle with salt and pepper. Heat the shortening in a large skillet, then add the rabbit and brown. Lower the heat and fry, turning often, for 25 minutes or until the juices run clear when a small slit is made in the thick part of the thigh.

Suggestions

The meat tastes very much like chicken, a little more dense and dry, and it would be worthwhile experimenting by substituting rabbit in some of the chicken dishes. Rabbit usually comes packaged, cut up in pieces, more often than not frozen. Defrost slowly in the refrigerator.

Lamb, Veal & Other Meats

Venison Steak and Chestnut Sauce

Submitted by: IDZI for Michael Smith.

Meal: Dinner
Prep Time: 45 minutes

Servings: 4
Cost: Moderate

Ingredients

3 tablespoon butter
1/2 onion, chopped
1/2 carrot, chopped
3 tablespoons flour
1-1/2 cups beef broth
1/2 bay leaf, crumbled

1 teaspoon coarsely ground black pepper
1 teaspoon salt
4 tablespoons Madeira
1 cup cooked, chopped chestnuts
1 or 2 venison steaks, 1-3/4 inch thick

Preparation

Melt the butter in a skillet, then add the onion and carrot and cook until lightly browned, about 5 minutes. Stir in the flour and cook until brown. Add the beef broth, bay leaf, pepper and salt. Simmer for 10 to 15 minutes. Strain, then add the Madeira and chestnuts and set aside. Preheat the broiler. Place the venison steaks on a rack 5 inches beneath the broiler element. Cook 5 minutes on each side. Remove to a hot platter and cover with the hot chestnut sauce.

Suggestions

With venison, always try to know the approximate age because it does make a difference when it is cooked. Tender young venison will need no marinating and can be cooked very briefly as in Broiled Venison Steak, or you may use some of the recipes for lamb-chops or roasts. Older venison should always be marinated before cooking.

Lamb, Veal & Other Meats

Marinated Leg of Venison

Submitted by: IDZI for Michael Smith.

Meal: Dinner
Prep Time: 2 days

Servings: 6
Cost: Moderate

Ingredients

5 pound leg of venison
2 cups dry red wine
1/2 cup olive oil
2 bay leaves
4 cloves garlic, chopped
2 teaspoons dry mustard

1 teaspoon rosemary, crumbled
1 teaspoon salt
1 teaspoon coarsely ground black pepper
4 slices bacon
3 tablespoons flour
1/2 cup red currant jelly

Preparation

Place the venison in a deep bowl. Combine the wine, oil, bay leaves, garlic, mustard, rosemary, salt, and pepper, and pour over the venison.Cover with foil and refrigerate for 2 days, turning often. Preheat the oven to 450 degrees. Drain the venison and reserve the marinade. Place the meat on a rack in a shallow pan and cover with the bacon strips. Roast for 30 minutes, basting several times with the marinade, then reduce the heat to 350 degrees. Continue roasting another 40 to 60 minutes (to an interior temperature of 130 degrees for rare, 140 degrees for medium). Put the venison on a platter and keep warm. Set the roasting pan over a burner, add the flour to the pan drippings, and cook until it is browned. Strain the reserved marinade and stir into the pan, cooking until smooth and thickened. Add the jelly, cook only until the jelly is melted and blended with the sauce. Carve at the table the way you would a roast of lamb, with the gravy in a sauceboat.

Lamb, Veal & Other Meats

Shirley's Partridge Chicken

Submitted by: Shirley Jones

Meal: Dinner   Servings: 8
Prep Time: 2 hours, 30 minutes   Cost: Moderate

Ingredients

1 pound cubed beef
1 pound cubed pork
1 pound cubed veal
Egg
Cracker meal

Butter
Herbs: garlic powder, lemon pepper,
    rosemary, salt, pepper, or others
    according to your taste

Preparation

Take 8 wooden skewers and alternate all meats until the skewer is full. Mix the egg and enough cracker meal to make a pasty consistency. Dip the skewers into the cracker meal until completely covered. May need to make up more cracker meal mixture. Brown on top of stove in butter until brown on all sides. Place in covered casserole dish with the herbs. Dot with butter. Bake in a preheated 300 degree oven for about 1 hour 45 minutes, baste a few times. Uncover and bake another 30 minutes. Serve with rice or noodles.

Potatoes & Vegetables

Recipe   **Page**

Vegetable Salad 8-1
Bean Burgers 8-2
Marinated Mushrooms 8-3
Vidalia Onion Tart 8-4
Picnic Potatoes 8-5
"Meaty" Black Bean Chili 8-6
Three Bean Salad 8-7
Italian Zucchini Fritters 8-8
Frijoles a La Mexicana 8-9
Mashed Potato Casserole 8-10
Haifa Baked Beans 8-11
Eggplant and Tomato Pie 8-12
Hot Slaw 8-13
Broccoli Casserole 8-14
Penne con Broccoli 8-15
Judge Wapner's au Gratin Potatoes 8-16
Potatoes Italiano 8-17
Seasoned Fried Cauliflower 8-18
Re-Baked Sweet Potatoes 8-19
Cottage Cheese Vegie Mix 8-20
Zucchini and Carrot Casserole 8-21
Carrot Salad 8-22
Scout's Own Hummus 8-23
Zucchini Pancakes 8-24
Seasoned Banana Peppers 8-25
Black Beans and Rice 8-26
Potato Casserole 8-27
Pea Casserole 8-28
Diane Ladd's Southern Japanese Dish 8-29
Keller's Green Tomato Relish 8-30
Summer Squash Casserole 8-31
Green Beans Vinaigrette 8-32
Potato and Apple Rosti 8-33
Italian Baked Tomatoes 8-34

Potatoes & Vegetables

Vegetable Salad
Submitted by: Lynette G. Zygmuntowicz

Meal: Lunch or Dinner   Servings: 4
Prep Time: 2 hours   Cost: Inexpensive

Ingredients

1 pound fresh carrots
3 to 4 pieces parsnips
2 medium granny smith apples, tart

2 hard boiled eggs
3 dill pickles
1 medium yellow onion

Preparation

Clean and cook whole carrots and parsnips in water until done, firm not hard. Cool carrots and parsnips until cold. Chop and dice all ingredients into small pieces, including the carrots and parsnips. Save the onion for last. Place all ingredients into a large bowl. Mix well with dressing recipe that follows. Chill and serve. Do not use a food processor to dice vegetables, it will make them too mushy.

Dressing Ingredients

1 to 1-1/2 cups mayonnaise, not
   dressing
2 teaspoons yellow mustard

Salt and pepper to taste

Potatoes & Vegetables

Bean Burgers
Submitted by: Cheryl Brugette

Meal: Lunch or Dinner   Servings: 8
Prep Time: 30 minutes   Cost: Inexpensive

Ingredients

1 (16-ounce) can kidney beans, drained
    and rinsed
2 cups cooked brown rice
2 tablespoons catsup
1/2 teaspoon garlic powder

1 teaspoon dried oregano
1/8 teaspoon dried thyme
1/4 teaspoon ground sage
Salt and pepper to taste
1/4 cup onion, finely chopped

Preparation

Combine all ingredients, except onions, in a large bowl. Mash with a fork or potato masher until beans are mashed well, the rice will be lumpy. Add onions and mix well. Divide mixture evenly and form into 8 burgers, 1/2 inch to 3/4 inch thick, wet hands slightly to keep from sticking. Lightly oil a non-stick griddle or skillet, preheat over medium heat. Place burgers on griddle and cook until browned on both sides, turning several times.

Marinated Mushrooms

Submitted by: Carol Le Bras

Meal: Dinner   Servings: 6 to 8
Prep Time: 2 hours, 15 minutes   Cost: Inexpensive

Ingredients

1 pound mushrooms, halved
1 cup celery, thinly sliced
1/2 cup green pepper, diced
1/2 cup onion, finely chopped
1 cup vegetable oil
1/4 cup dry red wine or red wine vinegar

2 teaspoons basil, crumbled
1 teaspoon salt
1/2 teaspoon garlic, finely minced
1/2 teaspoon coarse ground black pepper
1/2 teaspoon sugar

Preparation

Set all vegetables aside in a large bowl. Mix all remaining ingredients. Pour over vegetables, mix well. Refrigerate at least 2 hours.

Potatoes & Vegetables

Vidalia Onion Tart

Submitted by: Lois Ahlborn

Meal: Appetizer or Dinner   Servings: 6 to 8
Prep Time: 45 minutes   Cost: Inexpensive

Ingredients

1 pastry shell
2 large Vidalia onions, thinly sliced
8 ounces Cheddar cheese, thinly sliced

1/2 teaspoon salt
3 tablespoons milk

Preparation

Crimp pastry shell with a fork. Spread onions evenly on bottom of pastry shell. Top with cheese and salt. Sprinkle milk over top. Bake in a preheated 400 degree oven for 25 minutes or until cheese is lightly browned.

Potatoes & Vegetables

Picnic Potatoes

Submitted by: Judy Waldner in memory of Timmy.

Meal: Lunch or Dinner   Servings: 12
Prep Time: Overnight   Cost: Inexpensive

Ingredients

4 pounds pototes, unpeeled   1 can cream of celery soup
1 cup chopped onion   2 cups shredded cheddar cheese
1 stick butter   1 pint sour cream

Preparation

Boil the potatoes in their skins until just done. Pour off the boiling water and cover with cold water. Peel potatoes as soon as they can be handled. Grate them with a hand grater. A food processer could be used but with great care because it could mash the potatoes instead of grating them. Sauté the onions in the butter. When translucent, transfer the onions to a bowl. Mix the onions with the celery soup, cheese and sour cream. Add this mixture to the potatoes and mix well. Pour into a well greased 13x9-inch glass baking dish, glass is prefered for this particular dish. Refrigerate over night.

Topping Ingredients

1 cup corn flakes   3 tablespoons butter

Preparation

Sauté corn flakes quickly in the butter. Sprinkle over potatoes and bake for 1 hour in a preheated 350 degree oven.

Suggestions

Leftovers can be formed into patties and browned in butter the next day. You can substitute reduced fat soup, cheese and sour cream to lower the calories. It is not recommended to use oleo or the non-fat spreads to replace the butter it will effect the flavor. Will make enough for a small army, but can easily be doubled for larger crowds.

"Meaty" Black Bean Chili

Submitted by: Carina de Wit-Lord

Meal: Dinner   Servings: 4
Prep Time: 1 hour   Cost: Moderate

Ingredients

2 tablespoons olive oil
2 teaspoons cumin seeds
1 large yellow onion, chopped
1 medium red pepper, cut in squares
1 medium green pepper, cut in squares
2 stalks celery, chopped
2 cans black beans, drained and rinsed

1 (28-ounce) can peeled, whole tomatoes, undrained and broken up
2 tablespoons chili powder
2 teaspoons dried oregano
2 cups water or vegetable stock
1 cup Textured Vegetable Protein (TVP)
Salt and pepper to taste
Hot sauce, optional

Preparation

In a large soup pot or dutch oven, heat olive oil over medium heat. Add cumin seeds and sauté until they start to pop and smell fragrant, about 1 minute. Add onion and sauté until softened, about 5 minutes, stirring frequently. Add red pepper, green pepper and celery. Sauté another 5 minutes. Add black beans, canned tomatoes, chili powder, oregano and 1 cup of the water or stock. Stir to mix well and bring everything to a simmer. Turn heat to low and simmer, covered, for 20 to 30 minutes. Mixture should thicken somewhat, stir occasionally. Meanwhile, place TVP into a bowl. Bring remaining cup of water to a boil and pour over the TVP. Stir to mix. Cover and let sit for 5 minutes. Fluff TVP with a fork. Towards the end of the cooking time, add the TVP to the chili and stir to mix. Simmer another 5 minutes. Add more water if chili is to thick or a few teaspoons of tomato paste if chili is to thin. Season to taste with salt, pepper, and hot sauce.

Suggestions

Good served over cooked, brown rice or with cornbread and a green salad. TVP can be found in most health food stores and is available in flakes or chunks. TVP replaces beef in chili, sloppy joes, and spaghetti sauces.

Potatoes & Vegetables

Three Bean Salad

Submitted by: Joan Gamble

Meal: Lunch or Dinner   Servings: 8
Prep Time: Overnight   Cost: Inexpensive

Ingredients

1 (16-ounce) can each wax beans,
   green beans, and kidney beans,
   drained
1/2 green pepper, chopped
1 medium onion, finely chopped
1/3 cup oil
3/4 cup sugar

2 teaspoons rosemary
2/3 cup vinegar
1 teaspoon salt
1 teaspoon black pepper
1 teaspoon celery seed
Pinch of garlic powder

Preparation

Mix all above ingredients well. Refrigerate at least 24 hours before serving.

Potatoes & Vegetables

Italian Zucchini Fritters

Submitted by: Daniel Gamble
for all the mothers of Wellness who do so much.

Meal: Lunch or Dinner   Servings: 4
Prep Time: 1 hour   Cost: Inexpensive

Ingredients

1 medium zucchini (2 cups, peeled and
  diced into small cubes)
2 cups flour
1 tablespoon baking powder
1/4 cup grated Parmesan cheese
1 teaspoon salt

Clove garlic, minced
Black pepper to taste
3 eggs, slightly beaten
1/2 cup olive oil or vegetable oil
1/4 cup to 1/3 cup parsley

Preparation

Cook zucchini in about 1 quart of boiling water for 4 to 5 minutes, until tender. Drain and reserve 1 cup liquid. Let cool. Mix flour, baking powder, Parmesan cheese, salt, garlic and pepper. Make well in center of mixture. Mix in eggs and 1/2 of reserved liquid. Mix in zucchini and enough of remaining liquid to make a thick enough batter to hold onto a spoon. Heat oil in skillet. Drop by tablespoons into oil and brown on both sides. Drain on paper towels. Serve warm or cold. Sprinkle with chopped parsley

Potatoes & Vegetables

Frijoles a La Mexicana

Submitted by: Tim and Xavier Evans

Meal: Dinner
Prep Time: 1 hour

Servings: 2
Cost: Inexpensive

Ingredients

3 strips of bacon
1 can black beans

1 heaping teaspoon comino (cumin powder)
Toppings: shredded longhorn cheese, sour
cream, salsa

Preparation

Fry bacon crisp. Remove and reserve as another topping. Add beans and comino to the grease in the fry pan. Heat completely, stirring until beans break down. Serve with the toppings.

Suggestions

If you have extra cilantro, this makes an interesting garnish on the side.

Mashed Potato Casserole

Submitted by: Irene Kesling in memory of Joe

Meal: Dinner   Servings: 8
Prep Time: 1 hour, 30 minutes   Cost: Inexpensive

Ingredients

5 pounds potatoes, peeled and cut   1 teaspoon seasoned salt
1 (8-ounce) package cream cheese   Pepper
1/2 cup half and half   1/4 pound butter
1 teaspoon onion salt

Preparation

Cook, then mash the potatoes. Add above ingredients, except butter, and blend. Put in a greased 2 quart casserole dish and top with dots of butter. Bake in a preheated 350 degree oven for 30 minutes.

Potatoes & Vegetables

Haifa Baked Beans

Submitted by: William H. Fette in memory of Michael Smith.

Meal: Dinner	Servings: 6
Prep Time: 45 minutes	Cost: Inexpensive

Ingredients

3 cups cooked red beans
1-1/2 cups canned tomatoes
1 pimento, minced
1/4 teaspoon mustard
Dash pepper
3/4 teaspoon curry powder

1-1/2 teaspoons molasses
1-1/2 tablespoons sugar
1/4 teaspoon salt
1/4 cup deviled ham
6 strips Canadian bacon or corned beef

Preparation

Mix all ingredients, except meat. Turn into a greased casserole dish, arrange meat on top and bake in a preheated 350 degree oven for 30 minutes or until smoked.

Eggplant and Tomato Pie

Submitted by: Robin Leach

Meal: Dinner   Servings: 6
Prep Time: 2 hours   Cost: Inexpensive

Ingredients

6 eggplants, halved
4 large beefsteak tomatoes, each cut
   into 6 slices
Parmesan cheese, grated

Oil
Fresh lemon or lime juice
Pepper
Basil leaves

Preparation

In a preheated 375 degree oven, bake the eggplant in a baking dish for 20 to 30 minutes. Remove and let stand for 5 to 10 minutes. Slice the eggplant about the same thickness as the tomatoes. Layer into the baking dish the eggplant, tomatoes, Parmesan cheese, and drizzle with oil and the lemon juice. Sprinkle on pepper, and completely cover with basil leaves, as if it were pastry topping. Bake for 1 hour. Turn the oven off and let the pie sit for a few minutes before serving.

Potatoes & Vegetables

Hot Slaw
Submitted by: Pat Boone

Meal: Lunch or Dinner   Servings: 8
Prep Time: Overnight   Cost: Inexpensive

Ingredients

2 cups diced fresh tomatoes   1/2 cup sugar
1 large head cabbage, chopped   1/2 cup vinegar
1/2 cup green pepper, chopped   1/2 bottle catsup, medium size
1/2 cup celery, chopped   Hot sauce and salt to taste
1/2 cup onion, chopped

Preparation

Mix all together. Cover and refrigerate overnight.

Broccoli Casserole
Submitted by: Ada Rapp
in memory of our son Doug (1957 - 1990).

Meal: Dinner   Servings: 10
Prep Time: 45 minutes   Cost: Inexpensive

Ingredients

2 (20-ounce) bags of frozen cut broccoli   2 stacks of Ritz crackers, crumbled
1 cup butter   1 pound Velveta cheese, sliced

Preparation

Blanch the broccoli and drain well. Melt butter in pan then stir in crackers. Place 1/2 of the broccoli in a 9x12 pan. Cover with 1/2 of the cheese then cover with 1/2 of the cracker mixture. Repeat with remaining ingredients. Cover and bake in a preheated 350 degree oven for 25 to 30 minutes.

Penne con Broccoli

Submitted by: Connie Sellecca and John Tesh

Meal: Lunch or Dinner
Prep Time: 30 minutes

Servings: 6
Cost: Inexpensive

Ingredients

6 to 8 cloves fresh garlic, sliced
1/8 cup olive oil
1/2 stick butter
2 cups grated Parmesan cheese
1-1/2 cups tomato sauce
1-1/2 cups sliced fresh mushrooms

2 fresh Roma tomatoes, chopped
2 cups steamed broccoli, cooked al dente
1 cup raisins
3/4 cup pine nuts
1 (16-ounce) box Penne, cooked al dente

Preparation

In a large frying pan, sauté the garlic in olive oil then add butter. When melted, reduce heat to low and slowly add Parmesan cheese stirring constantly to get a thick soupy consistency. Add tomato sauce maintaining that consistency. Add mushrooms and tomatoes, and cook al dente. You may add more Parmesan cheese or tomato sauce to thicken or thin the sauce to your taste. Add 2 cups steamed broccoli, raisins and pine nuts. Allow to simmer for 5 minutes then pour entire contents over cooked Penne.

Judge Wapner's
au Gratin Potatoes

Submitted by: Judge Joseph Wapner

Meal: Dinner
Prep Time: 1 hour

Servings: 4 to 6
Cost: Inexpensive

Ingredients

4 medium-sized potatoes
Butter
Nutmeg

1 large onion
1/4 pound sharp Cheddar cheese, grated
Parmesan cheese

Preparation

Slice potatoes thin and par boil for 3 minutes. Place in butter greased pan and sprinkle with nutmeg. Add sliced onions and Cheddar cheese. Top with Parmesan cheese and bake in a preheated 350 degree oven for 40 minutes.

Potatoes & Vegetables

Potatoes Italiano

Submitted by: Most Reverend Anthony Bosco

Meal: Dinner
Prep Time: 45 minutes

Servings: 2
Cost: Inexpensive

Ingredients

3 or 4 tablespoons olive oil
2 or 3 large potatoes, 1/2 inch cubes
1/2 large onion, minced
4 cloves garlic, pressed or minced

1/4 cup fresh basil, chopped
4 tablespoons red wine vinegar
Salt and fresh ground black pepper

Preparation

In a cast iron skillet, add the oil. Add the potatoes and turn occasionally so they cook evenly. Add additional oil if needed. When the potatoes are slightly transparent, add the onions and continue cooking until the onions are transparent and the potatoes have begun to brown. Be careful not to burn the onions. Add the garlic and continue cooking. Towards the end of the cooking add the basil and cook for 1 minute, then add the wine vinegar and mix well. Cook about 2 minutes more to blend the flavors. Add salt and pepper as needed. Serve immediately.

Seasoned Fried Cauliflower

Submitted by: Mary Helen Hough in memory of Michael Norris.

Meal: Dinner
Prep Time: 30 minutes

Servings: 4 to 6
Cost: Inexpensive

Ingredients

1 large head cauliflower
1/2 stick butter

1/2 cup seasoned Italian bread crumbs

Preparation

Steam cauliflower until tender. Break into flowerettes. Melt butter in skillet and fry cauliflower. Sprinkle bread crumbs over top, toss and brown until crispy.

Re-Baked Sweet Potatoes

Submitted by: Lyndy Kelley

Meal: Dinner

Prep Time: 1 hour, 30 minutes

Servings: 6

Cost: Inexpensive

Ingredients

6 large sweet potatoes
1/4 cup sunflower oil
2 tablespoons unsweetened, shredded
  coconut

2 tablespoons butter
3 tablespoons dark rum
Salt to taste
Ground cinnamon to taste

Preparation

Wash the potatoes and rub them with the oil. Bake in a preheated 350 degree oven for 1 hour, or until done. Do not wrap the potatoes. Remove them from the oven and cut an "X" into the top of each potato. Press open with your fingers and scoop out the insides with a spoon. Place the insides into a mixing bowl with the remaining ingredients and mix well. Return the mixture to the shells and bake an additional 10 minutes or until heated through. Serve immediately.

Potatoes & Vegetables

Cottage Cheese Vegie Mix
Submitted by: Helen Szymanski

Meal: Lunch or Dinner   Servings: 6
Prep Time: 30 minutes   Cost: Inexpensive

Ingredients

1 large container cottage cheese
1 chopped onion
1 cup frozen peas, thawed in hot tap
   water

1 carrot, shredded
Garlic powder, salt, and pepper to taste
Lettuce and tomato, optional
Parsley to garnish, optional

Preparation

Mix all ingredients thoroughly. Serve as is, or on a bed of lettuce with a tomato wedge and the parsely.

Potatoes & Vegetables

Zucchini and Carrot Casserole

Submitted by: Nancy Phillips in memory of those who believed in the power of hope, believed in the strength of love, and believed all things are possible.

Meal: Dinner   Servings: 6
Prep Time: 1 hour, 15 minutes   Cost: Inexpensive

Ingredients

1/2 cup butter
8 ounce bag of stuffing, fine not cubed
1 pound zucchini, chopped or grated
1 cup carrots, chopped or grated
1 medium onion, chopped

1/2 cup celery, chopped
1 can cream of chicken soup or other cream soup, undiluted
1 cup (8-ounce carton) sour cream

Preparation

In a 2 quart baking dish, melt the butter. Toss the stuffing mix thoroughly with a fork. Take out 1/2 and reserve. Spread the remaining 1/2 of stuffing over bottom of dish. In separate bowl, mix zucchini, carrots, onion and celery together, then add the soup, and sour cream, blending all together. Pour into the dish, sprinkle the remaining stuffing over the top. Bake in a preheated 350 degree oven for 45 minutes to 1 hour, covered. For the last remaining 15 minutes, take cover off to brown a little.

Carrot Salad

Submitted by: Pat Zerega

Meal: Lunch or Dinner   Servings: 6
Prep Time: Overnight   Cost: Inexpensive

Ingredients

1 medium onion, sliced
1 small green pepper, chopped
1 (10-ounce) can tomato soup
1/2 cup oil
1 teaspoon salt
2/3 cup sugar
1/4 teaspoon pepper

1/4 cup vinegar
1 teaspoon celery seed
1 teaspoon mustard
1/2 teaspoon basil
1 teaspon Worcestershire sauce
5 cups carrots, cooked and sliced, not to
   soft

Preparation

Combine all ingredients in a glass or stainless bowl, except carrots. After carrots have cooled then add to the mix. Refrigerate at least 12 hours. Can be heated too.

Potatoes & Vegetables

Scout's own Hummus
Submitted by: Scout Thomas

Meal: Appetizer
Prep Time: 1 hour, 30 minutes

Servings: 6
Cost: Inexpensive

Ingredients

2 cans garbanzo beans (chick peas)
1/2 cup lemon juice
1/2 cup olive oil
1 to 2 cloves fresh garlic, to taste

1 teaspoon salt
Pepper to taste
Paprika for garnish

Preparation

In a food processor or blender combine all ingredients, except for paprika. Grind on grate setting in blender is ideal. Blend until smooth. In a blender you may need to stop and mix the hummus to keep it moving. If consistency seems to dry or chunky add, carefully, more olive oil, lemon juice and salt until the right consistency and taste is achieved. Place hummus in a bowl and sprinkle paprika on top for garnish. Let sit for at least an hour to let all flavors blend. Serve with pita bread or tortillas.

Zucchini Pancakes

Submitted by: Evelyn Brock

Meal: Lunch or Dinner   Servings: 6
Prep Time: 30 minutes   Cost: Inexpensive

Ingredients

1-1/2 cups grated, unpeeled zucchini,
    pressed dry between paper towels
2 tablespoons grated or finely chopped
    onions
1/4 cup Parmesan cheese
1/4 cup flour

2 eggs
2 tablespoons mayonnaise
1/4 teaspoon oregano
Salt and pepper to taste
1 teaspoon butter

Preparation

Mix all ingredients together, except butter. Melt 1 teaspoon butter in 8-1/2- to 10-inch skillet. Spoon batter by 2 heaping tablespoons into skillet. Flatten with spatula. Cook over medium heat until browned on both sides. Serve plain or with tomato sauce and grated cheese or sour cream and chives. Makes a terrific accompaniment for chicken or chops.

Potatoes & Vegetables

Seasoned Banana Peppers

Submitted by: Joyce Connors in memory of Susan Cannon.

Meal: Dinner

Prep Time: 30 minutes

Servings: 6

Cost: Inexpensive

Ingredients

10 banana peppers
1/2 cup olive oil
1 ounce wine vinegar
1/3 teaspoon basil
1/4 teaspoon oregano

1/4 teaspoon ground pepper
Pinch of salt
Splash of Tabasco sauce
1/2 teaspoon lemon juice

Preparation

Place peppers under the broiler. Broil until skins are blackened, turning frequently. Peel skins from peppers and cut into 1/2-inch strips. Mix the peppers with the oil and vinegar then add the basil, oregano, pepper, salt, Tabasco sauce and the lemon juice. May be served hot or cold.

Black Beans and Rice

Submitted by: Blake Mohler

Meal: Lunch or Dinner   Servings: 4
Prep Time: 30 minutes   Cost: Inexpensive

Ingredients

1 tablespoon olive oil
1 medium onion, chopped
1 small green pepper, chopped
1 teaspoon ground cumin
4 cups cooked black beans

1 (8-ounce) can tomatoes with liquid
2 hot peppers, minced (optional)
1 teaspoon salt
1 tablespoon red wine vinegar
Steamed rice

Preparation

Heat oil in large skillet and sauté onion and green pepper until tender. Stir in cumin and cook 1 minute. Add black beans, tomatoes, hot peppers, salt and vinegar. Cook for 10 minutes, stirring occasionally, breaking up tomatoes with a spoon. Serve over steamed rice.

Potatoes & Vegetables

Potato Casserole
Submitted by: Sally Stone

Meal: Dinner
Prep Time: 1 hour

Servings: 6
Cost: Inexpensive

Ingredients

1 (1- to 2-pound) package hash brown
   potatoes
8 ounce grated Parmesan cheese
1 can cream of chicken soup
1/2 cup chopped onion

1/2 cup melted butter
1 pint sour cream
Salt and pepper to taste
1/2 cup buttered bread crumbs

Preparation

Mix all ingredients, except bread crumbs, thoroughly. Place in a greased 9x13-inch pan, top with the bread crumbs. Bake uncovered in a preheated 350 degree oven for 1 hour.

Pea Casserole

Submitted by: Sally Stone

Meal: Dinner   Servings: 4
Prep Time: 1 hour   Cost: Inexpensive

Ingredients

1 package or 2 boxes frozen peas
1 can cream of mushroom soup
1/2 cup milk

1 can sliced chestnuts, drained
1 can Durkee onions
1 cup shredded Cheddar cheese

Preparation

Mix all ingredients thoroughly and place in a greased 9x13-inch pan. Bake in a 375 degree oven for 40 to 45 minutes.

Potatoes & Vegetables

Diane Ladd's
Southern Japanese Dish
Submitted by: Diane Ladd

Meal: Dinner   Servings: 6
Prep Time: 1 hour, 30 minutes   Cost: Moderate

Ingredients

3 tablespoons oil
1/3 cup BRAGG (amino acids substitute
   for soy), or Tamarai sauce, preferably
   non-wheat (may need more)
1/3 cup water
1 medium onion, chopped
1/2 green pepper, chopped
3 or 4 carrots, sliced
1 large handful green beans, chopped
1 Irish potato, scrubbed. Cut, keep and
   use the potato peel with 1/8 inch of
   potato skin left on for potassium.
   Slice, do not use middle of potato
1/2 rutabaga, peeled and sliced

1/2 turnip, peeled and sliced
3 cloves of garlic or more to taste
1/2 eggplant, cut into chunks
1 green zucchini, peeled and cut into
   chunks
2 yellow banana crooked-necked squash,
   cut up
1/4 head cabbage, cut in strips
1/4 head cauliflower, small florets
Tofu of choice (preferably silken and 1%),
   cut into chunks
Spinach leaves
Chunk Mozzarella cheese, thinly sliced

Preparation

In large skillet, add oil, BRAGG, and water. Add onion, green pepper, carrots, green
beans, potato, rutabaga, turnip and garlic. Bring to a boil and cook until tender, 15 to
20 minutes. Add more water, BRAGG and oil as needed. Add eggplant, zucchini,
squash, cabbage and cauliflower. Simmer until tender, about 10 to 15 minutes. Mix
thoroughly. Add tofu and mix thoroughly. Place spinach in a layer on top of dish.
Place slices of cheese on top of spinach layer. Turn to low and simmer until cheese
is melted.

Potatoes & Vegetables

Keller's Green Tomato Relish

Submitted by: Reverend David and Kathy Keller

Meal: Appetizer   Yields: 10 to 12 jars
Prep Time: 4 hours   Cost: Inexpensive

First Step Ingredients

12 large green tomatoes   3 large onions
5 large green peppers   1-1/2 tablespoons salt
1 sweet red pepper   4 cups cider vinegar

Preparation

Put the vegetables through a coarse food chopper or blender. Add the salt and let stand one hour. Add the vinegar.

Second Step Ingredients

1 cup flour   2 tablespoons celery salt
5 cups sugar (one cup may be brown if   1 tablespoon salt
   desired)   1 small jar yellow prepared mustard
2 tablespoons turmeric

Preparation

Add the above to the vegetables and mix in a large pot. Cook over medium heat. Bring just to boiling while stirring often. Color will change to dark yellow. Put into canning jars while very hot. They will seal themselves in several hours.

Potatoes & Vegetables

Summer Squash Casserole
Submitted by: Bishop McCoid

Meal: Dinner
Prep Time: 1 hour

Servings: 6
Cost: Inexpensive

Ingredients

2 pounds yellow squash
1/4 cup chopped onions
1 can condensed cream of chicken soup
1 cup dairy sour cream

1 cup shredded carrots
1 (8-ounce) package herb seasoned
  stuffing mix
1/2 cup melted butter

Preparation

In a saucepan, cook squash onions in salted water for 5 minutes. Drain and set aside. Combine soup and sour cream. Stir in carrots. Fold in squash and onion mixture. Combine stuffing mix and butter. Spread 2/3 of stuffing mix on bottom of 12x7-1/2x2-inch inch baking dish. Spoon vegetable mixture on top. Sprinkle remaining stuffing over vegetables. Bake in a 350 degree oven for 25 to 30 minutes.

Green Beans Vinaigrette

Submitted by: Cheryl Saunders in memory of Kerry Stoner.

Meal: Dinner   Servings: 4 to 6
Prep Time: 45 minutes   Cost: Inexpensive

Ingredients

1-1/2 pounds green beans   2 tablespoons red wine vinegar
1 gallon water   1/2 cup olive oil
1-1/2 teaspoons salt   1 teaspoon salt
1/2 cup parsley, chopped finely   1/4 teaspoon pepper
2 medium cloves garlic, chopped finely

Preparation

Trim and wash green beans. In a large pan, bring the water to a boil and add the salt. Add beans and boil gently for 8 to 10 minutes until "al-dente". Chop the parsley and garlic finely. Put into a small pan. Add vinegar, olive oil, salt and pepper. Bring just to a boil over medium heat, stirring constantly. Remove from heat immediately. Drain the beans and arrange on a serving platter. Pour hot vinegar mixture over bean whIle they are both still hot. Toss gently. Allow the beans to cool thoroughly so that flavors can fully develop. Serve at room temperature.

Potatoes & Vegetables

Potato and Apple Rosti
Submitted by: Julie Andrews

Meal: Lunch or Dinner
Prep Time: 45 minutes

Servings: 2
Cost: Inexpensive

Ingredients

2 medium-sized potatoes, Romano or
    Desiree
Salt
2 tablespoons lemon juice
2 medium-sized apples, Granny Smith

Fresh ground black pepper
Fresh grated nutmeg
1 tablespoon flour
1 ounce butter, melted

Preparation

Place scrubbed whole potatoes in saucepan, add salt and boiling water to cover. Boil for 8 minutes. Drain and let cool. Put lemon juice in a shallow dish. Peel, core, quarter and coarsely grate apples into the dish. Toss in lemon juice to prevent turning brown. Peel potatoes and grate in same manner over a large bowl. Add apple to potatoes leaving lemon juice behind. Season with salt, pepper and nutmeg, mixing thoroughly. Shape mixture into 8 small round cakes with rough edges about 2-1/2 inches in diameter. Place on a plate. Put flour on another plate and dust each rosti cake. Brush 10x14-inch baking tray with melted butter and place the rosti cakes inside also brushing the tops with melted butter. Place on top shelf in a preheated 425 degree oven and bake for 10 minutes. Turn cakes over and bake another 10 to 15 minutes. They are done when the cakes become crisp and golden brown on the outside.

Italian Baked Tomatoes

Submitted by: John F. Cerasini in memory of James Hanneken.

Meal: Lunch or Dinner   Servings: 4 to 6
Prep Time: 1 hour, 45 minutes   Cost: Inexpensive

Ingredients

Non-stick cooking spray
1/2 cup olive oil
4 to 6 fresh tomatoes, cut in half

2 to 3 cloves garlic, chopped fine
3 tablespoons dried oregano
Salt and pepper

Preparation

Coat a large baking pan with cooking spray. Pour half the olive oil in bottom and arrange tomatoes cut side up. Season with salt and pepper. Cover each half with garlic pieces pressing into tomato flesh. Sprinkle oregano over each tomato half then pour remaining oil over top. Bake in a preheated 350 degree oven for 1 hour, 30 minutes until tomatoes have collapsed and bottoms are brown. Juice from tomatoes will have infused the oil making a delicious sauce to spoon over them and for dunking with good, hearty bread. Serve as a side dish with roast meat or chicken.

Recipe   **Page**

Seafood Chowder.. 9-1
Cape Cod Fish Chowder 9-2
Caesar Salad... 9-3
Cranberry Jell-O Salad... 9-4
Speedy Minestrone Soup 9-5
Potato Dill Soup... 9-6
Ham Hock and Lima Beans.. 9-7
Hot Chicken Salad... 9-8
Salad for Lunch 9-9
Minestrone.. 9-10
Earl Campbell's Sausage Jambalaya.................................... 9-11
Lentil-Bulghur Salad 9-12
Broccoli Salad 9-13
Wonderful, Colorful Pasta Salad 9-14
Chicken Vegetable Soup.. 9-15
Kidney Bean and Potato Soup 9-16
Lima Bean Soup.. 9-17
Vegetable Soup with Coconut 9-18
Crôque Monsieur.. 9-19
Essence of Silver and Gold.. 9-20
Meredith's Malibu Nacho Salad.. 9-21
Broccoli and Cauliflower Salad... 9 22
Avgolemono Soup 9-23
Gaspacho.. 9-24
Soupe D'Etrilles... 9-25
Wild Strawberry Salad.. 9-26
Orange Chicken Salad 9-27
Tomato Basil Pie 9-28
Zucchini Relish 9-29
Vegan Stew... 9-30
Pistachio Pudding Salad... 9-31
Pretzel Salad... 9-32
Barbeque Sauce.. 9-33
Pasta Sauce 9-34
Whipped Cream Cole Slaw 9-35
Senate Bean Soup 9-36
Quick and Easy "Cream" of Broccoli 9-37
Pretzel Rasberry Jell-O Salad 9-38
Vegetarian Chili... 9-39
Lentil Soup with Turkey Kielbasa 9-40
Chicken Salad 9-41
Yorkshire Pudding 9-42

Seafood Chowder

Submitted by: Therese Lauth

Meal: Lunch or Dinner   Servings: 4
Prep Time: 3 hours, 30 minutes   Cost: Moderate

Ingredients

3 cloves garlic
1 medium onion
2 tablespoons olive oil
1 teaspoon basil
1 teaspoon oregano
1 teaspoon salt
1 teaspoon Italian seasoning

1 pound white fish (Pollack, Dolphin, or Walleye)
1 (28-ounce) can crushed tomatoes with puree
1 small can minced clams with juice
1 (14 1/2-ounce) can whole tomatoes
3 cups water

Preparation

Sauté garlic and onions in olive oil. Add basil, oregano, salt and Italian seasoning. Chop fish into 1 inch cubes and sauté with garlic and onion until white. Add tomatoes, puree, clams, and water. Simmer 3 hours, add additional water if needed.

Soups, Salads, Sandwiches & Sauces

Cape Cod Fish Chowder

Submitted by: Senator Edward M. Kennedy

Meal: Lunch or Dinner   Servings: 8
Prep Time: 1 hour, 30 minutes   Cost: Inexpensive

Ingredients

2 pounds fresh Haddock   1 bay leaf, crumbled
2 cups water   4 cups milk
2 ounces salt pork, diced   2 tablespoons butter
2 medium onions, sliced   1 tablespoon salt
1 cup celery, chopped   Freshly ground black pepper
4 large potatoes, diced

Preparation

Simmer Haddock in water for 15 minutes. Drain off and reserve the broth. Remove the skin and bones from the fish. Sauté the salt pork in a large pot until crisp. Remove the salt pork and sauté the onions in the pork fat until golden brown. Add the fish, celery, potatoes and bay leaf. Measure reserved fish broth, plus enough boiling water, to make 3 cups liquid. Add to the pot and simmer for 40 minutes. Add milk and butter, simmer for an additional 5 minutes, or until well heated. Season with salt and pepper.

Soups, Salads, Sandwiches & Sauces

Caesar Salad
Submitted by: Tom Atkins

Meal: Lunch or Dinner   Servings: 4
Prep Time: 15 minutes   Cost: Inexpensive

Salad Ingredients

1 head Romaine lettuce, washed, dried,   Caesar dressing
    and torn into bite size pieces   1 cup onion and garlic croutons
1 cup Parmesan cheese, freshly grated

Preparation

In a large salad bowl toss together the lettuce and 1/2 cup of Parmesan cheese. Pour dressing over lettuce to coat well. Add croutons and toss again. Serve remaining cheese on the side for individual use and any extra dressing there may be.

Caesar Dressing Ingredients

1 clove garlic, mashed to a paste   1/2 teaspoon Worcestershire sauce
1 egg, coddled   1/2 teaspoon fresh ground pepper
1 tablespoon lemon juice   1/4 teaspoon salt
1 teaspoon anchovy paste   1/2 cup olive oil

Preparation

In medium bowl combine the first 7 ingredients and mix well. Stir in olive oil.

Suggestions

To coddle egg: Bring a small pot of water to a boil, turn off heat. Slowly lower egg into the water, cover and let sit for 6 to 8 minutes. Plunge into cold water. Egg is less likely to crack if it is room temperature before placing it in the hot water.

Soups, Salads, Sandwiches & Sauces

Cranberry Jell-O Salad
Submitted by: Nancy Squibb

Meal: Lunch or Dinner   Servings: 10 to 12
Prep Time: 4 hours   Cost: Inexpensive

Ingredients

2 packages cherry Jell-O
2 cups hot water
1 cup cold water
1 cup black cherry juice, reserved from
   black cherries

1 can cranberry sauce, melted over low
   flame
1 large can crushed pineapple, drained
1 large can pitted black cherries
1 cup chopped nuts

Preparation

Dissolve Jell-O in hot water. Add cold water and juice, then add melted cranberry sauce. Pour into a 9x13-inch pan after it has thickened slightly. Add all other ingredients. Chill and serve.

Soups, Salads, Sandwiches & Sauces

Speedy Minestrone Soup
Submitted by: Peggy Hager
in memory of Chuck Johnston (8/20/65 - 6/11/92).

Meal: Lunch or Dinner   Servings: 6
Prep Time: 45 minutes   Cost: Inexpensive

Ingredients

3 beef bouillon cubes
2 cups boiling water
1 (12-ounce) can whole kernal corn
1/2 cup uncooked small macaroni or
   shells
1 (16-ounce) can whole or crushed
   tomatoes, undrained

1 (8-ounce) can lima beans, undrained
1 tablespoon instant minced onion
1/2 teaspoon salt
1/4 teaspoon dried basil leaves, crushed
Dash garlic powder
Dash pepper

Preparation

In large pan dissolve bouillon cubes in boiling water. Add remaining ingredients, cover and simmer for 30 minutes.

Potato Dill Soup
Submitted by: Senator Daniel Patrick Moynihan

Meal: Lunch or Dinner   Servings: 4
Prep Time: 1 hour   Cost: Inexpensive

Ingredients

7 large potatoes, peeled
2 onions, chopped
Bunch of scallions, chopped
Large amount of fresh dill
2 tablespoons butter

1 pint heavy cream
2 cups sour cream
Fresh ground black pepper
Parsley to garnish
Salt to taste

Preparation

Cook potatoes with onions in boiling water until they begin to fall apart. Strain. Add scallions, dill, butter, heavy cream, and cook 10 minutes. Stir in 1 cup sour cream and let it heat through for 2 minutes. Garnish each bowl with pepper, dill, parsley and 1 teaspoon sour cream.

Ham Hock and Lima Beans

Submitted by: Red Skelton

Meal: Lunch or Dinner   Servings: 4
Prep Time: Overnight   Cost: Inexpensive

Ingredients

1 pound package large, dried lima
   beans
1 large onion, diced
2 large stalks celery, diced
1 teaspoon salt

2 whole pepper corns
2 large sized carrots, diced
Pinch of nutmeg
1 good size smoked ham hock

Preparation

Place lima beans in a large bowl. Cover completely with water and let stand overnight. Save the water the lima beans were soaked in. Place the beans in a good sized pot. Take half of the water the beans were soaked in and combine them with the beans. Over a small flame, let beans cook for 15 minutes, covered. After the 15 minutes are up, add the vegetables, pepper corns, salt and nutmeg. Simmer for another 15 minutes. Wash the ham hock and add to the pot. Simmer for 1 hour. Add more water if necessary, use the water from when the beans were soaked.

Suggestions

Do not over season. The ham hock is already highly seasoned and will add spice to the recipe.

Hot Chicken Salad

Submitted by: Senator Robert F. Bennett

Meal: Lunch or Dinner   Servings: 6
Prep Time: 45 minutes   Cost: Inexpensive

Ingredients

2/3 cups slivered almonds (may be toasted)
4 cups cooked, diced chicken (approximately 5 breasts)
2 tablespoons lemon juice
3/4 cup mayonnaise

2 cups finely chopped celery
1 cup cream of chicken soup
1 teaspoon minced onion
1 cup grated Cheddar cheese
1-1/2 cups crushed potato chips or corn flakes

Preparation

Toast almonds on cookie sheet in a 350 degree oven for 5 to 7 minutes, watch carefully. Mix all ingredients except cheese and potato chips. Add cheese, then chips to top of mixture. Bake at 400 degrees for 20 minutes.

Soups, Salads, Sandwiches & Sauces

Salad for Lunch

Submitted by: Art Linkletter

Meal: Lunch   Servings: 2 to 4
Prep Time: 15 minutes   Cost: Moderate

Ingredients

2 heads of romaine hearts, cut up   Italian dressing
1/2 pound small defrosted shrimp   Garlic toast
Handful of crumbled up Bleu or Stilton
   cheese

Preparation

Combine first 3 ingredients. Toss with dressing and serve with the garlic toast.

Minestrone

Submitted by: Brian Rohleder in memory of Jim Hanneken.

Meal: Lunch or Dinner   Servings: 4
Prep Time: Overnight   Cost: Inexpensive

Ingredients

1 box mixed, dried beans   1 pound soup meat, cut up
1 large onion, chopped   2 soup bones
2 cloves garlic, minced   Salt and pepper to taste
1 large can tomato sauce   Fresh grated Parmesan cheese

Preparation

Soak beans overnight. Rinse and place beans with rest of ingredients in a Dutch oven. Fill pot 3/4 full with water. Cook over medium heat 3-1/2 to 4 hours. Serve with freshly grated Parmesan cheese.

Soups, Salads, Sandwiches & Sauces

Earl Campbell's
Sausage Jambalya
Submitted by: Earl Campbell

Meal: Lunch or Dinner
Prep Time: 1 hour

Servings: 4
Cost: Inexpensive

Ingredients

1-1/2 cups onion, chopped
1-1/2 cups celery, chopped
1 cup green pepper, chopped
1-1/2 teaspoons garlic, minced
4 tablespoons butter

1 pound EARL CAMPBELL SMOKED
   SAUSAGE, diced
2 cups rice, uncooked
4 cups chicken stock
4 bay leaves

Spice Mix Ingredients

1 teaspoon salt
1/2 teaspoon ground black pepper
1/2 teaspoon ground cayenne pepper

1/2 teaspoon ground white pepper
1 teaspoon dry mustard
1/2 teaspoon dried thyme leaf

Preparation

In a small bowl, combine spice mix ingredients. Mix well and set aside. Combine the onion, green pepper, celery and garlic in a medium bowl and set aside. Heat butter in a large heavy skillet over high heat. Add the diced sausage and cook 5 minutes, stirring occasionally. Add the onion, pepper, celery and garlic. Add the spice mix. Stir well, scraping the pan bottom. Cook until browned, about 10 to 12 minutes. Add the rice. Again, stir well and scrape the pan bottom. Cook 5 minutes. Add stock and bay leaf, stirring well. Bring mixture to a boil, reduce heat and simmer, stirring occasionally until rice is just tender, about 20 minutes. Remove bay leaf and serve.

Lentil-Bulghur Salad

Submitted by: Carina de Wit-Lord

Meal:	Lunch or Dinner	Servings: 4
Prep Time:	2 hours, 30 minutes	Cost: Inexpensive

Ingredients

1 cup French lentils
3-1/2 cups water
1 cup bulghur wheat, finely cracked wheat
3/4 cup walnut pieces, toasted
1/3 cup extra virgin olive oil
2 tablespoons freshly squeezed lemon juice
2 tablespoons red wine vinegar, garlic flavor
1 large clove garlic, crushed

1 teaspoon salt
1/4 teaspoon black pepper
1/2 red bell pepper, seeded and finely chopped
1/2 green bell pepper, seeded and finely chopped
1/2 red onion, finely chopped
2 stalks celery, finely chopped
10 radishes, finely chopped
1/2 cucumber, seeded and finely chopped
10 sprigs parsley, finely chopped

Preparation

Place lentils in a sieve and rinse thoroughly. Place lentils in a sauce pan with 2-1/2 cups water and bring to boil. Reduce heat to low and simmer 30 to 45 minutes until lentils are tender but not mushy. Lentils should hold their shape. While lentils are simmering, place bulghur wheat in a bowl. Boil the remaining cup of water and pour over bulghur wheat, cover, let stand until all water has been absorbed, about 15 minutes. Fluff bulghur wheat with a fork. When the lentils are done, pour off any remaining liquid and let cool. Heat an iron-cast skillet over high heat. Add walnut pieces and move them around constantly with a wooden spoon until they begin to brown. Turn off heat and set aside. In a small bowl, mix olive oil, lemon juice, vinegar, garlic, salt and pepper with a fork, until you obtain a dressing. Place lentils in a large bowl, preferably glass. With a wooden spoon, carefully mix in bulghur wheat, followed by the chopped vegetables and the toasted walnuts. Pour dressing evenly over salad and mix in with a fork. Refrigerate salad at least 1 hour to allow the flavors to blend.

Suggestions

French lentils are small, dark green lentils which can be found in most health food stores. If they are unavailable, you may substitute brown lentils. Bulghur wheat can also be found in health food stores. It comes in several different degrees of coarseness. For this recipe, you want to use the finely cracked variety.

Soups, Salads, Sandwiches & Sauces

Broccoli Salad

Submitted by: Dana Magnone

Meal: Lunch or Dinner   Servings: 6
Prep Time: 30 minutes   Cost: Inexpensive

Ingredients

2 (10-ounce) packages frozen broccoli   1 medium tomato, divided
1 can chick peas   1/2 pound Provolone cheese, divided
1 medium onion, divided   1 large bottle Italian dressing

Preparation

Cook broccoli until just tender. Cool, mix all other ingredients, except dressing. If making ahead of time put dressing on just before serving.

Wonderful, Coloful Pasta Salad

Submitted by: Mardi Isler

Meal: Lunch or Dinner   Servings: 6
Prep Time: 1 hour, 30 minutes   Cost: Inexpensive

Ingredients

1 pound tri-colored rotini
1/8 cup olive oil
Vinaigrette
1/4 cup mayonnaise
1 diced green pepper
1 diced red pepper
1 can of black olives

Can of green olives
Sugar snap peas (optional), cut on the
   diagonal
Small Vidalia onion (optional), diced
1/2 cup Parmesan cheese
Salt and pepper to taste

Preparation

Cook rotini according to directions. Toss immediately with olive oil. Toss again with vinaigrette, just until moist. Add the 1/4 cup mayonnaise, or even more to taste. Add the peppers, olives and sugar snap peas, and onion, if using them. Sprinkle with Parmesan cheese and mix well. Taste after an hour and add salt and pepper to taste. Let sit out of the refrigerator for 1/2 an hour before serving.

Chicken Vegetable Soup

Submitted by: Anne Davis

Meal: Lunch or Dinner
Prep Time: 1 hour, 30 minutes

Servings: 6
Cost: Inexpensive

Ingredients

1 large onion, diced
1 clove garlic, crushed
1 rib celery
4 chicken breasts
Salt and pepper to taste

3 quarts water
1 carrot, diced
1 cup peas
3 potatoes, diced

Preparation

In a soup pot, add the onion, garlic, celery, chicken, salt and pepper. Cover and let simmer 1/2 hour, stirring once or twice. When vegetables look soft, add the water and simmer 1/2 hour. Boil until chicken is done, about 1/2 hour.

Kidney Bean and Potato Soup
Submitted by: Anne Davis

Meal:　　　Lunch or Dinner　　　　Servings: 8
Prep Time:　3 hours　　　　　　　Cost:　　Inexpensive

Soup Ingredients

1 package dried, dark kidney beans,
　rinsed
3 quarts water

1 smoked neck bone
3 medium potatoes, diced
Salt and pepper to taste

Preparation

Add the beans, water and neck bone. Simmer until beans are done, about 2-1/2 hours. Add potatoes, salt and pepper when beans are done. Simmer another 15 minutes or until potatoes are no longer hard. Serve with polenta.

Polenta Ingredients

1 cup yellow cornmeal

3 cups water

Preparation

Mix cornmeal with water and stir. Cook over medium heat, stirring constantly until very thick. Pour into a dish. Add polenta in spoonfuls to soup.

Lima Bean Soup
Submitted by: Anne Davis

Meal: Lunch or Dinner   Servings: 6
Prep Time: 3 hours   Cost: Inexpensive

Ingredients

1 pound baby lima beans   2 tablespoons shortening
1 smoked neck bone   1 medium onion, diced
1 carrot, grated   2 tablespoons flour
1 medium potato, diced   Salt and pepper to taste

Preparation

Rinse lima beans in cold water. Add smoked neck, and the carrot. Simmer until beans are done. Add the potato and simmer until done, set aside. In large skillet sauté onion in the shortening until light brown. Add the flour and make light brown. Bring soup back to a boil and add soup broth to skillet mixture. Stir constantly until smooth. Add salt and pepper to taste.

Vegetable Soup with Coconut

Submitted by: Victor Wahome

Meal: Lunch or Dinner   Servings: 4
Prep Time: 1 hour   Cost: Inexpensive

Ingredients

1 tablespoon butter
1/2 red onion, finely chopped
6 ounces each, turnip, sweet potato,
   and pumpkin, diced, medium-size
1 teaspoon dried marjoram
1/2 teaspoon ginger
1/4 teaspoon cinnamon
1 tablespoon chopped scallions

Salt and pepper to taste
4 cups vegetable stock
2 tablespoons sliced almonds
1 fresh chili, seeded and chopped
1 teaspoon sugar
1/2 cup coconut cream
Fresh, chopped cilantro, to garnish

Preparation

Melt the butter in a large skillet and fry the onion for 5 minutes. Add the vegetables and fry another 5 minutes. Add the marjoram, ginger, cinnamon, scallions, salt and pepper. Fry over low heat for 10 minutes, stirring frequently. Add the vegetable stock, almonds, chili and sugar and stir well to mix. Cover and simmer gently for 10 to 15 minutes or until the vegetables are tender. Add the coconut cream and stir. Sprinkle with the cilantro and serve in warm bowls.

Crôque Monsieur
Submitted by: The Author

Meal: Lunch or Snack
Prep Time: 10 minutes

Servings: 1 or 2
Cost: Inexpensive

Ingredients

2 pieces of bread
Butter
Mustard to taste

4 slices deli ham
2 slices deli cheese, your choice

Preparation

Toast bread until golden brown. Spread butter and mustard onto toast to taste. Layer each slice with deli ham and top with cheese. Bake in a toaster oven using the Top Brown setting until cheese becomes bubbly and slightly browned.

Suggestions

This recipe can become a Crôque Madame by simply adding a fried egg to the top of the finished sandwich.

Soups, Salads, Sandwiches & Sauces

Essence of Silver and Gold
Submitted by: Robin Leach

Meal: Dinner   Yields: 4 cups
Prep Time: Overnight   Cost: Expensive

Ingredients

2 (1-pound) pieces bottom round of
  veal, boned and tied
2 whole chicken breasts, about 1 pound
  each, bone in
4 pounds veal bones
2 leeks, trimmed, washed thoroughly,
  and coarsely chopped
2 celery stalks, thickly sliced
2 medium carrots, halved, and thickly
  sliced

3 to 4 branches fresh thyme, 2 teaspoons
  dried
2 bay leaves
2 large onions, stuck with 2 whole cloves
2 teaspoons salt
20 whole black peppercorns
12 cups water
4 cups good-quality dry, white wine

Preparation

Trim the veal and chicken of any fat. Have the butcher chop the veal bones into 3 to 4 large pieces. Combine all ingredients in a large, nonreactive stockpot. Bring to a boil over moderately high heat, then reduce heat to moderate and simmer, uncovered, 2 to 3 hours or until the liquid measures about 4 cups. Periodically skim off any residue that rises to the top. Line a large sieve or colander with a double layer of cheesecloth or coarse muslin and set it inside a large bowl. Carefully ladle in the hot stock, discarding the solids. Let the stock cool to room temperature, then cover and refrigerate. Remove any fat that hardens on top.

Suggestions

Use your best wine for this sauce. Spare not and the results will pay off.

Soups, Salads, Sandwiches & Sauces

Meredith's Malibu Nacho Salad

Submitted by: Burgess Meredith

Meal: Lunch or Dinner   Servings: 4
Prep Time: 30 minutes   Cost: Inexpensive

Ingredients

1 can black beans   Lime juice
1 cup yellow corn   Salt and pepper
1 cup cooked rice   1 head lettuce
1 onion, chopped   1 bag tortilla chips
1 bunch cilantro, chopped   Grated cheese and sour cream, optional
3 medium tomatoes, chopped   Fresh salsa
Olive oil

Preparation

Mix beans, corn, rice, onion, cilantro and tomatoes. Marinate with olive oil, lime juice, salt and pepper to taste. Use a little lime juice at a time, adding more as needed for your taste. Serve on a bed of lettuce and corn chips. Top with grated cheese, sour cream, and salsa.

Broccoli and Cauliflower Salad
Submitted by: Irlene Mandrell

Meal: Lunch or Dinner   Servings: 6
Prep Time: 2 hours   Cost: Inexpensive

Ingredients

2 cups broccoli, cut in small pieces   1/2 cup chopped walnuts
2 cups cauliflower, cut in small pieces   1/2 cup raisins
3 to 4 green onions, chopped   8 slices fried bacon or bacon chips

Preparation

Mix all ingredients together and toss with the dressing that follows.

Dressing Ingredients

3/4 cup mayonnaise   2 tablespoons vinegar
1/4 cup sugar

Preparation

Mix thoroughly. Toss with above salad ingredients and chill.

Soups, Salads, Sandwiches & Sauces

Avgolemono Soup

Submitted by: Mathieu Wahrung

Meal: Lunch or Dinner
Prep Time: 45 minutes

Servings: 4
Cost: Inexpensive

Ingredients

1/4 cup ground rice
1 quart chicken stock
2 egg yolks
1 cup lemon juice

Salt and Szechuan pepper
1 lemon, sliced thin
Parsely, chopped

Preparation

Cook the rice in the chicken broth. Mix egg yolks and lemon juice, set aside. Once the rice is cooked, take 2 cups of the hot broth and pour it on the mixed egg yolks. Whip constantly and pour into the soup mixture. Heat on low, stirring constantly. Do not let the soup boil. Adjust seasonings and serve decorated with the lemon slices and parsley.

Soups, Salads, Sandwiches & Sauces

Gaspacho
Submitted by: Mathieu Wahrung

Meal: Lunch or Dinner   Servings: 4
Prep Time: 1 hour   Cost: Moderate

Ingredients

Fistful of bread, without crust
1 tablespoon olive oil
3 tablespoons vinegar
3 pounds tomatoes, peeled and seeded
  (do this carefully to save the juices)
1 cucumber, peeled, seeded and
  coarsely chopped

1 green pepper, peeled, seeded and
  coarsley chopped
1 onion, peeled and coarsley chopped
2 cloves garlic
Espelette capsicum or a few drops of
  tabasco
1/2 teaspoon paprika
Salt and pepper to taste

Preparation

Soak the bread in the oil and vinegar, then wring out. Put all ingredients in a blender
and puree. Pass through a strainer, correct the seasonings and chill.

Suggestions

The pepper is easily peeled with a potato-peeler or blanch it for 5 minutes and then
just peel off the skin. Add the liquid from the tomatoes to get the right consistency.
Gaspacho can be served with diced tomatoes, cucumbers, peppers and onions.
Sprinkled with chopped basil. Use old sherry vinegar. If you prefer a stronger taste,
use balsamic or wine vinegar instead.

Soupe D'Etrilles
Submitted by: Mathieu Wahrung

Meal: Lunch or Dinner   Servings: 4
Prep Time: 2 hours   Cost: Expensive

Ingredients

3-1/2 cups fish stock
6 etrilles, this is a velvet swimming crab
  but any crab should do, these are
  about the size of a fist
1 cup crème fraiche
1 cup white wine
1/2 cup Cognac or Armagnac
3/4 stick butter, divided
1 shallot, finely chopped

1 clove garlic, finely chopped
2 tomatoes, peeled, seeded and cut into
  chunks
1 teaspoon sage
1/2 teaspoon paprika
Salt and pepper to taste
Dash Cayenne pepper
1 bay leaf

Preparation

Boil the fish stock. Kill the crabs by dipping them briefly in the fish stock. Do not cook them, just kill them. Open them, eliminate the gills. Separate the coral and mix with the cream, set aside. Take out as much flesh as you can, set aside. Flambé white wine and Cognac. The idea here is to burn away the volatile acids not eliminate the alcohol that would cook away anyhow. Put the mortal remains of the crab in a blender and crush. Brown them in 1/2 the butter and set aside. In a big saucepan, melt the rest of the butter and cook the shallots and garlic. Add the tomatoes, sage, paprika, salt, pepper and Cayenne pepper. Over a brisk heat, stirring vigorously, add the crushed crabs. Add the wine, Cognac and fish stock. Bring to a boil, skim and let simmer for 1/2 an hour. Strain the mixture, retrieving as much of the juice as possible. Just before serving, bind the liquid with the mixture of cream and coral. Do not boil the soup again after that. Add the crab meat, the soup should be hot enough to cook the crab meat. Sprinkle the soup with chopped coriander leaves for a different flavor. Can also be garnished with stewed seashells (cockles, clams...).

Wild Strawberry Salad

Submitted by: Robert Keith Eros and Louis Paul Eros

Meal: Lunch or Dinner   Servings: 6
Prep Time: 2 hours   Cost: Moderate

Ingredients

2 cups boiling water
2 small packages strawberry gelatin
2 mashed, over-ripe bananas
2 (10-ounce) packages frozen
   strawberries

2 cups crushed pineapple, well drained
2-1/2 cups chopped pecans
1 small container sour cream

Preparation

Mix 1 cup boiling water with 1 package gelatin. Add 1 banana, 1 package
strawberries, 1 cup pineapple and 1/2 cup pecans, mix together. Pour into a bundt
pan and refrigerate until set. After this has set, add a layer of sour cream (use whole
container or to your preference). Mix together all remaining ingredients and pour on
top of the sour cream. Put the pan back in the refrigerator until fully set.

Soups, Salads, Sandwiches & Sauces

Orange Chicken Salad
Submitted by: Senator Michael Enzi

Meal: Lunch or Dinner   Servings: 6
Prep Time: 30 minutes   Cost: Moderate

Salad Ingredients

6 cups iceberg lettuce, cut in bite size
   pieces
2 small cans mandarin oranges, drained
3 green onions, sliced thin
3/4 cup diced celery

1 (12-1/2-ounce) can white chicken packed
   in water, drained
3/4 cup slivered almonds, optional
Honey Mustard Dressing (see below)
1 (12-ounce) bag Chinese noodles

Preparation

In large bowl, toss the lettuce, oranges, onions, celery, chicken, and almonds until
well mixed. Add 1/2 cup Honey Mustard Dressing and toss again. Serve over the
noodles and serve the remaining dressing at the table.

Honey Mustard Dressing Ingredients

3/4 cup olive oil
1/3 cup vinegar or lemon juice
6 tablespoons honey

1 teaspoon garlic
1 teaspoon dry mustard
1/2 to 1 teaspoon dill weed

Preparation

Blend all ingredients thoroughly.

Tomato Basil Pie

Submitted by: Susan Martin Fink

Meal: Lunch or Dinner   Servings: 8
Prep Time: 1 hour   Cost: Inexpensive

Ingredients

1/2 of pie crust
1-1/2 cups shredded Mozzarella cheese
5 Roma or 4 medium tomatoes, cut into
  wedges
1 cup loose basil leaves

4 cloves garlic
1/2 cup mayonnaise
1/4 cup Parmesan cheese
1/8 teaspoon ground white pepper

Preparation

Place crust in 9-inch quiche pan and pre-bake. Remove from oven and sprinkle with 1/2 cup Mozzarella cheese. Layer tomatoes over Mozzarella cheese. In food processor, process and combine basil and garlic until coarsely chopped. Sprinkle over tomatoes. In mixing bowl, combine remaining Mozzarella cheese, mayonnaise, Parmesan cheese and pepper. Spoon cheese mixture over top of pie. Bake in a preheated 375 degree oven for 35 to 40 minutes or until golden and bubbly. Serve warm.

Zucchini Relish

Submitted by: William T. and Anne E. Timmins

Meal: Lunch or Dinner   Yields: 7 pints
Prep Time: Overnight   Cost: Inexpensive

Ingredients

10 cups ground zucchini, about 5
    pounds
4 large onions, ground
4 large green bell peppers, ground
4 large red bell peppers, ground
1/2 cup pickling salt
2-1/2 cups cider vinegar

4 cups sugar
2 tablespoons cornstarch
1 teaspoon ground turmeric
1 teaspoon ground nutmeg
2 teaspoons celery seed
1/4 teaspoon pepper

Preparation

Put zucchini, onions, green peppers and red peppers in a food processor or food grinder to obtain a medium coarseness. Sprinkle with pickling salt and let sit overnight. In the morning, drain and rinse well with cold water. Mix together vinegar, sugar, cornstarch, turmeric, nutmeg, celery seed and pepper. Bring to a boil in a large kettle. Add the ground vegetables and simmer for 30 minutes. Ladle into hot jars, leaving 1/2-inch head space. Process in boiling water bath for 15 minutes.

Vegan Stew
Submitted by: Danielle and Steve Barczykowski

Meal: Lunch or Dinner   Servings: 6
Prep Time: 1 hour, 30 minutes   Cost: Inexpensive

Ingredients

8 cups vegetable stock or water
1 cup dry lentils
1/2 cup pearled barley
1 large onion, peeled and chopped fine.
2 medium carrots, peeled and sliced into
   1/4 inch rounds
2 stalks celery, diced into 1/4 inch
   pieces

4 or 5 medium potatoes, chopped into 1
   inch cubes
8 ounces fresh white mushrooms, sliced
2 to 4 tablespoons soy sauce
Salt and pepper to taste

Preparation

Add stock to large stock pot over high heat. While the stock is coming to a boil, rinse the lentils, checking for stones or other foreign matter. Add the cleaned lentils and barley to the stock. Add onions, carrots, celery and potatoes to the stock and bring up to a boil. When the stew begins to boil, turn the heat to low and partially cover with a lid. Stir occasionally. Add extra stock or water a cup at a time, if needed, to keep the vegetables just barely covered with liquid. Simmer for 50 minutes or until the potatoes are tender and the lentils break down to create a sauce. Add the mushrooms and the soy sauce. If using stock, use 2 tablespoons soy sauce; if using water, use 4 tablespoons soy sauce. Continue cooking for another 10 minutes. The finished stew should be fairly thick and saucy. Season with salt and pepper. Serve in bowls with crusty French bread on the side.

Soups, Salads, Sandwiches & Sauces

Pistachio Pudding Salad
Submitted by: Barbara Shearer

Meal: Lunch or Dinner   Servings: 8
Prep Time: 2 hours   Cost: Inexpensive

Ingredients

2 cups Ritz crackers, crushed   4 cups vanilla ice cream, softened
1 stick melted butter   2 large boxes pistachio pudding
2 cups milk   Frozen whipped topping

Preparation

Mix together the crackers and the butter in a 9-inch pie pan, press down to make a crust. Mix the milk, ice cream and dry pudding mix. Pour into crust, top with frozen whipped topping. Chill for an hour.

Pretzel Salad

Submitted by: Barbara Shearer

Meal: Lunch or Dinner   Servings: 10
Prep Time: 2 hours   Cost: Inexpensive

Ingredients

2 cups crushed pretzel, not to fine
3/4 cup melted butter
3 tablespoons sugar
1 (8-ounce) package cream cheese,
   softened
1 cup sugar

1 medium-size frozen whipped topping
2 boxes strawberry gelatin
2 cups boiling water
2 (10-ounce) bags frozen strawberries,
   thawed

Preparation

Mix together pretzel, butter and sugar. Press into a 9x13-inch pan and bake in a
preheated oven for 10 minutes. Do not overbake. Cool completely. Mix together
cream cheese and sugar. Fold in frozen whipped topping. Spread over pretzel crust
and refrigerate. Mix together gelatin, water and strawberries, refrigerate for 20
minutes. Pour gelatin mixture over cheese and refrigerate.

Barbeque Sauce
Submitted by: Pat Crawford in memory of Ed Crawford, Jr.

Meal:　　　　Lunch or Dinner　　　　Servings: 6
Prep Time: 1 hour　　　　　　　　　　Cost:　　Inexpensive

Ingredients

1 cup catsup
1/4 cup sugar
1/8 cup Worcestershire sauce
1 teaspoon white vinegar

Salt and pepper to taste
A little minced onion, optional
Kolbassi

Preparation

Mix all ingredients, except Kolbassi, and heat thoroughly. Boil Kolbassi and slice into rounds. Cover with barbecue sauce and bake in a preheated 350 degree oven for 20 minutes. Serve with toothpicks. This barbecue sauce is great with a variety of other meats as well.

Pasta Sauce
Submitted by: Jill Kornberg

Meal: Lunch or Dinner   Yields: Sauces 1 pound pasta
Prep Time: 1 hour   Cost: Inexpensive

Ingredients

1 (28-ounce) can whole tomatoes
1 (15-ounce) can tomato sauce
1 teaspoon sugar
1 teaspoon cinnamon
1 tablespoon butter

1 tablespoon tomato paste, optional
2 tablespoons oil
1 teaspoon salt
1 teaspoon pepper
1 teaspoon garlic

Preparation

Mix all above ingredients thoroughly. Simmer over low heat very slowly for 30 to 45 minutes. Serve over your favorite pasta.

Soups, Salads, Sandwiches & Sauces

Whipped Cream Cole Slaw

Submitted by: Wilma Eyman

Meal: Lunch or Dinner
Prep Time: 2 hours

Servings: 8 to 10
Cost: Inexpensive

Ingredients

2 pounds shredded cabbage
3/4 cup sugar
1/2 teaspoon salt

Pepper
1/2 cup vinegar
1 cup whipping cream

Preparation

Alternate cabbage and dry ingredients in layers and pound down with the bottom of a glass. Pour vinegar over and refrigerate until ready to use. Whip the cream and fold into cabbage.

Senate Bean Soup

Submitted by: Senator Carl Levin

Meal:	Lunch or Dinner	Servings: 8	
Prep Time:	4 hours	Cost:	Inexpensive

Ingredients

2 pounds small Michigan Navy Beans
4 quarts of hot water
1-1/2 pounds smoked ham hocks

1 medium onion, chopped
Butter
Salt and pepper to taste

Preparation

Wash the beans. Run hot water through the beans until they are white again. Boil four quarts of water with the beans. Add the ham hocks and let simmer on a slow boil for three hours covered. Braise the onion in butter until light brown. Add to the soup. Season with salt and pepper. Do not add the salt until ready to serve.

Senatorial Record

Whatever uncertainties may exist in the Senate of the United States, one thing is sure; Bean Soup is on the menu of the Senate Restaurant everyday. The origin of this culinary decree has been lost to antiquity, but there are several oft repeated legends. One story has it that Senator Fred Thomas DuBois of Idaho, who served in the Senate from 1901 to 1907 when the Chairman of the Committee that supervised the Senate Restaurant, gaveled through a resolution requiring the bean soup be on the menu every day. Another account attributes the bean soup mandate to Senator Knute Nelson of Minnesota, who expressed a fondness for it in 1903. In any case, Senators and their guests are always assured of a hearty, nourishing dish; they know they can rely upon its delightful flavor and Epicurean qualities.

Quick and Easy "Cream" of Broccoli

Submitted by: Mary Ann Gubish

Meal: Lunch or Dinner

Prep Time: 40 minutes

Servings: 6

Cost: Inexpensive

Salad Ingredients

1 cup onions or leeks, sliced
1/4 cups of butter
1 cup potatoes, diced
2 cups broccoli (zucchini or cauliflower
   can be substituted)

1/2 cup carrots, sliced
1 quart chicken stock
1 teaspoon salt
1/4 cup pepper

Preparation

Sauté the onions in butter. Add vegetables, stock, salt and pepper. Simmer 30 minutes until the vegetables are tender. Puree in blender. Serve hot.

Pretzel Raspberry Jell-O Salad

Submitted by: Dorothy Lakatos
in memory of my dear nephew John J. Pingree.

Meal: Dessert   Servings: 10 to 12
Prep Time: Overnight   Cost: Inexpensive

First Layer Ingredients

2 cups crushed pretzels   2 tablespoons sugar
3/4 cup soft butter

Preparation

Mix all together until crumbly and press into 13x9x2-inch pan. Preheat oven to 350 degrees and bake 8 to 10 minutes. Cool.

Second Layer Ingredients

1 (8-ounce) soft cream cheese   1 cup granulated sugar
1 (8-ounce) container frozen whipped
   topping

Preparation

With an electric mixer, beat until creamy, then pour over the first layer and refrigerate.

Third Layer Ingredients

1 large package raspberry Jell-O   2 packages frozen raspberries
2 cups hot water

Preparation

Dissolve the Jell-O in the water and add the berries. Refrigerate until it just begins to set. Pour the mixture over the second layer. Cover and refrigerate overnight.

Vegetarian Chili
Submitted by: Reverend Renée Waun

Meal: Lunch or Dinner   Servings: 8 to 10
Prep Time: Overnight   Cost: Inexpensive

Ingredients

1 cup each of three or four types dried
   beans
3 to 4 onions, chopped
1 cup each uncooked lentils and brown
   rice
3 carrots

3 potatoes (cut into 1 inch chunks)
1 (12-ounce) can tomato paste
1 or 2 cans stewed tomatoes
Salt and pepper to taste
Chili powder to taste

Preparation

Soak the beans in a giant soup pot overnight in enough water to cover by at least 2 inches. Remove the beans from the pot, drain the water and rinse the beans in a colander. In the pot, sauté the onions in a little water until soft. Add the beans, lentils, rice and enough water to cover and boil until beans are soft. Add remaining ingredients and simmer until the vegetables are cooked.

Suggestions

Serve with a simple salad and some wonderful whole grain bread. This chili provides complete protein. Freezes very well in individual servings.

Lentil Soup
with Turkey Keilbasa
Submitted by: Michael Dukakis

Meal: Lunch or Dinner   Servings: 8 to 10
Prep Time: 8 hours   Cost: Moderate

Ingredients

2 cups lentils
10 cups water
2 carrots, sliced
1 stalk celery
1 onion, diced
1 cup peeled, diced potatoes
1/2 teaspoon thyme

2 tablespoons soy sauce
1 tablespoon Worcestershire sauce
1/2 teaspoon savory
1 pound turkey kielbasa
3 tablespoons wine vinegar
Salt and pepper to taste

Preparation

Soak the lentils in water for 3 hours. Do not drain. Bring to a boil and add carrots, celery and onions. Cover and simmer for 3 hours. Add potatoes, thyme, soy sauce, Worcestershire sauce, savory, and kielbasa. Cook an additional hour. Stir in vinegar, salt and pepper. Sprinkle with parsley.

Soups, Salads, Sandwiches & Sauces

Chicken Salad

Submitted by: The Rusty Nail Restaurant

Meal: Lunch or Dinner   Servings: 10 to 15
Prep Time: 4 hours   Cost: Moderate

Ingredients

5 pounds cooked chicken, cubed
2 cups celery, chopped fine
12 hard boiled eggs, grated

1 tablespoon salt
1 tablespoon pepper
Mayonnaise to taste

Preparation

In a large bowl, combine all ingredients. Mix and chill several hours.

Yorkshire Pudding

Submitted by: John Yelland

Meal:	Dessert	Servings: 6 to 8
Prep Time:	40 minutes	Cost: Inexpensive

Ingredients

1 cup sifted flour
3/4 teaspoon salt
2 eggs, beaten

1 cup milk
1/4 cup beef drippings

Preparation

Sift together the flour and salt. Beat the eggs add the milk to a large mixing bowl. Slowly add the flour and salt mixture beating constantly. Place 1 teaspoon of beef drippings in each custard dish. Place approximately 3 tablespoons into each dish. Bake at 400 degrees for 20 minutes.

Bread & Breakfast

Recipe	Page
Zucchini Bread	10-1
Griddle Drop Scones	10-2
1/2 Recipe Buns	10-3
Onion Biscuits	10-4
Banana Bread	10-5
Whole Wheat Pancakes	10-6
Corn Cakes	10-7
Poor Man's Dumplings	10-8
Paula Poundstone's Recipe for an Airport Breakfast	10-9
Tropical Fruit Pancakes	10-10
Southern Corn Bread	10-11
Sticky Buns	10-12
Cornflakes (Breakfast Dish)	10-13
Cherry Nut Bread	10-14
Jewish Holiday Bread	10-15
Oatyurt™ Summer Breakfast Cooler	10-16
Ashley Judd's Perfect Biscuits	10-17
Polish "Paczki"	10-18
David's Old Fashioned Bread	10-19
Grandma's Stuffing	10-20
Pina (Easter Bread)	10-21
Cranberry Nut Bread	10-22
Crêpes	10-23
Biscotti	10-24
Eggs Benedict Foie Gras	10-25

Bread & Breakfast

Zucchini Bread

Submitted by: Nancy Squibb

Meal: Any
Prep Time: 1 hour, 30 minutes

Servings: 2 loaves
Cost: Inexpensive

Ingredients

3 eggs
1 cup oil
1 cup brown sugar
1 cup sugar
3 teaspoons maple flavoring
2 cups zucchini, coarsely chopped
2-1/2 cups unsifted flour

1/2 cup toasted wheat germ
2 teaspoons baking soda
2 teaspoons salt
1/2 teaspoon baking powder
1 cup finely chopped nuts
1/3 cup sesame seeds

Preparation

Mix eggs to blend, add oil, sugars and maple flavoring, beat until thick and foamy. Using a spoon, stir in zucchini. Combine the zucchini with the flour, wheat germ, baking soda, salt, baking powder and nuts. Grease and flour two bread pans and pour mixture in. Sprinkle with sesame seeds and bake at 350 degrees for 1 hour or until pick inserted comes out clean.

Griddle Drop Scones
Submitted by: David Edwards

Meal: Any
Prep Time: 30 minutes

Servings: 20 scones
Cost: Inexpensive

Ingredients

1 cup self rising flour
1/2 cup sugar
1/2 teaspoon salt
1-1/2 to 2 ounces unsalted butter,
  softened

2 eggs
1/4 pint milk
1/4 teaspoon lemon juice

Preparation

Mix the flour, sugar and salt in a bowl, then gently cut in 1 ounce of the butter until the mixture resembles fine breadcrumbs. Make a well in the center. Beat the eggs, milk and lemon juice together thoroughly, then pour into the well in the flour. Stir the flour slowly into the liquid until you have a smooth batter. Heat a griddle or heavy-based cast-iron frying pan, and grease it with some of the remaining butter. Using a dessert spoon, drop three blobs of the mixture on the griddle or pan at a time. Cook for a few minutes until the undersides are golden, check by lifting the scones up with a spatula, then flip them over and cook the other side until golden. Remove the scones from the griddle as they cook and wrap them in a clean cloth to keep warm. Re-grease the griddle with butter between cooking each batch of scones.

Suggestions

For a different flavor, stir a peeled, cored, and grated eating apple, and a generous pinch of ground cinnamon into the batter before cooking.

Bread & Breakfast

1/2 Recipe Buns
Submitted by: Randy Milne

Meal: Any
Prep Time: 2 hours

Servings: 18 buns
Cost: Inexpensive

Ingredients

1 small cake yeast, or 1 package dry
    yeast
2 cups warm water
6 tablespoons sugar

1/4 cup shortening
2 teaspoons salt
6 cups flour

Preparation

Break yeast into water and dissolve. Add sugar, shortening and salt, mix well. Add flour and knead until stretchy. Let rise until double in bulk. Push down and roll out thick. Cut as for large biscuits. Let rise on cookie sheet until double in bulk. Bake in a preheated 400 degree oven for 18 to 20 minutes.

Onion Biscuits

Submitted by: Paul Gerhardt

Meal: Any   Servings: 6
Prep Time: 30 minutes   Cost: Inexpensive

Ingredients

1 stick butter   1 can buttermilk biscuits, quartered
2-1/2 tablespoons dry onion soup mix

Preparation

Melt the butter and then add the onion soup mix. Add the biscuits and brown in the skillet for 15 to 20 minutes.

Bread & Breakfast

Banana Bread

Submitted by: Fred Rogers

Meal: Any
Prep Time: 1 hour, 15 minutes

Servings: 1 loaf
Cost: Inexpensive

Ingredients

4 over-ripe bananas (3 if large)
1 cup sugar
1 egg
1-1/2 cups flour

1 teaspoon baking soda
1 teaspoon salt
1/4 cup melted butter (3 tablespoons if
   solid)

Preparation

In a medium bowl, mash bananas with a fork. Stir in other ingredients as given, makes it easier to mix. Pour into a buttered 8-1/2x3-1/2x2-1/2-inch loaf pan. Bake in a preheated 325 degree oven for 1 hour.

Suggestions

Notes: Really over-ripe bananas are the best. Black bananas give a real banana flavor for any baked recipe. Bananas that are just right for eating can barely be tasted when added to breads and cakes. Bananas can be frozen as is, no additional wrapping (other than the natural skin) is necessary. Let them get to be solid black, then freeze. Thaw when ready to use. You can add 1/2 cup of pecans or your favorite nuts for banana nut bread. I use a 10-3/4x4-1/4x3-inch loaf pan, this bakes in slightly less than an hour. Two small loaves can be made, they will not be as high, obviously, and will need to be baked for approximatey 35 minutes. Time depends on the size of your pans. When using T-Fal lower temperature by about 10 degrees. Freezes well for up to 2 months.

Bread & Breakfast

Whole Wheat Pancakes

Submitted by: John & Samantha Williams

Meal: Breakfast   Servings: 2
Prep Time: 30 minutes   Cost: Inexpensive

Ingredients

1 egg
1 cup non-fat plain yogurt
1 tablespoon butter
1 tablespoon maple syrup
1 teaspoon vanilla
1 cup whole wheat pastry flour

1 teaspoon baking powder
3/4 teaspoon salt or less
1/2 teaspoon baking soda
Nutmeg, optional
Non-fat powdered milk

Preparation

Beat together egg, yogurt, butter, maple syrup and vanilla. Add flour, baking powder, salt, baking soda and nutmeg. Whisk until fully blended. Add non-fat powdered milk to achieve desired consistency. Use a non-stick griddle.

Corn Cakes

Submitted by: Pat Boone

Meal: Any	Servings: 6
Prep Time: Overnight	Cost: Inexpensive

Ingredients

3 cups cornmeal, preferably white
1 teaspoon salt
1 tablespoon sugar

Boiling water
Fat

Preparation

In a bowl mix the dry ingredients. Pour in enough water to make a thick paste, stirring vigorously. Cover and refrigerate over night. When ready to fry, make into cakes the size of the palm of your hand. Fry in deep hot fat until golden brown, turning once. Serve at once.

Poor Man's Dumplings

Submitted by: Robert Sankey

Meal: Dinner
Prep Time: 6 hours, 15 minutes

Servings: 6
Cost: Inexpensive

Ingredients

1 loaf white bread
3 medium potatoes, peeled
1 medium onion
1 egg, beaten

3 tablespoons flour
1/2 teaspoon pepper
1 teaspoon salt

Preparation

Break apart bread on a towel and let sit out until semi-hard, about 6 hours. Process potatoes and onion in a food processor until liquified. Mix all ingredients in a large bowl until well blended. Form into balls. With slotted spoon, lay balls into boiling water for 10 minutes, serve. Freeze leftover dumplings. Slice down and fry in bacon drippings as an alternative to homefries or put in a bowl of chicken soup. They have a million uses and are very hearty.

Bread & Breakfast

Paula Poundstone's Recipe for an Airport Breakfast

Submitted by: Paula Poundstone

Meal:	Breakfast	Servings:	1
Prep Time:	5 minutes	Cost:	Inexpensive

Ingredients

1 airport
1 hot dog

1 medium diet soda
2 carry-on bags

Preparation

Although, for environmental reasons as well as occasional unwelcome pangs of conscience, I generally try to avoid meat. At breakfast time in an airport I do truly enjoy an airport hot dog and medium diet soda. Mr. Blanchard, my junior high history teacher, read us an article which claimed that 14% of hot dogs are rodent hairs and insect parts and so I comfort myself with the thought that they may even be meat-free. As an added benefit, on the many days that I have a carry-on bag on each shoulder, getting the food, paying for it, restoring the change to my pocket, applying the condiments to the dog and lumbering with the works to a seat at the gate to dine can, I think, count as a weight loss program.

I go with a medium diet soda, as opposed to the large tankard available, because I don't like to use the bathroom on the plane if I can avoid it. The temptation to tamper with the smoke detector is too great (and, no, I do not smoke). Besides, whether you ask for Diet Pepsi and they say they only have Diet Coke, or you ask for Diet Coke and they only have Diet Pepsi, at the airport the soda is the kind dispensed with a gun from the tanks and they've managed to make it taste uniformly equi-wretched. I only even get the diet soda there in case the hot dog happens to be hot and I burn my tongue. The diet soda is a safety measure. The plastic lids can be recycled and I carry them home to do so.

Sometimes the hot dog is actually hot making applying the condiments particularly important. By the way, a dog properly bunned does not require a Styrofoam plate. The first few steps from the cash register to the condiment counter with a hot dog in one hand, a medium diet soda in the other, and a 30 pound bag on each shoulder are not easy and it may be wise to practice in the home either substituting with plastic fruit or using real food but confining the practice to a stain proof area. Ideally the ketchup is in a large dispenser so you can get a plastic knife right near it, slice the dog down the center, hold it beneath the spout of the dispenser and depress the big ketchup button applying distinctive tomato flavored coolant right up the middle of the dog. Although, I often have to use the little foil pouches of condiments, they are messy and wasteful and difficult to open. Sometimes it takes so long to open those foil condiment pouches (and squeeze out precious little hot dog coolant from each) using my teeth, trying not to wear it, balancing my 40 pounds of carry-on luggage on each shoulder, that a big line of impatient condiment-seeking businessmen will form behind me and cause me to reflect on the poor quality of my entire life.

By now the luggage straps, bearing 50 pounds apiece, have usually worked their way off my shoulders to my upper arms and can only be maintained by extending my elbows out from my sides. Of course, after all this work, it's important not to spill so I try to sip at the beverage while shuffling slowly towards the gate in this posture -- I've never seen myself from the back, but I suppose, when I do it right, I look like a big chicken perhaps headed for a cruise.

Once at the gate, I generally find a place to dine on the floor. I kneel slowly, as if balancing an ornate tribal headdress, in order to lower my 60 pound bags and food. Of course, in cooking, presentation is very important so I try to place the hot dog and beverage on the floor in a decorative fashion to please the eye before pleasing the palate.

I can't help it, cooking is in my blood.

Tropical Fruit Pancakes

Submitted by: Victor Wahome

Meal: Breakfast   Servings: 4
Prep Time: 30 minutes   Cost: Inexpensive

Ingredients

1 cup self-rising flour
Pinch of grated nutmeg
1 tablespoon sugar
1 egg
1-1/4 cups milk
1 tablespoon melted butter, plus extra
    for frying
1 tablespoon fine dried coconut, optional

8 ounces ripe, firm mango, diced
2 bananas, coarsley chopped
2 kiwi fruit, sliced
1 large orange, peeled and segmented
1 tablespoon lemon juice
2 tablespoons orange juice
1-1/2 tablespoons honey
3 tablespoons orange liqueur, optional

Preparation

Sift flour, nutmeg and sugar together, set aside. In a separate bowl beat egg and most of the milk. Slowly add to the flour mixture and beat well with a wooden spoon to make a thick, smooth batter. Add the remaining milk, butter and coconut, if using. Beat until the batter is a smooth pourable consistency. Melt a little butter in a large frying pan, swirl to cover whole pan. Pour a little batter to cover the bottom of the pan. Fry until golden brown then turn with spatula. Continue with remaining batter, making about 8 pancakes. Place the fruit in a bowl and mix with the lemon juice, orange juice, honey and orange liqueur, if using. Mix well. Spoon a little fruit mixture into the center of each pancake and fold. Serve warm with cream.

Southern Corn Bread

Submitted by: Johnny Mathis

Meal: Any   Servings: 8
Prep Time: 45 minutes   Cost: Inexpensive

Ingredients

1-1/2 cups yellow cornmeal
1/2 cup flour
1 teaspoon baking soda
1/2 teaspoon salt

1-1/2 cups buttermilk
2 tablespoons shortening, melted
1 egg

Preparation

Combine cornmeal, flour, baking soda and salt. Add the buttermilk, shortening and egg. Stir to blend well. Pour into a greased 9x9x2-inch pan. Bake in a preheated 400 degree oven for 20 minutes.

Bread & Breakfast

Sticky Buns

Submitted by: John Jarrett

Meal: Breakfast   Servings: 16 buns
Prep Time: 3 hours   Cost: Inexpensive

Ingredients

1 package yeast   1 teaspoon salt
1/4 cup warm water   3-1/4 cups sifted flour, may need more
1 cup milk, scalded   1 egg, beaten
1/4 cup shortening   Brown sugar
1/4 cup sugar   Butter

Preparation

Soften yeast in warm water, set aside. Combine hot milk, shortening, sugar and salt. Cool to luke warm. Add 1 cup flour to milk, beat well. Beat in yeast and egg. Gradually add remaining flour to form a soft dough, beating well. Brush lightly with soft shortening. Cover and let rise until doubled, about 1-1/2 to 2 hours. Punch down and turn out onto a floured surface then divide in half. Roll each piece out to be 12x8 inches. Brush dough with butter and spread with brown sugar. Roll up and cut in slices and bake in a preheated 375 degree oven for 25 minutes.

Cornflakes (Breakfast Dish)

Submitted by: John Cleese

Meal: Breakfast   Servings: 1
Prep Time: 5 minutes   Cost: Inexpensive

Preparation

1. Buy a packet of cornflakes.

2. Open the cardboard box.

3. Open the sort of plastic packet inside the box.

4. Pour the contents (sort of yellowy, brownish bits of things) onto a plate.

5. Buy a bottle of milk.

6. Take the top of the thin end of the bottle.

7. Invert the bottle gently over the cornflakes making sure that the milk does not go over the edge of the plate.

It's very simple to make and absolutely delicious. An alternative is to use Coca-Cola instead of milk. Add basil as required.

Cherry Nut Bread

Submitted by: Senator and Mrs. Tim Johnson

Meal: Any   Servings: 8
Prep Time: 1 hour, 45 minutes   Cost: Inexpensive

Ingredients

8 ounces cream cheese
1 cup butter
1-1/2 cups sugar
1-1/2 teaspoons vanilla
4 eggs

2-1/4 cups flour
1-1/2 teaspoons baking powder
3/4 cup cherries
1/2 cup chopped pecans

Preparation

Thoroughly blend cream cheese, butter, sugar and vanilla. Add eggs 1 at a time, beating well after each addition. Gradually add 2 cups flour sifted with baking powder. Combine remaining flour, cherries and nuts. Fold in batter. Pour batter into a greased 10-inch loaf or bundt pan. Bake in a preheated 325 degree oven for 1 hour and 20 minutes. Cool for 5 minutes and remove from pan. Drizzle following glaze all over cake.

Glaze Ingredients

1-1/2 cups powdered sugar   2 tablespoons milk

Preparation

Combine thoroughly.

Bread & Breakfast

Jewish Holiday Bread
Submitted by: Terry G. Gouchnour

Meal: Any   Servings: 4 loaves
Prep Time: 4 hours   Cost: Inexpensive

Ingredients

1-1/2 cups water or milk, warm to touch
   wrist
1/2 cup sugar
1-1/2 teaspoons salt
2 packages yeast

1/2 cup warm water
8 cups flour
1/2 cup melted butter
4 large eggs, save part for tops of bread

Preparation

Combine yeast and the 1/2 cup warm water to soften. In a separate bowl Pour water or milk over sugar and salt in large bowl. Cool to lukewarm and add yeast mixture. Beat in 4 cups flour, add butter and eggs, blend thoroughly. Add remaining flour. Knead until smooth and satiny, about 8 minutes. Place in greased bowl and grease the top. Let rise until double in size, about 1 hour. Punch down and shape according to the following directions. Divide dough in 4 even parts. Each part will be divided into thirds. Roll each portion into 12-inch strands, 1/4-inch in diameter. Place 3 strands on a board and braid together, pinching ends together and tucking them. Two loaves can be placed on a greased baking sheet. Repeat for second braid. The last 2 loaves can be placed in regular bread pans. Cover the loaves and let rise until nearly double in size, about 1 hour 15 minutes. Brush with egg. Bake in a preheated 350 degree oven for 35 to 45 minutes or golden on top. Cool on racks.

Bread & Breakfast

Oatyurt™ Breakfast Cooler

Submitted by: Jackson Brower

Meal: Breakfast   Servings: 1
Prep Time: 30 minutes   Cost: Inexpensive

Ingredients

1/2 cup oatmeal   1/2 cup low-fat fruit yogurt
1 cup water   1/2 cup low-fat milk

Preparation

Cook oatmeal according to directions. Add yogurt and milk, mix well. Oatyurt™ can then be chilled in the refrigerator or mixed with electric blender with ice. It makes a delicious, nutritious breakfast that goes down cool and fast.

Bread & Breakfast

Ashley Judd's Perfect Biscuits

Submitted by: Ashley Judd

Meal: Any   Servings: 24
Prep Time: 45 minutes   Cost: Inexpensive

Ingredients

2 cups self-rising flour   7/8 cup non-fat milk
1/4 cup shortening

Preparation

Sift flour, cut in shortening with your fingers until mixture is coarse beads. Make a dent in flour, a well, and pour milk into the hole. Using your first 2 fingers, stir flour and milk together, letting the dough collect into a shiny ball. Pat out onto a floured surface, about 1/2 inch thick. Cut into biscuits. Bake in a preheated 450 degree oven for 12 to 15 minutes.

Suggestions

Do not overwork dough. The less you handle it the lighter and fluffier the biscuits will be. Dough refrigerates well. Using the exact amount of milk is very important. These biscuits are very low in fat.

Bread & Breakfast

Polish "Paczki"

Submitted by: Pope John Paul II

Meal: Any   Servings: 8 to 10
Prep Time: 2 hours   Cost: Inexpensive

Ingredients

1 kilogram flour   Juice and rinds of 2 large lemons
3 teaspoons ground vanilla beans   Dash of salt
100 grams leaven   1 vodka glass of spirit
1/2 liter milk   5 to 6 teaspoons olive oil or butter
100 to 150 grams sugar   400 grams jam
7 egg yolks   2 to 2-1/2 liters cooking oil
1 whole egg   Confectioner's sugar

Preparation

Sift flour and vanilla beans. Melt leaven in lukewarm milk with a spoonful of sugar and pour it in 200 grams of flour until it becomes creamy. Allow leaven to rise in a warm place. Blend egg yolks, egg, and remaining sugar until the mixture becomes white. Add the rest of the flour, vanilla beans, lemon juice, lemon rind, remaining milk, a dash of salt, the leaven mixture and the spirit. Blend the mixture until smooth, bright and so that it does not stick to the hands. Add olive oil or melted butter to the mixture and blend. Cover the mixture with a clean table napkin and allow to rest in a warm place for 15 minutes. When the mixture rises to about twice its original size, take a small portion and spread the dough with a rolling pin until approximately 1/4 inch thick. Cut circles in the dough with a drinking glass. Place a teaspoon of jam on one circle and cover it with another sealing the sides well. Arrange "paczkis" on a floured board and allow to rise some more. Heat cooking oil in a large pan. Arrange "paczkis" in the pan top side down spacing evenly. Cover and fry until brown on the bottom. Turn over and fry uncovered until completely browned. Remove from pan and drain on paper towels to remove extra fat. Allow to cool and powder with confectioner's sugar.

Bread & Breakfast

David's Old Fashioned Bread

Submitted by: Lou Danilovics and David Wiser
in memory of Michael Smith.

Meal: Any   Servings: 2 loaves or 18 rolls
Prep Time: 5 hours   Cost: Inexpensive

Ingredients

2-1/4 cups milk
3 tablespoons butter
3 cups all-purpose flour and also 2-3/4
   to 3-1/4 cups all-purpose flour

2 packages active dry yeast
2 tablespoons sugar
2 tablespoons salt

Preparation

Heat milk and butter to 120 degrees. In large mixer bowl, combine 3 cups flour, yeast, sugar, salt and milk mixture. Blend until smooth. Add 2-3/4 cups flour or more depending on consistency. Knead about 6 minutes or until smooth and elastic. Shape into a ball and place in a greased bowl. Cover with a clean towel and let rise until double in size, about 2 hours. Punch dough down and shape into loaves or make rolls. Place in a greased loaf pan or on a cookie sheet. Bake in a preheated 375 degree oven for 10 minutes, reduce heat to 350 degrees and bake another 30 to 35 minutes. Remove from pans and let cool on racks.

Bread & Breakfast

Grandma's Stuffing
Submitted by: Jennifer Stone

Meal: Dinner   Servings: 6
Prep Time: Overnight   Cost: Inexpensive

Ingredients

1 large loaf bread   1 cup potatoes, cubed
1-1/2 quarts water   1 cup onion, chopped
Turkey giblets   1 cup celery, diced

Preparation

Break bread into pieces and let stand while preparing the rest of the ingredients. Put the water into a large pot and add the giblets, potatoes, onion and celery. Simmer for 6 to 8 hours. Add 1-1/2 quarts of this to the bread and stuff the turkey immediately before roasting. This should be quite moist but very tasty.

Bread & Breakfast

Pina (Easter Bread)
Submitted by: David and Julia Buccilli

Meal: Any   Yields: 4 loaves
Prep Time: 4 hours   Cost: Inexpensive

Ingredients

12 eggs   1 tablespoon anise oil
2 cups sugar   Milk, enough to hold dough
3 dry packets yeast, proof yeast in some   Flour
  warm milk

Preparation

Combine all ingredients thoroughly, using just enough flour to form a dough not to moist and not to dry, knead. Butter and flour tube or bundt pans. Shape dough into rings and place in pans. Let rise to the top of the pans, about 2 to 3 hours. Bake in a preheated 375 degree oven until hollow when tapped and golden brown, about 25 minutes. Cool and then slice and serve.

Cranberry Nut Bread

Submitted by: "The Shepherd Boys" Steel City Softball League

Meal: Any
Prep Time: 1 hour

Yields: 2 large or 4 small loaves
Cost: Inexpensive

Ingredients

2 eggs, beaten
2 cups sugar
4 tablespoons butter, melted
1-1/2 cups orange juice
1 teaspoon orange extract
4 cups flour

3 teaspoons baking powder
1 teaspoon salt
1 teaspoon baking soda
2 cup walnuts
2 cups fresh cranberries, cut in half

Preparation

Mix all ingredients together in the order listed. Pour into greased loaf pans, fill 2/3 full. Bake in a preheated 350 degree oven for 40 to 45 minutes or until toothpick inserted in center comes out clean.

Bread & Breakfast

Crêpes

Submitted by: Stephanie Kyc

Meal: Breakfast or dessert   Servings: 8
Prep Time: 5 hours   Cost: Inexpensive

Ingredients

3 cups flour
1/2 cup sugar
1 heaping teaspoon salt
Water (as needed)

3 eggs
1 stick butter, melted
1 cup milk

Preparation

Place flour, sugar and salt into a mixing bowl. Add enough water to moisten until smooth, but not runny. Add the eggs and continue to mix. Add the milk to the melted butter to cool to lukewarm. Beat with a wooden spoon or whisk until smooth. Heat frying pan until hot. Using a 1/4 measuring cup or small ladle, pour into frying pan. When batter looks dry on top, turn using fork or tongs and brown the other side.

Suggestions

You can fill this with Mozzarella cheese for lunch, jelly for breakfast, or with fruit or ice cream and dust with powdered sugar for dessert.

Biscotti

Submitted by: Stephanie Kyc

Meal: Dessert
Prep Time: 30 minutes

Servings: 8 to 10
Cost: Inexpensive

Ingredients

6 eggs, beaten
1 cup sugar
1/4 teaspoon salt

1 cup oil
1/4 cup anise oil
3 cups flour

Preparation

Mix well and pour into 4 greased and floured bread pans. Bake at 350 degrees for 20 minutes. Let cool and slice diagonally. Toast both sides.

Eggs Benedict Foie Gras

Submitted by: Roger Taylor in memory of Freddie Mercury.

Meal: Breakfast
Prep Time: 20 minutes

Servings: 6
Cost: Expensive

Ingredients

3 English muffins
1 ounce of butter
6 slices cooked ox tongue
Pinch of salt
1 teaspoon white wine vinegar

6 eggs
6 tablespoons Hollandaise sauce
Chopped fresh parsley to garnish
Foie Gras

Preparation

Split the muffins and toast them Butter them lightly and put a slice of tongue on each half, trimming it to fit. In a shallow pan of boiling water add the pinch of salt and the vinegar. Stir this round and lightly poach the eggs in it, one at a time for 2 to 3 minutes. Place an egg on each slice of tongue and spoon over a tablespoon of Hollandaise sauce. You can warm the sauce gently in a heavy based pan if you prefer. Sprinkle a little chopped parsley on top of the eggs to garnish and serve immediately with Foie Gras on the side.

Pies, Cakes & Frostings

Recipe	**Page**
Thanksgiving Cheesecake	11-1
Easy Pineapple Squares	11-2
Kevin Gessler's Poppy Seed Cake	11-3
Sour Cream Pound Cake	11-4
Frozen Lime Pie	11-5
Glazed Apple Coffee Crown	11-6
Deep Dish Apple Crisp	11-7
Southern Coconut Pie	11-8
Lemon Flip Cake	11-9
Angel Food Cake	11-10
Senator James Jeffords' Maple Syrup Cake	11-11
Current River Chocolate Sheet Cake	11-12
Angel Food Dessert	11-13
Easy, Wonderful Cheesecake	11-14
Hawaiian Wedding Cake	11-15
Italian Prune-Plum Cake	11-16
Chocolate Pecan Cake	11-17
Caramel Pineapple Cake Roll	11-18
Carrot Cake	11-19
Banana Cake	11-20
Oreo Ice Cream Cake	11-21
Ruth Thompson's Coconut Cream Pie	11-22
Ruth Thompson's Fresh Coconut Cake	11-23
Easy Strudel	11-24
Dolly's Mud Pie	11-25
Apple Dumplings	11-26
Chocolate Soufflé	11-27
Blackberry Cake	11-28
Rhubarb Crunch	11-29
Apple and Blackberry Tart	11-30
Berry Banana Trifle	11-31
Audrey Landers' Strawberry Cheesecake	11-32
Coffee Cake	11-33
Fruit Torte	11-34
Blueberry Buckle	11-35
Aliette's Apricot Buzz	11-36
One-Step Pound Cake	11-37
Fruit Filled Coffee Cake	11-38
Rhubarb Cake	11-39

continued

Section 11
Pies, Cakes & Frostings

Recipe   **Page**

Tom Daschle's Famous Cheesecake 11-40
Marnie's "Red" Velvet Cake 11-41
Mexican Fruit Cake 11-42
Fruit Crisp 11-43
Francesca's Ricotta Cake 11-44
Fresh Apple Cake 11-45
Mom's Chocolate "Mayonnaise" Cake
   with Almond Buttercream Icing 11-46
Fresh Apple Cake 11-47
Dairy and Sugar Free Pumpkin Pie.. 11-48
Sour Cherry Crumb Cake 11-49
Rice Pie.. 11-50
Deep Oatmeal Pie.. 11-51
Hot Fudge Walnut Pudding Cake... 11-52
Lemon Verbena Soufflé 11-53
Brenda Vaccaro's Cheesecake Fantasy 11-54
Pineapple Dream Cake 11-55
No-Bake Strawberry Pie... 11-56
Carrot Cake.. 11-57
Pineapple Noodle Ring 11-58
Chocolate Walnut Pie... 11-59
Jewish Apple Cake... 11-60
Nana's Peach Pie... 11-61
Elegant Simple Dessert.. 11-62

Pies, Cakes & Frostings

Thanksgiving Cheesecake

Submitted by: Dennis Estes for my friend Chuck.

Meal: Dessert   Servings: 10
Prep Time: 7 hours   Cost: Inexpensive

Sweet Crust Ingredients

1/2 cup butter
1/2 cup sugar
1/2 teaspoon pure vanilla extract
1 egg, beaten

1-1/2 cups all-purpose flour
1 teaspoon baking powder
2 to 3 tablespoons milk

Preparation

In a large bowl, cream butter then add the sugar and vanilla until well blended. Add the egg and beat until fluffy. Sift the flour and baking powder and add to the butter mixture in small amounts until well blended. Moisten with the milk until a dough is formed. Form into a ball and wrap with plastic wrap and refrigerate for 1 hour. Line the bottom of a 9-inch spring form pan with foil, grease and flour it. Divide the dough into 2 parts. Use half to line the bottom of the pan and form the other half into a roll, slice into 1/8-inch thickness to form the walls of the pan. Press the dough all the way around the pan smoothly so that it joins the bottom. Place in the refrigerator until ready for the filling.

Pie Filling Ingredients

2 (8-ounce) packages cream cheese,
    room temperature
1 (1-pound) can solid-pack pumpkin
1-1/2 cups sugar
4 eggs, slightly beaten
1 teaspoon pure vanilla extract
1/2 teaspoon salt
1/2 teaspoon ground cinnamon

1/2 teaspoon apple pie spice
1/2 teaspoon pumpkin pie spice
1/4 teaspoon ground cloves
1 to 3 tablespoons flour
2 or 3 tablespoons cornstarch
1/3 cup butter, melted
1 pint sour cream

Preparation

In a large bowl, cream the cheese with an electric mixer at low speed, adding the pumpkin gradually. Continue beating until well mixed. Add the sugar and eggs until well mixed then add the vanilla, set aside. Mix together the salt, cinnamon, apple pie spice, pumpkin pie spice, cloves, flour and cornstarch. After mixing, slowly add the flour mixture to the cream cheese mixture at low speed. Add the butter and the sour cream. Combine until smooth. Pour the mixture into the pan. Bake in a preheated 350 degree oven for 1 hour or until cheesecake is firm in the center. When cheesecake is done turn oven off and let it sit in the oven for 2 hours. Remove from pan and let cool completely. Refrigerate for several hours before serving.

Pies, Cakes & Frostings

Easy Pineapple Squares

Submitted by: Cheryl Brugette

Meal: Dessert

Prep Time: 1 hour

Servings: 10

Cost: Inexpensive

Cake Ingredients

2 eggs
2 cups sugar
1 (20-ounce) can crushed pineapple,
   undrained

2 cups flour
2 teaspoons baking soda
1 teaspoon vanilla
1/2 cup walnuts, chopped (optional)

Preparation

Mix all ingredients, except nuts. Stir in nuts, if using them. Place mixture in a greased 9x13-inch baking pan. Bake at 350 degrees for 25 to 35 minutes. It will turn very brown. Make sure to bake fully. Cool and frost.

Frosting Ingredients

1 (8-ounce) package cream cheese,
   softened
1 stick butter, softened

1-3/4 cup confectioners sugar
1 teaspoon vanilla
1/2 cup walnuts, chopped (optional)

Preparation

Mix all ingredients, except nuts, if using them. Spread on bars and sprinkle with nuts.

Suggestions

Two (11-ounce) cans of Mandarin oranges can be used to replace the pineapple for Mandarin Orange Squares. Coarsely chop fruit, reserving syrup. Add both to batter. Omit the nuts, although 1/2 cup of shredded coconut can be added to the batter as an option. Add 1 teaspoon orange juice concentrate to the frosting ingredients, omitting nuts.

Kevin Gessler's Poppy Seed Cake

Submitted by: Tricia Nowalk in memory of Kevin Gessler.

Meal: Any   Servings: 8
Prep Time: 1 to 2 days   Cost: Inexpensive

Ingredients

1 cup sour cream   2 sticks butter
1 teaspoon baking soda   1/3 cup poppy seeds
4 eggs, separated   2 cups flour
1-1/2 cups sugar   Powdered sugar

Preparation

Stir baking soda into sour cream, set aside. Beat egg whites until stiff, set aside. Cream together sugar and butter until fluffy, but do not over work the butter. Beat the egg yolks and add with the poppy seeds to the butter mixture. Mix in alternately the flour and sour cream. Carefully fold egg whites into the batter. Grease and flour bundt pan and pour mixture in. Bake in a preheated 350 degree oven for 40 to 60 minutes, depending on the pan used. Watch carefully. Remove cake from pan immediately after it comes out of the oven. Cool, then store in an airtight container for a day or two to allow flavors to mature. To serve, dust with powdered sugar.

Pies, Cakes & Frostings

Sour Cream Pound Cake

Submitted by: Lois Ahlborn

Meal: Any
Prep Time: 2 hours

Servings: 8 to 10
Cost: Inexpensive

Ingredients

1/2 pound butter
3 cups sugar
6 eggs, separated
1 (8-ounce) container sour cream

2 teaspoons vanilla extract
1-1/2 teaspoons almond extract
1/4 teaspoon baking soda
3 cups flour, sifted twice

Preparation

Cream butter and sugar together until light and fluffy. Beat in egg yolks until well blended. Beat in sour cream, vanilla extract and almond flavoring. Sift flour and baking soda together then beat into butter mixture 1 cup at a time. Beat until well blended. Gently fold in stiffly beaten egg whites. Pour batter into a greased and floured 10-inch pan. Preheat an oven to 325 degrees and bake for 1-1/2 hours or until done.

Frozen Lime Pie

Submitted by: Karen Tritten

Meal: Dessert	Servings: 6
Prep Time: 1 hour	Cost: Inexpensive

Ingredients

5 large eggs, separated
3/4 cups sugar
2/3 cup lime juice
Finely grated rind of 2 limes

1/8 teaspoon salt
1 graham cracker crust or
   frozen/refrigerated pie shell
1 tablespoon graham cracker crumbs

Preparation

In a small mixing bowl, beat the yolks with 1/2 cup of the sugar at high speed for 5 minutes, until mixture is very pale and thick. Reduce speed to low and gradually add the lime juice. Stir in the grated lime rind. Turn the mixture into the top of a large double boiler over shallow hot water on moderate heat. Cook 6 to 7 minutes stirring constantly with a wooden spoon, scraping sides and bottom. Mixture should reach between 175 and 180 degrees and is thick enough to coat the spoon. Remove the top of the double boiler and pour mixture into a large mixing bowl, stirring occasionally until cool. In a large mixing bowl, add the salt to the egg whites and beat until soft peaks form. Reduce speed and gradually add 1/4 cup of the sugar. Increase speed and beat until the mixture holds a definite shape, but is not stiff or dry. Gradually, in 3 additions, fold the egg yolk mixture into the egg white mixture. Handle very carefully and very little. Turn the mixture into the crust. It may look too full, but just mound it high. Sprinkle top with graham cracker crumbs. Bake for 15 minutes in a preheated 350 degree oven. Cool on a rack to room temperature, then freeze. When frozen, wrap with plastic. May be kept frozen for up to 3 weeks.

Pies, Cakes & Frostings

Glazed Apple Coffee Crown

Submitted by: John Jarrett

Meal: Breakfast   Servings: 8
Prep Time: 2 hours, 30 minutes   Cost: Inexpensive

Cake Ingredients

4 to 5 cups all purpose flour or
    unbleached flour
1/3 cup sugar
1 teaspoon salt

1 package active dry yeast
1 cup milk
1/2 cup water
1/4 cup butter

Preparation

Lightly spoon flour into measuring cup, level off. In large bowl, combine 2 cups flour, sugar, salt and yeast. In small sauce pan, heat milk, water and butter until very warm, 120 to 125 degrees. Add warm liquid and egg to flour mixture. Blend at low speed until moistened. By hand, stir in 2 cups flour. On floured surface, knead in 1/2 to 1 cup flour until smooth and elastic, about 5 to 8 minutes. Place dough in greased bowl, cover loosely with plastic wrap and cloth towel. Let rise in warm place until light and doubled in size, about 1 hour.

Filling Ingredients

3/4 cups sugar
1-1/2 teaspoons cinnamon
1/4 cup butter, softened

1 (3-ounce) package cream cheese
2-1/2 cups chopped, peeled apples
1/3 cup firmly packed brown sugar

Preparation

In small bowl, combine sugar, 1 teaspoon cinnamon, butter and cream cheese. Blend until smooth. In small bowl, combine apples, brown sugar, and 1/2 teaspoon cinnamon. Divide dough in half. On lightly floured surface, roll out half of dough into 18x18 rectangle. Spread with 1/2 of cream cheese mixture to within 1/2 inch of edges, then spread with half of the apple mixture. Starting at larger side, roll up tightly, pinch ends and edges to seal. Repeat with other remaining half of dough. Place both rolls in a greased 12-cup fluted tube pan or 10-inch wide tube pan. Cover, let rise in warm place until light and doubled in size, about an hour. Heat oven to 350 degrees and bake 45 to 55 minutes or until light brown. Remove from pan immediately. Combine glaze ingredients thoroughly and drizzle with mixture (see below).

Glaze Ingredients

1 cup powdered sugar
1 tablespoon milk

1 tablespoon butter, softened
1 teaspoon lemon juice

Pies, Cakes & Frostings

Deep Dish Apple Crisp

Submitted by: Mario & Nathalie Lemieux
in memory of Bill Goldsworthy.

Meal: Dessert   Servings: 6
Prep Time: 1 hour   Cost: Inexpensive

Ingredients

3 pounds apples   1 cup flour
Juice of 1 lemon   1/2 cup brown sugar
1 tablespoon cornstarch   Salt
1/2 cup sugar   6 tablespoons unsalted butter
1/4 teaspoon cinnamon, more if desired   1/4 cup sliced almonds
1/8 teaspoon nutmeg

Preparation

Peel, core, and slice apples and toss with the lemon juice. Mix cornstarch, sugar, cinnamon and nutmeg. Add to the apples and toss. Arrange in a baking dish. Add flour, brown sugar, salt, butter and sliced almonds, mix until crumbly. Sprinkle on top of the apples and bake in a preheated 400 degree oven for 45 minutes.

Suggestions

Serve hot with ice cream.

Southern Coconut Pie

Submitted by: Marvin Hamlisch

Meal: Dessert
Prep Time: 1 hour

Servings: 6
Cost: Inexpensive

Ingredients

3 eggs, beaten
1-1/2 cups sugar
1/2 cup butter, melted
4 teaspoons lemon juice

1 teaspoon vanilla extract
1 (3-1/2 ounce) can or 1-1/2 cups flaked
  coconut
1 unbaked 9-inch pastry shell

Preparation

Thoroughly combine eggs, sugar, butter, lemon juice and vanilla extract. Stir in coconut. Pour filling into unbaked pastry shell. Bake in moderate oven, 350 degrees, for 40 to 45 minutes or until knife inserted in the center comes out clean. Cool before serving.

Lemon Flip Cake

Submitted by: Senator Richard Lugar

Meal: Dessert

Prep Time: 1 hour

Servings: 8

Cost: Inexpensive

Ingredients

1 tablespoon butter
2 tablespoons flour
3/4 cup sugar

2 eggs, separated
1/4 cup fresh lemon juice
1 cup milk

Preparation

Cream butter, flour and sugar. Beat egg yolks and add to the sugar. Add lemon juice and milk. Beat egg whites until stiff then fold them into sugar mixture. Put in an 8-inch ungreased pan set in a pan of water. Bake in a preheated 350 degree oven for 35 minutes. When cool, flip cake over onto a plate. Sauce, custard consistency, is now on top.

Pies, Cakes & Frostings

Angel Food Cake
Submitted by: Richard & Lynda Petty, Car #43
in memory of Tim Richmond.

Meal: Dessert   Servings: 8 to 10
Prep Time: 1 hour, 30 minutes   Cost: Inexpensive

Ingredients

1-1/2 cups egg whites   1-1/2 cups sugar
1 teaspoon cream of tartar   1 teaspoon vanilla
1/4 teaspoon salt   1 cup sifted flour, then sift 4 times

Preparation

Beat eggs until foamy, add cream of tartar and salt. Beat until stiff but not dry.
Gradually beat in sugar. Add vanilla, then fold in flour as gently as possible. Bake in
angel food cake pan at 325 degrees for 1 hour and 15 minutes or until top is nicely
browned.

Senator James Jeffords' Maple Syrup Cake

Submitted by: Senator James Jeffords

Meal: Dessert
Prep Time: 1 hour, 15 minutes

Servings: 8
Cost: Inexpensive

Ingredients

1/2 cup shortening
1/2 cup white sugar
2 eggs, beaten lightly
1 cup maple syrup
1/4 cup water

2-1/2 cups cake flour
1/2 teaspoon ginger
1/4 teaspoon baking soda
2 teaspoons baking powder

Preparation

Cream the shortening, gradually add the sugar. Add the eggs beaten without separating the white and the yolks. Add maple syrup and water, then the flour which has been sifted, measured and sifted again with the ginger, soda and baking powder added. Bake in a tube loaf pan about 50 minutes at 325 degrees. Cover with maple icing and decorate with halved nuts.

Current River
Chocolate Sheet Cake
Submitted by: Senator Christopher Bond

Meal: Dessert   Servings: 20 to 24
Prep Time: 30 minutes   Cost: Inexpensive

Cake Ingredients

1 cup butter
1/2 cup cocoa
1 cup water
2 cups sugar
2 cups flour, unsifted

1 teaspoon baking soda
2 eggs, slightly beaten
1/2 cup sour cream
2 teaspoons vanilla extract

Preparation

Combine butter, cocoa and water in a saucepan, bring to a full boil. While still hot, pour mixture over combined sugar, flour and baking soda, mix well. Add eggs, sour cream and vanilla extract, mix well. Pour batter into a greased 15-1/2x10-1/2-inch jelly roll pan. Bake in a preheated 350 degree oven for 15 minutes, do not over bake. Ice cake immediately after removing from oven with icing that follows.

Icing Ingredients

1/2 cup butter
1/4 cup cocoa
6 tablespoons evaporated milk

1 (16-ounce) box confectioners sugar
1 cup chopped nuts
1 teaspoon vanilla extract

Preparation

Mix butter, cocoa and milk in a saucepan, heat to boiling point. Add confectioners sugar, nuts and vanilla, mix well. Additional milk may be needed to make icing more spreadable.

Pies, Cakes & Frostings

Angel Food Dessert

Submitted by: Barb Loesch

Meal: Dessert
Prep Time: 1 hour

Servings: 10
Cost: Inexpensive

Ingredients

1 angel food cake
1 large box vanilla pudding

1 large container whipped topping, thawed
3 Butterfinger bars

Preparation

Prepare pudding according to directions and set aside. Break angel food cake up into pieces in a 9x13-inch pan. Pour the pudding over the cake. Pour whipped topping over cake and pudding. Crush the Butterfingers and sprinkle on top. Refrigerate until ready to eat.

Easy, Wonderful Cheesecake

Submitted by: Isabel Bloom in memory of Warren Truitt.

Meal: Dessert   Servings: 8
Prep Time: 2 hours, 15 minutes   Cost: Inexpensive

Ingredients

1 (8-ounce) package cream cheese, softened
1 carton whipping cream
3 tablespoons sugar

1 can pie filling, blueberry or strawberry
1 pie shell, graham or baked

Preparation

Put soft cream cheese, whipping cream and sugar in a bowl and whip until stiff. Spoon into pie shell. Spread pie filling on top and refrigerate for 2 to 3 hours before serving.

Hawaiian Wedding Cake
Submitted by: Ada Rapp
in memory of our son Doug (1957 - 1990).

Meal: Dessert
Prep Time: 1 hour

Servings: 15
Cost: Inexpensive

Cake Ingredients

2 cups sifted flour
2 cups sugar
2 teaspoons baking soda
2 eggs, beaten

1 cup nuts, ground
1 cup coconut
1 (20-ounce) can crushed pineapple,
    undrained

Preparation

Sift together flour, sugar and baking soda. Add remaining ingredients and combine well, do not beat. Turn batter into a greased and floured 9x13-inch pan. Bake in a preheated 350 degree oven for 45 minutes. Let cool then frost with icing below.

Frosting Ingredients

1 (8-ounce) package cream cheese
1/2 cup butter

1 teaspoon vanilla
1-1/2 cups powdered sugar

Preparation

Mix all ingredients with electric mixer until well blended.

Pies, Cakes & Frostings

Italian Prune-Plum Cake

Submitted by: Richard Goldman

Meal: Dessert
Prep Time: 1 hour

Servings: 6 to 8
Cost: Inexpensive

Ingredients

1/4 pound butter, softened
1/2 cup sugar
1 egg
1 cup flour (1/2 white, 1/2 whole wheat pastry), sifted
1 teaspoon baking powder

1/8 teaspoon salt
1 teaspoon almond extract
20 Italian prune-plums (firm, fresh, halved and pitted), with skins left on
1 cup cinnamon sugar

Preparation

In a bowl, cream butter and sugar. Add egg, beat in dry ingredients then add almond extract. Mix well and push batter into an 8x8-inch square, or 9-inch round oiled and floured baking dish (glass preferably). Push plums skin side down all over into batter. Sprinkle generously with cinnamon sugar and bake in a preheated 350 degree oven for 30 minutes to 1 hour until edges are browned (average baking time=40 minutes).

Joan Specter's
Chocolate Pecan Cake
Submitted by: Senator Arlen Specter

Meal: Dessert   Servings: 6 to 8
Prep Time: 45 minutes   Cost: Inexpensive

Ingredients

1/2 cup butter, divided
1/2 cup firmly packed dark brown sugar
1/2 cup shredded coconut
2/3 cup chopped pecans
1/2 cup semi-sweet chocolate chips
1 tablespoon milk
1 cup flour

1/2 cup sugar
1-1/2 teaspoons baking powder
1/4 teaspoon salt
1/2 teaspoon vanilla extract
1/3 cup water
1 egg
Vanilla ice cream

Preparation

Melt 1/4 cup butter in saucepan. Remove from heat and stir in brown sugar, coconut, pecans, chocolate chips and milk, blending well. Spread mixture in bottom of 9-inch round baking pan and set aside. Combine flour, sugar, baking powder and salt. Add remaining 1/4 cup butter, vanilla extract, water and egg to dry ingredients and mix thoroughly. Pour batter over coconut pecan mixture. Bake in a preheated 350 degree oven for approximately 30 minutes or until a wooden pick inserted near the center of the cake comes out clean. Cool cake in pan for 5 minutes, then invert on serving plate. If coconut-pecan mixture does not separate from pan easily, use spoon or spatula to remove and spread on cake. Serve warm or cold with ice cream.

Joan Specter's
Caramel Pineapple Cake Roll

Submitted by: Senator Arlen Specter

Meal: Dessert   Servings: 6 to 8
Prep Time: 2 hours   Cost: Inexpensive

Ingredients

2 (20-ounce) cans crushed pineapple,   4 large eggs, separated
   drained   3/4 cup sugar
1/2 cup dark brown sugar   2 teaspoons vanilla extract
3/4 cup cake flour   1 teaspoon grated lemon rind
1 teaspoon baking powder   Confectioner's sugar
1/2 teaspoon salt

Preparation

Butter well a 10x15-inch jelly roll pan. Spread drained fruit evenly over bottom of pan and sprinkle with brown sugar. Sift flour with baking powder and salt. In a bowl, beat egg whites until foamy and add 3/4 cup of white sugar gradually, beating until stiff. Beat egg yolks into stiffened whites, and add vanilla extract and lemon rind. Sprinkle flour over all and gently fold in. Spread batter evenly over the pineapple and brown sugar. Bake in a preheated 375 degree oven for 18 to 20 minutes. Turn upside down on a damp towel and sprinkle lightly with confectioner's sugar. Roll up in towel and cool. Remove towel when cool. Place cake on platter and ice.

Icing Ingredients

1 cup heavy cream   3 tablespoons confectioner's sugar

Preparation

Beat heavy cream with sugar until stiff.

Pies, Cakes & Frostings

Carrot Cake
Submitted by: David Doorley
in memory of Jim Hanneken

Meal: Dessert   Servings: 10 to 12
Prep Time: 1 hour   Cost: Inexpensive

Ingredients

4 eggs
3 cups raw carrots, coarsely grated
1-1/2 cups salad oil
2 cups sugar
1 teaspoon vanilla extract
2 cups whole wheat flour, sifted

2 teaspoons baking soda
2 teaspoons cinnamon
1/2 teaspoon salt
1 cup chopped nuts
Powdered sugar

Preparation

In a bowl, beat eggs, carrots, sugar and oil until well mixed. Beat in rest of
ingredients. Pour into well oiled and floured bundt or loaf pan. Bake in a preheated
350 degree oven for 40 to 45 minutes or until cake springs back in center when lightly
touched with finger. Cool in pan for 20 minutes before turning out. Dust with powdered
sugar.

Banana Cake

Submitted by: John Jarrett

Meal: Dessert
Prep Time: 1 hour

Servings: 6 to 8
Cost: Inexpensive

Ingredients

2 cups flour
1 teaspoon baking powder
1 teaspoon baking soda
1 teaspoon salt
1/2 cup shortening

1-1/2 cups sugar, divided
1 cup mashed bananas
3 eggs, separated
2 teaspoons vanilla extract
1/4 cup sour milk

Preparation

Sift together flour, baking powder, baking soda and salt, set aside. In a bowl, cream shortening with sugar, reserving 3 tablespoons of the sugar. Add banana, then egg yolks one at a time while mixing. Mix in vanilla extract and dry ingredient mixture alternating with milk. Whip egg whites stiff with 3 tablespoons of sugar. Fold, not whip, into batter 3 times. Bake in greased round pans in a preheated 350 degree oven for 30 minutes.

Suggestions

To convert this recipe into banana bread, add nuts to the ingredients and place into a bread pan.

Pies, Cakes & Frostings

Oreo Ice Cream Cake
Submitted by: Dana Magnone

Meal: Dessert   Servings: 6 to 8
Prep Time: 3 hours   Cost: Inexpensive

Ingredients

1 (1-pound) package Oreo cookies
1 stick butter
1/2 gallon French vanilla ice cream

1 can chocolate syrup
1 (8-ounce) container whipped topping

Preparation

Crush cookies into crumbs. Place most of them in a 9x13-inch pan reserving some crumbs for topping. Melt butter and mix with crumbs in pan. Layer ice cream on top of crumbs. Pour chocolate syrup on top. Spread whipped topping over top and sprinkle with reserved cookie crumbs. Freeze and serve.

Pies, Cakes & Frostings

Ruth Thompson's
Coconut Cream Pie
Submitted by: Senator Fred Thompson

Meal: Dessert
Prep Time: 1 hour

Servings: 6 to 8
Cost: Inexpensive

Filling Ingredients

1 cup sugar
2 tablespoons corn starch
2 cups milk
1 teaspoon vanilla extract

2 egg yolks
1 can flaked coconut
1 pie shell, baked

Preparation

In a bowl, mix together sugar, corn starch, milk and vanilla extract. Beat egg yolks and add to mixture. Cook over medium heat, stirring constantly, until mixture thickens. Remove from heat and add 1/2 can flaked coconut. Place into baked pie shell.

Meringue Ingredients

2 egg whites
1/4 cup sugar

1/2 teaspoon cream of tartar
1/2 teaspoon vanilla extract

Preparation

In a bowl, beat egg whites until stiff. Add sugar, cream of tartar and vanilla extract and beat until mixture peaks. Spread meringue over top of the pie and sprinkle with remaining 1/2 can flaked coconut. Lightly brown in a preheated 325 degree oven.

Pies, Cakes & Frostings

Ruth Thompson's Fresh Coconut Cake

Submitted by: Senator Fred Thompson

Meal: Dessert   Servings: 6 to 8
Prep Time: 1 hour, 30 minutes   Cost: Inexpensive

Cake Ingredients

1/2 cup vegetable shortening   1 cup milk
1-1/4 cups granulated sugar   1 teaspoon vanilla extract
2 cups cake flour, sifted   3 egg whites
2-1/2 teaspoons baking powder   1 fresh coconut
1/4 teaspoon salt

Preparation

In a bowl, cream shortening and sugar until fluffy. Sift together flour, baking powder and salt. Sift 3 times. Then add milk, a small amount at a time, beating after each addition until smooth. Add vanilla extract. Beat egg whites until they peak, then stir into batter. Bake in 2 greased and floured 8-inch or 9-inch cake pans in a preheated 350 degree oven for 30 minutes, or until done. Let cool. Grate fresh coconut and reserve milk. Dribble coconut milk over each layer before frosting.

Fluffy White Frosting Ingredients

1-2/3 cups granulated sugar   1/4 teaspoon cream of tartar
1/2 cup water   1/2 cup egg whites

Preparation

Combine sugar, water and cream of tartar in a small sauce pan, stirring over low heat until sugar is dissolved. Boil mixture without stirring until syrup threads from spoon. Beat egg whites until stiff. Add syrup gradually, beating all the time until cool enough to spread. Frost top and sides of cake. Sprinkle coconut on top and sides.

Vegetarian?: Yes

Pies, Cakes & Frostings

Easy Strudel

Submitted by: Lou Danilovics and David Wiser
in memory of Michael Smith.

Meal: Any
Prep Time: Overnight

Servings: 3 strudels
Cost: Inexpensive

Ingredients

1/2 pound butter
2 cups flour, divided
3 egg yolks
2 tablespoons vinegar
1/4 cup water

9 tablespoons sugar
1-1/2 teaspoons cinnamon
3 apples, peeled and sliced
1/2 cup raisins
Confectioner's sugar

Preparation

Cut butter into flour, reserving 3 tablespoons of flour. Add egg yolks, vinegar and water, mixing well. Cover and refrigerate overnight (at least 3 hours). Divide dough into 3 parts. Roll out onto floured cloth to fit 10-1/2x15-1/2-inch cookie sheet. Sprinkle each portion with 1 tablespoon flour, 3 tablespoons sugar and 1/2 teaspoon cinnamon. Arrange apples with raisins on long side of dough and roll up guiding with the cloth in each hand. Place on ungreased cookie sheet and bake in a preheated 375 degree oven for 35 to 45 minutes. Serve sprinkled with confectioner's sugar.

Pies, Cakes & Frostings

Dolly's Mud Pie

Submitted by: Bill Keane

3 Tbl spoons dirt
1 mouthful water
Blend ~~ingridience~~ ~~ingreedent~~ the stuff together. Then squish around for two minutes, and serve to your little ~~brother~~.

Apple Dumplings

Submitted by: Brad Beachem

Meal: Any   Servings: 8
Prep Time: 1 hour, 45 minutes   Cost: Inexpensive

Dumpling Ingredients

2 boxes pie crust mix   3 teaspoons cinnamon
8 teaspoons sugar   8 Granny Smith apples, peeled and cored

Preparation

Make crust according to directions. Combine sugar and cinnamon. Roll and cut dough to fit around apples. Place apples on dough and sprinkle with sugar mixture. Wrap apples and place in cake pan. Do not grease pan. Pour the following sauce over apples.

Sauce Ingredients

1 cup sugar   2 teaspoons cinnamon
2 cups water   3 tablespoons butter

Preparation

In a small pan, mix ingredients and boil for 4 minutes, stirring constantly. Pour sauce over dumplings, it will be watery. Bake in a 350 degree oven for 1 hour, sauce will thicken as it cooks. Wait 15 minutes before serving.

Chocolate Soufflé

Submitted by: Marlo Thomas

Meal: Dessert   Servings: 8
Prep Time: 1 hour, 15 minutes   Cost: Inexpensive

Ingredients

2 tablespoons butter
2 tablespoons flour
3/4 cup milk
Pinch of salt
2 squares unsweetened chocolate
1/3 cup sugar

2 tablespoons cold coffee
1/2 teaspoon vanilla extract
3 egg yolks, lightly beaten
4 egg whites, stiffly beaten
Whipped cream

Preparation

In a saucepan, melt the butter. Add the flour and stir with a whisk until blended. Meanwhile, bring the milk to a boil in another saucepan. Add, at once, to the butter-flour mixture, stirring vigorously with the whisk. Add the salt. Melt the chocolate with the sugar and coffee in a double boiler. Stir the melted chocolate mixture into the sauce and add the vanilla extract. Beat in the egg yolks, one at a time, and cool. Fold in the stiffly beaten egg whites and turn the mixture into a buttered 2-quart casserole sprinkled with sugar. Bake in a preheated 375 degree oven for 35 to 45 minutes, or until puffed and brown. Serve immediately with whipped cream.

Blackberry Cake
Submitted by: Faye Allen Bell

Meal: Dessert   Servings: 12 to 15
Prep Time: 1 hour, 30 minutes   Cost: Inexpensive

Cake Ingredients

2 cups sugar
1 cup butter
3 cups flour
1 teaspoon allspice
1 teaspoon cloves
1 teaspoon cinnamon

1/2 teaspoon nutmeg
1/2 teaspoon salt
3 eggs
1 teaspoon soda
1 cup buttermilk
2 cups blackberries, if canned, drained

Preparation

Cream sugar and butter, set aside. Sift flour and add allspice, cloves, cinnamon, nutmeg and salt. Add eggs, one at a time, set aside. Add soda to buttermilk, watch it does not bubble over. Add buttermilk to creamed sugar. Gradually add flour mixture to this. Fold in blackberries. Grease and flour a tube pan and pour mixture in. Bake in a preheated 350 degree oven for 1 hour, test with a toothpick for doneness. This is a moist cake but may need an extra 10 minutes depending on the oven. Ice with the following icing.

Icing Ingredients

1 cup water
1 cup sugar
1/2 cup butter

Powdered sugar
Butterscotch flavoring

Preparation

Boil water, sugar and butter to soft stage, test a drop in cold water. Put in a mixer and add powdered sugar and butterscotch flavoring to a spreadable consistency. Frost cake after it has cooled.

Rhubarb Crunch

Submitted by: Joseph Lesnick
in memory of George W. Goss (1953 - 1995).

Meal: Dessert   Servings: 8
Prep Time: 1 hour   Cost: Inexpensive

Ingredients

4 cups cut rhubarb
1-3/4 cups sugar
1 cup plus 2 tablespoons flour
1 tablespoon butter

1 teaspoon baking powder
1/4 teaspoon baking soda
1 large egg, beaten

Preparation

Mix rhubarb, 3/4 cup sugar and 2 tablespoons flour, place in baking dish and dot with butter. Mix all remaining ingredients and sprinkle over the rhubarb, shake to settle crumbs. Bake in a preheated 350 degree oven for 40 minutes. Serve with cream or ice cream.

Apple and Blackberry Tart

Submitted by: Brian May in memory of Freddie Mercury

Meal: Dessert
Prep Time: 45 minutes

Servings: 6
Cost: Inexpensive

Ingredients

4 ounces shortcrust pastry
1 pound cooking apples, cored and
  sliced
2 ounces butter
1 egg yolk

2 ounces brown sugar
1 ounce sultanas
8 ounces blackberries
1/2 teaspoon ground cinnamon

Preparation

Roll out pastry and line an 8-inch flan ring. Arrange apples in the pan. Melt the butter and remove from heat to cool. In separate bowl beat together egg yolk and sugar. Add sultanas, blackberries, cinnamon, and melted butter. Mix well and pour over apples in flan dish. Bake in a preheated 400 degree oven for 30 to 35 minutes.

Pies, Cakes & Frostings

Berry Banana Trifle
Submitted by: Lynn Abram in memory of Bob Brooks.

Meal: Dessert   Servings: 8 to 10
Prep Time: 30 minutes   Cost: Inexpensive

Ingredients

1 (10-ounce) package frozen
  raspberries in syrup, thawed and
  drained, reserve 2/3 cup syrup
1/4 cup red currant or strawberry jelly
1 tablespoon cornstarch
1 (14-ounce) can condensed milk
1-1/2 cups cold water
1 small package instant vanilla pudding
  and pie filling mix

2 cups whipping cream, whipped
1 (3-ounce) package ladyfingers or 1 (10-
  3/4-ounce) loaf pound cake, cut into 12
  slices then each slice cut in half
  vertically
3 medium bananas, sliced and dipped in
  lemon juice
1 cup coarsely chopped toasted walnuts

Preparation

In small saucepan, combine raspberry syrup, jelly and cornstarch. Cook and stir until thickened and clear, stir in raspberries. Cool. In large bowl, combine condensed milk and water, add pudding mix and beat well. Chill for 5 minutes. Fold in whipped cream. Spoon half of pudding mixture into a 2-1/2- to 3-quart glass serving bowl. Line side of bowl with ladyfingers. Arrange remaining ladyfingers on top of pudding. Top with half each of the bananas, raspberry sauce and walnuts. Repeat again with remaining ingredients. Garnish as desired. Refrigerate.

Audrey Landers'
Strawberry Cheesecake

Submitted by: Audrey Landers

Meal: Dessert   Servings: 6
Prep Time: 45 minutes   Cost: Inexpensive

Ingredients

1 cup graham cracker crumbs
1 tablespoon butter
3 tablespoons water
2 cups low-fat cottage cheese

Whipped cream
6 cherries
Chocolate syrup

Preparation

Combine graham cracker crumbs, butter and water. Form in pie pan for crust. Mix remaining ingredients and blend until smooth. Pour into crust and bake in a preheated 375 degree oven for 15 minutes.

Topping Ingredients

1 cup sour cream
4 tablespoons sugar

1 tablespoon vanilla extract
1 cup fresh strawberries

Preparation

Combine topping ingredients. Blend until smooth. Pour on top of baked pie then bake in the oven for 10 additional minutes. Cool then refrigerate. Decorate with sliced strawberries.

Coffee Cake

Submitted by: Ina Leasure

Meal: Any   Servings: 15
Prep Time: 1 hour   Cost: Inexpensive

Ingredients

1/2 cup butter
1 cup sugar
2 eggs
1 cup sour cream
2 cups flour

1 teaspoon baking soda
1 teaspoon baking powder
1 teaspoon vanilla
1/4 teaspoon salt

Topping Ingredients

1/3 cup brown sugar
1/4 cup granulated sugar

1 teaspoon cinnamon
1 cup finely chopped nuts

Preparation

Mix in order given alternately, cream and dry ingredients. Add 1/3 of the topping mixture to the batter and mix well. Grease and flour a 13x9x2-1/2-inch pan. Spread 1/2 of the batter in pan, well up into the corners. Sprinkle on a 1/3 of the topping mix evenly. Add the rest of the batter, and again sprinkle the final 1/3 of the topping mix. Bake in a preheated 350 degree oven for 30 minutes.

Fruit Torte

Submitted by: Bishop and Nara Duncan

Meal: Dessert   Servings: 6
Prep Time: 1 hour, 15 minutes   Cost: Inexpensive

Ingredients

1/2 cup butter
1 cup sugar
1 cup sifted flour
1 teaspoon baking powder
2 eggs

Dash salt
1 pint blueberries, sliced apples or sliced
  peaches
Sugar

Preparation

Cream together butter and sugar. Add the flour, baking powder, eggs and salt. Mix well. Place in a 9-inch springform pan. Cover with fruit then sprinkle with the sugar. Bake in a preheated 350 degree oven for 1 hour. Great served with ice cream or whipped topping.

Pies, Cakes & Frostings

Blueberry Buckle

Submitted by: Nancy Phillips in memory of those who believed in the power of hope, believed in the strength of love, and believed all things are possible.

Meal: Dessert
Prep Time: 1 hour

Servings: 15
Cost: Inexpensive

Ingredients

3/4 cup sugar
1/2 cup soft shortening
1 egg
1/2 cup milk

2 cups flour
1/2 teaspoon salt
2 teaspoons baking powder
2-1/2 cups blueberries

Preparation

Cream the sugar, shortening and egg. Stir in the milk and dry ingredients. Fold in the berries. Spread into a greased 13x9-inch pan. Sprinkle with topping below. Bake in a preheated 350 degree oven for 35 to 45 minutes.

Topping Ingredients

1/2 cup sugar
1/2 teaspoon cinnamon

1/3 cup flour
1/4 cup soft butter

Preparation

Mix all ingredients thoroughly.

Aliette's Apricot Buzz

Submitted by: Aliette

Meal: Dessert
Prep Time: 5 minutes

Servings: 2
Cost: Inexpensive

Ingredients

2 old fashioned doughnuts
4 shots apricot brandy
4 marshmallows

2 small golden apples, cored
2 scoops of your favorite ice cream

Preparation

Place doughnuts on individual microwaveable dishes. Sprinkle 1 shot of brandy on each doughnut to moisten, microwave for 45 seconds. Place an apple on each doughnut and stuff with the marshmallows. Microwave for 3 to 4 minutes. Top with the ice cream and the rest of the brandy, serve immediately.

One-Step Pound Cake
Submitted by: Michael Schultz

Meal: Dessert   Servings: 12
Prep Time: 1 hour, 30 minutes Cost: Inexpensive

Ingredients

2-1/4 cups flour
2 cups sugar
1/2 teaspoon baking soda
1/2 teaspoon salt
1 teaspoon grated lemon peel

1 teaspoon vanilla
1 cup butter
1 cup (8-ounce) carton yogurt or sour
  cream
3 eggs

Preparation

In large bowl, combine all ingredients. Blend at low speed, then beat for 3 minutes at medium speed, scraping bowl occasionally. Pour batter into a greased 10-inch bundt or tube pan. Bake in a preheated 325 degree oven for 60 to 65 minutes or until top springs back when lightly touched. Cool completely then drizzle with glaze that follows.

Lemon Glaze Ingredients

1 cup powdered sugar
1 teaspoon grated lemon peel

1 tablespoon butter
2 to 3 tablespoons lemon juice

Preparation

In a bowl, combine all ingredients until mixed well.

Pies, Cakes & Frostings

Fruit Filled Coffee Cake

Submitted by: Terry G. Gouchnour

Meal: Breakfast
Prep Time: 1 hour

Servings: 15
Cost: Inexpensive

Cake Ingredients

3 cups sifted flour
4 teaspoons baking powder
1 teaspoon salt
1/2 cup sugar
1/2 cup shortening

1 egg, slightly beaten
3/4 cup milk
Fruit filling

Preparation

Sift flour once, measure, then add baking powder, salt and sugar, sift again. Cut in shortening. Combine egg and milk. Add to flour mixture and stir until soft dough is formed. Turn out onto lightly floured board and knead for 30 seconds to shape. Place dough on baking sheet and pat or roll into a 15x10 rectangle. Place fruit filling down center of dough in a 2-inch strip. Cut dough in 1-inch strips from filling to outside edge. Lace strips over filling by lifting 1 strip from each side and crossing in center. Bake in a preheated 375 degree oven for 45 minutes. After removing cake from oven immediately brush lightly with the icing. Serve warm.

Icing Ingredients

4 tablespoons confectioners sugar

1-1/2 teaspoons hot water

Preparation

Mix together confectioners sugar and water.

Pies, Cakes & Frostings

Rhubarb Cake

Submitted by: Peter Chapman in memory of Phil. May your garden continue to flourish and grow. You're missed!

Meal: Dessert
Prep Time: 1 hour

Servings: 8 to 10
Cost: Inexpensive

Ingredients

1/2 cup shortening
1-1/2 cups sugar
2 eggs
Vanilla, splash
1 cup buttermilk
1/4 teaspoon salt
1 teaspoon baking soda

2 cups flour, full not level
2 cups diced rhubarb, fresh is preferred
    but frozen will do, never use canned
Several tablespoons brown sugar
1/4 cup white sugar
Cinnamon

Preparation

Cream shortening, 1-1/2 cups sugar, eggs, vanilla and buttermilk, set aside. Mix salt, baking soda and flour then add to the sugar mixture. Add rhubarb last. Fold mixture into baking pan, if using metal, use foil to prevent discoloration. Bake in a preheated 350 degree (metal) or 325 degree (glass) oven for 45 minutes or until toothpick inserted in center comes out clean. Mix together the sugars and cinnamon. After the cake has cooled use this mixture as a topping.

Pies, Cakes & Frostings

Tom Daschle's Famous Cheesecake

Submitted by: Senator Tom Daschle

Meal: Dessert   Servings: 6 to 8
Prep Time: 4 hours   Cost: Inexpensive

Cake Ingredients

1/3 box crushed graham crackers   4 eggs, beaten
1 stick melted butter   1-1/2 cups sour cream
1/4 cup sugar   Juice from 1 whole lemon
1/2 cup sugar   1 teaspoon vanilla extract
2 large packages cream cheese   1 teaspoon almond extract

Preparation

Combine graham crackers, butter and 1/4 cup sugar. Press into a springform pan. Cream the 1/2 cup sugar and cream cheese. Fold in eggs. Add the sour cream and remaining ingredients. Pour mixture into springform pan. Bake in a preheated 375 degree oven for 20 minutes. After 20 minutes, set oven to 350 degrees and bake for another 25 to 30 minutes or until cheesecake rises and turns golden brown. Let cool at room temperature and then refrigerate for several hours before serving. Delicious served by itself or with your favorite fruit.

Marnie's "Red" Velvet Cake
Submitted by: Tippi Hedren

Meal: Dessert   Servings: 8
Prep Time: 1 hour, 30 minutes   Cost: Inexpensive

Ingredients

1/2 cup shortening
1-1/2 cups sugar
2 eggs
2 cups all-purpose flour
2 tablespoons cocoa

1/2 teaspoon salt
1 cup buttermilk
2 ounces red food coloring
1 teaspoon baking soda
1 tablespoon vinegar

Preparation

Cream the shortening and sugar together until light and fluffy. Beat in eggs and set aside. Sift together flour, cocoa and salt, and add alternately with the buttermilk and food coloring to the creamed mixture. Dissolve the baking soda in the vinegar and fold in. Pour batter into 3 greased and floured 8-inch layer cake pans. Bake in a preheated 350 degree oven for 25 minutes or until cake tester comes out clean. Cool on racks and frost with following frosting.

Frosting Ingredients

1 cup milk
4-1/2 tablespoons flour
3/4 cup butter
4-1/2 tablespoons shortening

1-1/4 cups sugar
1/8 teaspoon salt
3 teaspoons vanilla

Preparation

Gradually add the milk to the flour to make a smooth mixture. Bring to a boil, stiring until the mixture thickens. Cool. Cream the butter, shortening, sugar and salt together. Beat in the vanilla. Combine the cooked milk mixture with the creamed mixture. Chill and then use to fill and frost cakes. Makes about 3 cups frosting.

Vegetarian?: Yes

Mexican Fruit Cake

Submitted by: Anthony and Sandra Cardenas

Meal: Dessert
Prep Time: 5 minutes

Servings: 12
Cost: Inexpensive

Ingredients

2 cups flour
2 cups sugar
2 teaspoons baking soda
2 eggs

1/2 teaspoon salt
1 cup chopped nuts
1 (20-ounce) can crushed pineapple with
   juice

Preparation

Combine all ingredients. Mix well with a wooden spoon until blended. Pour batter into a greased and floured 13x9-inch pan. Bake in a preheated 350 degree oven for 30 to 40 minutes. When cool, frost with following.

Frosting Ingredients

1 (8-ounce) package cream cheese
1 stick butter

2 cups powdered sugar
1 teaspoon vanilla

Preparation

Mix together all ingredients with electric mixer until well blended. Spread on cooled cake and refrigerate.

Pies, Cakes & Frostings

Fruit Crisp

Submitted by: Brad Beachem

Meal: Dessert
Prep Time: 1 hour

Servings: 10
Cost: Inexpensive

Ingredients

4 cups oatmeal
2 cups flour
1 cup sugar
1/2 cup brown sugar

1/2 teaspoon salt
1 stick butter
4 cups of fresh fruit (your choice), or 2
   cans fruit

Preparation

Mix all dry ingredients. Melt butter and mix in. On a greased cake pan sprinkle 1/2 of the mixture. Then add the fruit and sprinkle remaining topping on top. Bake in a preheated 350 degree oven for 35 minutes, let sit for 15 minutes before serving. Excellent served with ice cream.

Pies, Cakes & Frostings

Francesca's Ricotta Cake

Submitted by: Frances Hanneken

Meal: Dessert   Servings: 10
Prep Time: 1 hour, 30 minutes   Cost: Inexpensive

Ingredients

1 package yellow butter recipe cake mix
6 eggs
20 ounces Ricotta cheese
1/2 cup sugar

Dash of vanilla extract
1 package frozen whipped topping
1 pint strawberries or other seasonal fruit

Preparation

Mix cake mix according to directions using 3 eggs, set aside. In a separate bowl, mix
Ricotta cheese, 3 eggs, sugar and vanilla extract, using the highest speed to liquefy.
Pour cake mix into a 13x9-inch pan. Pour cheese mixture on top, do not stir. Bake in
a preheated 350 degree oven until cake is done, cheese will sink to the bottom during
cooking. Cool cake and pour frozen whipped topping on top and add the berries.

Fresh Apple Cake

Submitted by: Louise Banyasz

Meal: Dessert
Prep Time: 1 hour

Servings: 8
Cost: Inexpensive

Ingredients

3 cups finely sliced apples
1-1/4 cups oil
2 cups sugar
2 eggs, beaten
3 cups flour

2 teaspoons cinnamon
1 teaspoon baking soda
2 teaspoons vanilla extract
1 cup chopped nuts

Preparation

Mix ingredients as listed. Pour into sheet cake pan or 2 (9-inch) cake pans. Bake in preheated 350 degree oven for 45 minutes. A nice added touch is to top with whipped topping.

Mom's Chocolate "Mayonnaise" Cake with Almond Buttercream Icing

Submitted by: Ivann in memory of the Ophelia Street "family".

Meal: Dessert
Prep Time: 1 hour

Servings: 8
Cost: Inexpensive

Cake Ingredients

1 cup plus 2 tablespoons sugar
1 cup mayonnaise
4 tablespoons cocoa
1 cup cold water

1 teaspoon vanilla
2 cups flour
2 teaspoons baking soda
1/4 teaspoon salt

Preparation

In large bowl, cream sugar, mayonnaise and cocoa. Add water and vanilla, set aside. Mix flour, baking soda and salt then slowly add to wet ingredients. Pour into greased 9-inch baking pan. Bake in a preheated 350 degree oven for 40 minutes. Let cool then ice with following icing.

Icing Ingredients

1/2 cup softened butter
1-1/2 cups powdered sugar
2 teaspoons milk or cream

1 teaspoon real vanilla extract
1 teaspoon almond extract

Preparation

In small bowl, cream butter. Sift powder sugar then slowly add to creamed butter and cream until almost white. Add milk as mixture thickens. Beat in vanilla and almond extract.

Fresh Apple Cake

Submitted by: Cathy Peters
for all of God's children struck down by HIV/AIDS.

Meal: Dessert
Prep Time: 2 hours

Servings: 10
Cost: Inexpensive

Ingredients

3 eggs
1 cup oil
1 teaspoon vanilla
2 cups sugar
3 cups flour

1 teaspoon baking soda
1 teaspoon cinnamon
1 teaspoon salt
2-1/2 to 3 cups fresh apples
1 cup chopped nuts, optional

Preparation

Beat together eggs, oil and vanilla then add the sugar, flour, baking soda, cinnamon and salt. Mix well with a wooden spoon. Batter will be very stiff. If too stiff, add a little applesauce. Grease and flour a tube pan or a bundt pan, pour batter in. Bake in a preheated 350 degree oven for 1 hour.

Pies, Cakes & Frostings

Dairy and Sugar Free Pumpkin Pie

Submitted by: Chef Robert Sendall

Meal: Dessert   Servings: 8
Prep Time: 1 hour, 30 minutes   Cost: Inexpensive

Pie Ingredients

16 ounces firm tofu   1 teaspoon grated fresh ginger root
2 cups canned or cooked pumpkin   1/4 teaspoon grated fresh nutmeg.
2/3 cup honey   1/8 teaspoon ground cloves
1 teaspoon vanilla extract   Grated rind of 1 orange
1-1/2 teaspoons ground cinnamon   1 (9-inch) unbaked pie crust or paté brisée

Preparation

Blend tofu in food processor or blender until creamy and smooth. Add pumpkin, honey, vanilla, cinnamon, ginger root, nutmeg, cloves and orange rind. Blend well in food processor. Pour into a deep dish pie shell or the paté brisée. Bake in a preheated 400 degree oven for about 1 hour or until toothpick inserted in center comes out almost clean. Cool and serve with stewed apples and pears with a spoon of yogurt.

Paté Brisée Ingredients

2 cups all-purpose flour   Salt to taste
4 ounces cold butter, cut in small pieces   About 1/4 to 1/3 cup water
1-1/2 ounces shortening

Preparation

In a medium-size mixing bowl, mix flour, butter, shortening and salt. Slowly cut the fats into the flour with a pastry blender. The mixture should look like a crumbled topping mixture. Slowly add enough water to pull the dough together but not to wet. The mixture should still be loose. Place the dough onto a piece of plastic wrap and wrap up. Slowly massage it to form a flat, round mass. Refrigerate until firm. Roll out as you would any pie dough and place in a 9-inch pie dish. Finish the edges as desired.

Suggestions

Sprinkle diced, candied ginger on top of yogurt.

Sour Cherry Crumb Cake

Submitted by: Catherine Huber

Meal: Dessert	Servings: 12
Prep Time: 1 hour	Cost: Inexpensive

Ingredients

1 box yellow cake mix, with pudding in batter
1 (16-ounce) can sour cherries, drained
1 stick butter
2 cups flour

2/3 cups sugar
Pinch salt
1/4 teaspoon cinnamon
1/8 teaspoon nutmeg

Preparation

Prepare cake mix according to directions. Add the cherries to the cake mix. Grease and sugar two 9-inch springform pans, distribute batter and cherries evenly between the 2 pans. Melt the butter and blend in with a fork the flour, sugar, salt, cinnamon and nutmeg. Sprinkle topping evenly over the 2 pans. Bake in a preheated 350 degree oven for 40 minutes or until it tests done. Remove to racks to cool and then remove sides to serve.

Pies, Cakes & Frostings

Rice Pie

Submitted by: David and Julia Buccilli

Meal: Dessert
Prep Time: 3 hours

Servings: 24
Cost: Inexpensive

Filling Ingredients

1 pound raw rice
1 quart milk
1 to 2 cups sugar, to taste
1 pound Ricotta cheese

Cinnamon and nutmeg to taste
Citron, 1/3 of a small container or 1 to 2 ounces
3 to 4 prepared pie shells or traditional pie
   shells (see below)

Preparation

Cook rice until firm but not mushy, it will cook more in the oven. When cool, mix rice with milk, sugar, cheese, cinnamon, nutmeg and citron. Pour into pie shells, the amount of pies depends on deepness of the pan. Bake in a preheated 325 degree oven for 1 hour, 30 minutes or until pie looks creamy on top but not dry. It will dry out more as it cools. If it doesn't jiggle too much, it's firm. Cool, refrigerate and serve.

Pie Crust Ingredients

2-1/2 cups flour
12 tablespoons shortening
1 teaspoon baking powder

1 tablespoon sugar
1 egg

Preparation

Combine all ingredients thoroughly. May need to use a little more flour for a flaky crust. Roll out on a floured surface and place in a pie pan then pour in batter.

Pies, Cakes & Frostings

Deep Oatmeal Pie

Submitted by: Peggy Farnan

Meal: Dessert
Prep Time: 1 hour

Servings: 8
Cost: Inexpensive

Ingredients

3/4 cup sugar
3/4 cup packed brown sugar
1/4 teaspoon salt
3 eggs, beaten light and fluffy
3/4 cup milk

3/4 cup oatmeal
3/4 cup coconut
1 teaspoon vanilla extract
1 unbaked 9-inch deep dish pie shell

Preparation

Combine sugar, brown sugar and salt. Add eggs and milk, mix well. Add oatmeal and coconut and vanilla extract, mix well. Pour into pie shell. Bake in a preheated 350 degree oven for 35 to 40 minutes.

Pies, Cakes & Frostings

Hot Fudge Walnut Pudding Cake

Submitted by: Shelia Omecene
in loving memory of my brother Kevin Gessler.

Meal: Dessert   Servings: 8
Prep Time: 1 hour, 15 minutes   Cost: Inexpensive

Cake Ingredients

1-1/4 cups sugar   1/3 cup butter, melted
1 cup flour   1-1/2 teaspoons vanilla
7 tablespoons cocoa   1 cup semi-sweet chocolate bits
2 teaspoons baking powder   1/2 cup walnut pieces
1/4 teaspoon salt   1/2 cup light brown sugar, packed
1/2 cup milk   1-1/4 cups hot water

Preparation

In a bowl, stir together 3/4 cup sugar, flour, 3 tablespoons cocoa, baking powder and salt. Stir in milk, butter and vanilla and beat until smooth. Stir in chocolate bits and walnuts. Pour batter into an 8- or 9-inch pan. Stir together remaining sugar, brown sugar and remaining cocoa. Sprinkle mixture evenly over the top. Pour hot water over the top, do not stir. Bake in a preheated 350 degree oven for 35 to 40 minutes. Let stand 15 minutes. Spoon into desert dishes, spooning sauce from bottom over the top. Serve with vanilla ice cream or whipping cream.

Lemon Verbena Soufflé
Submitted by: Chef Robert Sendall

Meal: Dessert	Servings: 6 to 8
Prep Time: 1 hour, 15 minutes	Cost: Inexpensive

Ingredients

2/3 cups sugar
2/3 cups flour
2 cups milk
2 tablespoons butter
1/2 cup chopped lemon verbena, this is
  a fresh herb and is grown in most
  climates

2 lemon rinds, grated
9 egg whites
3 tablespoons sugar
Powdered sugar, for dusting

Preparation

Prepare a 6-cup soufflé dish with a collar by wrapping a double strength foil around the dish and overlapping slightly. Tie a piece of string around the dish to keep the foil from opening. Lightly wipe the inside of the dish and the foil with butter and dust with white sugar. In a small mixing bowl, place the 2/3 cup sugar, flour and 1/2 cup milk. Beat with a wire whisk until smooth. In a medium saucepan, place the remainder of the milk and warm slowly over medium heat. When the milk is warmed, slowly pour into the flour mixture and whisk until smooth. Place mixture back into saucepan and heat on medium heat until thick, do not scorch. Remove from heat and stir in butter. Fold in the lemon verbena and lemon rind. This procedure can be done up to this point the day before and refrigerated. If this is done, be sure to let the mixture come to room temperature before continuing with remaining steps. Preheat oven to 425 degrees. In a very clean mixing bowl, place the egg whites and beat until frothy. Slowly add the 3 tablespoons sugar and beat until they become firm but not dry. Fold in the lemon verbena mixture in 3 parts. Pour into the soufflé dish and place on a baking dish. Place in the preheated oven and immediately turn the temperature down to 375 degrees and bake for 50 minutes to 1 hour or until knife inserted in center comes out clean. Serve immediately dusted with the powdered sugar.

Brenda Vaccaro's
Cheesecake Fantasy

Submitted by: Brenda Vaccaro

Meal: Dessert   Servings: 8
Prep Time: 3 hours   Cost: Inexpensive

Cake Ingredients

1 (8-ounce) package cream cheese,
   room temperature
1-1/2 cups sugar
6 eggs

1 tablespoon vanilla extract
2 (16-ounce) pints sour cream
1 package Pepperidge Farms bread
   cookies, crushed

Preparation

Beat cream cheese until light and fluffy. Add sugar and mix well, add eggs one at a time. Add vanilla and then fold in sour cream. Beat at medium speed for 2 minutes. Lavishly butter a springform pan. Dust pan with crushed cookies, shake out excess. Pour batter into pan. Bake in a preheated 350 degree oven for 1 hour. After baking, turn oven off and leave cake in the oven for 30 minutes. Open oven door and leave cake in the oven for another 30 minutes. Remove from oven and let cool for 30 minutes. Wrap in tin foil and refrigerate. Top with your favorite fruit.

Pineapple Dream Cake

Submitted by: David Binder
in memory of my cousin, Thomas E. Truscello.

Meal: Dessert   Servings: 10
Prep Time: 1 hour   Cost: Inexpensive

Cake Ingredients

2 cups flour
2 cups sugar
2 eggs

2 teaspoon baking soda
1 cup chopped walnuts
1 (20-ounce) can crushed pineapples

Preparation

In a large bowl, mix together flour, sugar, eggs, baking soda, walnuts and pineapple by hand. Pour into a greased and floured 9x13-inch pan. Bake in a preheated 350 degree oven for 35 to 45 minutes, check in 25 minutes. While still warm, frost with following icing.

Frosting Ingredients

1 (8-ounce) package cream cheese,
  softened
1 stick butter, softened

1 teaspoon vanilla
1 cup chopped walnuts
2 cups confectioners sugar

Preparation

Beat cream cheese, butter, vanilla, walnuts and confectioners sugar until smooth. Spread over cake.

No-Bake Strawberry Pie

Submitted by: Wilma Eyman

Meal: Dessert
Prep Time: 3 hours

Servings: 6
Cost: Inexpensive

Cake Ingredients

3/4 cup sugar
3 tablespoons cornstarch
1-1/2 cups water

1 (3-ounce) package, strawberry Jell-O
1 quart fresh strawberries
1 (9-inch) pie shell, baked

Preparation

Place sugar and cornstarch in a saucepan. Add the water and stir well. Cook over medium heat until thickened. remove from heat and add Jell-O. Cool, then fold in sliced strawberries. Pour in baked pie shell. Place in refrigerator until set. Cover with whipped cream or frozen whipped topping.

Pies, Cakes & Frostings

Carrot Cake
Submitted by: Senator Carl Levin

Meal: Dessert   Servings: 8
Prep Time: 90 minutes   Cost: Inexpensive

Ingredients

1 cup flour   5/8 cup oil
3/4 cup sugar   1 cup grated carrots
1 teaspoon baking powder   1 small can crushed pineapple, drained
1/2 teaspoon salt   1/2 cup roughly chopped walnuts
2 eggs

Preparation

Put all dry ingredients in a food processor and mix 5 to 10 seconds. Add eggs and oil and mix for 30 seconds. (this mixture will be very thick). Add the carrots and pineapple and mix thoroughly. Add the nuts and mix only to distribute. Bake in a greased pan about one hour at 350 degrees.

Frosting Ingredients

3 ounces butter   3 ounces cream cheese
1/2 teaspoon vanilla   3 heaping tablespoons confectioners sugar

Preparation

Process the butter, vanilla and cheese for about 20 seconds in a food processor. Slowly add the sugar and continue mixing. When the cake is cold, pat over the top.

Pies, Cakes & Frostings

Pineapple Noodle Ring

Submitted by: Ellie Pingree
in memory of my dear son, John J. Pingree.

Meal: Dessert   Servings: 10-12
Prep Time: 1 hour, 30 minutes   Cost: Inexpensive

Ingredients

1 (1-pound) package wide noodles
1/2 pound melted butter
4 eggs, beaten
1 cup sugar

1 pint sour cream
1 pound carton creamy cottage cheese
1 teaspoon salt
1 (1-pound) can crushed pineapple

Preparation

Cook the noodles according to package directions, drain and set aside. Melt the butter and blend in the beaten eggs, sugar, sour cream, cottage cheese, salt and pineapple. Add the noodles and mix well. Put the mixture in a slightly greased pan. Cover with foil and place in a preheated 350 degree oven for 20 minutes. Remove the foil and bake for another 40 minutes making sure the ends do not get too well done.

Chocolate Walnut Pie

Submitted by: Bishop McCoid

Meal: Dessert   Servings: 6 to 8
Prep Time: 1 hour, 30 minutes   Cost: Inexpensive

Ingredients

3 large eggs
1-1/2 cups sugar
3/4 stick butter, melted and cooled
2 teaspoons vanilla extract

3/4 cup flour
1-1/2 cups semi-sweet chocolate chips
1-1/2 cups chopped walnuts
Vanilla ice cream

Preparation

In a large bowl, combine eggs sugar butter and vanilla extract and beat until blended. Add the flour chocolate and nuts. Mix well. Pour filling into pie shell and bake in a 350 degree oven for up to 1 hour. The top should be light in color and crusty.

Suggestions

This is best served warm with vanilla or coffee ice cream and topped with shaved chocolate.

Jewish Apple Cake

Submitted by: Anna Milko
in memory of my dear nephew John J. Pingree.

Meal: Dessert	Servings: 8
Prep Time: 2 hours	Cost: Inexpensive

Cake Ingredients

5-6 apples (cut thin)	4 eggs
3 teaspoons cinnamon	1/4 cups orange juice
4 tablespoons sugar	3 cups sifted flour
1 cup oil	3-1/2 teaspoons baking powder
2 cups sugar	2-1/2 teaspoons vanilla

Preparation

Mix apples, cinnamon and sugar together in a bowl and set aside. Beat remaining ingredients together until smooth. Grease and flour a tube pan. Alternate layers starting with second bowl first and ending with batter. Bake at 350 degrees for an hour and a half. Sprinkle with powdered sugar if desired.

Nana's Peach Pie
Submitted by: Reverend Dr. Helen B. Cochrane

Meal: Dessert   Servings: 8
Prep Time: 1 hour   Cost: Inexpensive

Ingredients

1 cup sugar   2 cups peaches
1 tablespoon flour   1 egg, beaten

Preparation

Mix the sugar and flour. Add peaches, mix then add beaten egg and mix. Pour into unbaked pie shell. Bake at 425 degrees for 20 minutes then at 325 degrees for 20 more minutes.

Elegant Simple Dessert
Submitted by: Don Baratie

Meal: Dessert   Servings: 6
Prep Time: 5 minutes   Cost: Inexpensive

Ingredients

1 (12-ounce) package frozen (or fresh)   Whipped cream
  strawberries   6 cherries
6 (1/2-inch) slices pound cake   1 packet chocolate syrup
Vanilla ice cream

Preparation

Puree the strawberries. Dab 3 tablespoons of the fruit in the center of a dessert plate. Place a slice of the pound cake slightly off center. Add a scoop of vanilla ice cream opposite the pound cake. Top with a small amount of whipped cream and add a cherry. From a height of about 12 inches, open the end of the chocolate syrup packet and allow it to drizzle. Step back and admire your creation, but not too long because you should serve immediately.

Suggestions

Do not attempt to wipe any misdirected syrup. It will only smear on the plate.

Recipe   **Page**

7-Layer Cookie Bars 12-1
Chocolate Tapioca 12-2
Party Cookies... 12-3
Sesame Cookies 12-4
Dog Bones 12-5
Walnut Squares 12-6
Poor Man Cookies 12-7
Double Chocolate Brownies.. 12-8
Fruit Pizza 12-9
French Mint 12-10
Million Dollar Fudge 12-11
Brownies 12-12
Pineapple Nut Bars 12-13
Buckeyes 12-14
Caramels... 12-15
Boston Drops 12-16
Nut Filled Tortes.. 12-17
Starlight Mints 12-18
Chocolate Peanut Butter Chip Cookies.............................. 12-19
Annie Glenn's Baked Fruit 12-20
Cathy's Can't Fail Fudge... 12-21
Lime Nuts 12-22
White Trash... 12-23
Birds Nest Cobbler 12-24
Cherry Tarts 12-25
Alcoholic Jell-O 12-26
Lady Locks.. 12-27
Dirt 12-28
Esbat Crescent Cakes 12-29

Vegetarian?: Yes

Cookies & Candies

7-Layer Cookie Bars
Submitted by: The Author

Meal: Dessert
Prep Time: 1 hour

Servings: 25
Cost: Inexpensive

Ingredients

1/2 cup butter
1 cup graham cracker crumbs
1 cup flaked coconut
1 cup butterscotch chips

1 cup chocolate chips
1 can sweetened condensed milk
1 cup pecans or walnuts, chopped

Preparation

Preheat oven to 350 degrees. Melt butter in 9x13-inch baking pan. Evenly spread graham cracker crumbs across bottom of pan. Layer coconut, butterscotch and chocolate chips. Swirl top with condensed milk. Sprinkle nuts on top. Pat down ingredients in pan to form an even layer. Bake for 30 minutes and allow to cool thoroughly.

Suggestions

7-Layer Cookie Bars may be refrigerated or frozen once cooled. They make excellent additions to your holiday cookie trays, or pleasing snacks for the kids.

Cookies & Candies

Chocolate Tapioca

Submitted by: Peggy Hager
in memory of Chuck Johnston (8/20/65 - 6/11/92).

Meal: Dessert   Servings: 4
Prep Time: 1 hour   Cost: Inexpensive

Ingredients

1 egg, beaten
1 cup sugar
3 tablespoons minute tapioca
1/8 teaspoon salt

3-2/3 cup milk
2 squares unsweetened chocolate
1 teaspoon vanilla

Preparation

Mix egg, sugar, tapioca, salt and milk in a saucepan. Let stand for 5 minutes. Add chocolate, cook and stir over medium heat until mixture comes to a full boil and is blended well, about 15 minutes. Remove from heat. Stir in vanilla, cool 20 minutes. Stir and spoon into dishes, serve warm or chill.

Cookies & Candies

Party Cookies
Submitted by: Peggy Hager
in memory of Chuck Johnston (8/20/65 - 6/11/92).

Meal: Dessert   Servings: 6 dozen
Prep Time: 1 hour   Cost: Inexpensive

Ingredients

1 cup butter, softened   2-3/4 cups flour
1 cup brown sugar, packed   1 teaspoon baking soda
1/2 cup white sugar   1 teaspoon salt
2 eggs (room temperature)   1-1/2 cups M&M plain chocolate candies
2 teaspoons vanilla extract

Preparation

Beat together butter and brown and white sugars until light and fluffy. Blend in eggs and vanilla extract. Sift flour, baking soda and salt together, and combine with mixture, stirring well. Stir in 1/2 cup of the candies. Drop dough by rounded teaspoonfuls onto ungreased cookie sheet. Press 2 to 3 additional candies into each cookie. Bake in a preheated 375 degree oven for 10 to 12 minutes or until golden brown.

Cookies & Candies

Sesame Cookies

Submitted by: Louise Ketchum

Meal: Dessert
Prep Time: 1 hour

Servings: 6 to 7 dozen
Cost: Inexpensive

Ingredients

2-1/2 cups flour
1/2 teaspoon salt
3/4 teaspoon baking powder
2 sticks butter, softened
1-1/2 cups sugar

1 egg
1 tablespoon water
1 teaspoon vanilla or almond flavoring
1/2 cup toasted sesame seeds, see below
Almonds

Preparation

To toast sesame seeds: Preheat oven to 350 degrees. Place sesame seeds in a shallow baking dish and bake for 20 to 25 minutes. Sift dry ingredients. Cream sugar and butter. Add egg, water, and vanilla or almond flavoring, mix well. Add dry ingredients and sesame seeds. Roll dough into small balls and place on greased cookie sheet. Press cookie with a fork or the bottom of a glass dipped in flour or sugar. Place an almond on top of each cookie. Bake in a 350 degree oven for up to 15 minutes, check in 10 minutes.

Cookies & Candies

Dog Bones
Submitted by: Fido

Meal: Snack
Prep Time: Overnight

Servings: 24 bones
Cost: Inexpensive

Ingredients

1 package dry yeast
1/4 cup water
2 cups canned chicken stock
3-1/2 cups white flour
2 cups whole wheat flour
1 cup rye flour

1 cup corn meal
2 cups cracked wheat
1/2 cup non-fat dry milk
4 teaspoons salt
2 eggs
1 tablespoon milk

Preparation

Dissolve yeast in water then add to chicken stock, set aside. Mix all dry ingredients then add the yeast mixture. Knead for 3 minutes by hand. Dough will be heavy and dry. Add 1 egg. Roll out to 1/4-inch thick and cut with a cookie cutter. Place on an ungreased cookie sheet. Mix last egg with the milk. Brush bones with egg and milk mixture.Bake in a preheated 350 degree oven for 45 minutes, turn oven off and leave bones in overnight.

Cookies & Candies

Walnut Squares
Submitted by: Elizabeth Le Bras

Meal: Dessert   Servings: 12
Prep Time: 1 hour   Cost: Inexpensive

Ingredients

2 cups butter, softened
1-1/2 cups packed brown sugar
1/4 cup sugar
1 egg yolk

1 teaspoon vanilla extract
1/2 teaspoon salt
1 cup chopped walnuts
2 cups all purpose flour

Preparation

In a bowl beat 1 cup of the butter, 3/4 cup of the brown sugar and the sugar until creamy. Add vanilla, egg yolk and salt. Stir in 1/2 cup of the nuts and then the flour. Press dough evenly into a 15x10x1-inch baking pan. Bake in a preheated 350 degree oven for 15 minutes. Meanwhile, combine remaining butter and brown sugar. Bring to a boil over high heat and boil for 3 minutes, stirring constantly. Remove pan from oven and prick dough all over with a fork. Pour sugar syrup evenly over dough and bake an additional 5 minutes. Remove pan from oven and place on a wire rack and immediately sprinkle with the remaining nuts. Let cool completely before cutting.

Cookies & Candies

Poor Man Cookies
Submitted by: Randy Milne

Meal: Dessert
Prep Time: 30 minutes

Servings: 25
Cost: Inexpensive

Cookie Ingredients

1 cup raisins
1-1/4 cups water
1/2 cup shortening
1 egg
1 cup sugar
1/2 teaspoon salt

2 cups flour
1 teaspoon cinnamon
1 teaspoon nutmeg
1 teaspoon baking soda
1 teaspoon cloves
1/2 cup chopped walnuts, optional

Preparation

Boil the raisins in the water for 20 minutes. Add the shortening and let cool. After cooling the raisins add the egg. Sift dry ingredients together. Then add dry ingredients and walnuts to raisin mixture. Spread on a cookie sheet and bake in a preheated 375 degree oven for 15 to 20 minutes. Ice with either of the icings below.

Butter Cream Icing Ingredients

3 cups powdered sugar, sifted
1/3 cup butter

3 to 4 tablespoons milk or cream
1-1/2 teaspoons vanilla

Preparation

Beat all ingredients together until creamy.

Easy Cream Icing Ingredients

2 cups powdered sugar, sifted
1/2 teaspoon salt

1 teaspoon vanilla
2 tablespoons water or 3 tablespoons cream

Preparation

Beat all ingredients until creamy.

Cookies & Candies

Double Chocolate Brownies

Submitted by: Mardi Isler

Meal: Dessert   Servings: 25
Prep Time: 1 hour   Cost: Inexpensive

Ingredients

1 cup butter
2 squares unsweetened chocolate
2 cups sugar
4 eggs, slightly beaten

1-1/2 cups flour
1 teaspoon baking powder
2 teaspoons vanilla
1 cup chocolate chips

Preparation

In a large pot melt butter and chocolate over low heat. Remove pan from heat. Add sugar, mix well. Add eggs, quickly, mix well. Add flour and baking powder to chocolate mixture. Stir in vanilla, add chocolate chips. Stir until well blended. Preheat oven to 350 degrees. Bake in a greased 13x9x2-inch pan for 35 to 40 minutes. These are very easy since everything is mixed right in the pot.

Cookies & Candies

Fruit Pizza

Submitted by: Terri Gamble

Meal: Dessert
Prep Time: 2 hours

Servings: 8
Cost: Inexpensive

Ingredients

1 roll sugar cookie dough
8 ounces cream cheese
1/3 cup sugar
1 teaspoon vanilla extract

Any preferred or available fruit
   (blueberries, kiwi, strawberries, and
   Mandarin oranges are some
   suggestions)

Preparation

Slice cookie dough into 1/4-inch rounds and put on the bottom of a cookie sheet. Roll out to fill baking sheet completely and bake as directed. Let cool. Beat cream cheese, sugar and vanilla until creamy. Spread mixture evenly onto cooled cookie dough. Arrange fruit on top of cream cheese. For optional glaze see below. Chill at least 1 hour before serving but do not let chill overnight.

Glaze Ingredients

2 cups orange marmalade

2 tablespoons warm water

Preparation

Mix thoroughly, then drizzle over pizza.

French Mint
Submitted by: Senator Orrin Hatch

Meal: Dessert   Servings: 24
Prep Time: 3 hours, 45 minutes Cost: Inexpensive

Ingredients

4 squares (1-ounce) unsweetened chocolate, or 6 ounces chocolate chips
1 cup butter, softened
2 cups confectioners sugar

4 eggs
1 teaspoon vanilla
1 teaspoon peppermint extract
Chopped nuts

Preparation

Melt chocolate and set aside to cool. Using an electric beater, beat butter while gradually adding sugar, about 15 minutes. Add cooled, melted chocolate, beat another 5 minutes. Beat in eggs, one at a time. Mix in vanilla and peppermint. Sprinkle chopped nuts on the bottom of 24 paper cupcake holders. Fill each cupcake holder 1/2 full and sprinkle more nuts on top. Freeze for at least 3 hours.

Cookies & Candies

Million Dollar Fudge

Submitted by: Dennis Ferrell
in memory of Hubert Osborne.

Meal: Dessert   Servings: 12
Prep Time: 1 hours, 30 minutes   Cost: Inexpensive

Ingredients

1 pint (7-1/2 ounces) marshmallow
   cream
1-1/2 cups chocolate morsels
4-1/2 cups sugar

1/2 pound butter
1-1/2 cups evaporated milk, undiluted
Pinch of salt
1 tablespoon vanilla

Preparation

Place marshmallow cream and chocolate morsels in large mixing bowl, set aside. In large, heavy saucepan, combine sugar, butter, milk and salt. Bring to a boil and cook hard for 12 minutes, stirring constantly. Pour boiling mixture over morsels and marshmallow cream and beat until well blended. Stir in vanilla. Pour into a large buttered pan. Cool completely then cut into serving pieces.

Cookies & Candies

Brownies
Submitted by: Senator John Ashcroft

Meal: Dessert   Servings: 24
Prep Time: 30 minutes   Cost: Inexpensive

Ingredients

1 box brownie mix, your choice
Chocolate syrup

1 cup chocolate chips
1 cup walnuts

Preparation

Prepare brownies according to the directions on the box except substitute chocolate syrup for one-fourth of the liquid ingredients. Combine mixture thoroughly and add chocolate chips and walnuts. Pour mixture into a pan two-thirds the recommended size. Preheat oven to 320 degrees. Place in oven, but be advised the brownies will require extended baking time.

Cookies & Candies

Pineapple Nut Bars

Submitted by: Representative Patsy T. Mink

Meal: Dessert
Prep Time: 1 hour

Servings: 20 to 24
Cost: Inexpensive

Ingredients

1/2 cup butter, melted
1-1/2 cups sugar
4 eggs
1-1/2 cup flour, sifted
1/2 teaspoon salt

1/2 teaspoon baking soda
1 (2-pound) can crushed pineapple,
   drained well
1 cup chopped nuts
Powdered sugar

Preparation

Mix butter and sugar well. Add eggs one at a time, beating well. Add sifted flour, salt and baking soda to mixture, stirring well. Add pineapple and nuts, mix well. Grease 9x13-inch pan and bake in a preheated 350 degree oven for 45 minutes or until nice and brown. Sprinkle with powdered sugar, cool and cut into bars.

Suggesstions

Cans of pineapple are marked "100% Hawaiian" if grown in Hawaii.

Buckeyes
Submitted by: Barb Rodebaugh

Meal: Dessert   Servings: 15
Prep Time: 1 hour   Cost: Inexpensive

Ingredients

2 pounds peanut butter   24 ounces chocolate chips
1 pound butter, softened   1/2 bar parafin
3 pounds confectioners sugar

Preparation

Mix peanut butter, butter and confectioners sugar well. Roll into balls, about walnut size, set aside. Melt in double boiler the parafin and chocolate chips. Place toothpick in center of balls and dip in chocolate, cool on wax paper.

Cookies & Candies

Caramels

Submitted by: Barb Rodebaugh

Meal: Dessert
Prep Time: 1 hour

Servings: 20
Cost: Inexpensive

Ingredients

2 cups sugar
1 cup butter
1 cup light corn syrup

1 can condensed milk
2 teaspoons vanilla
Chopped pecans, optional

Preparation

This is a microwave dish. Combine sugar, butter and corn syrup in an 8 cup bowl, microwave on high for 3 to 4 minutes. Whisking constantly, add condensed milk. Microwave on high for 18 minutes. During the last 1/3 of cooking time whisk every 2 minutes. Mixture will be golden brown and thick. Add vanilla and nuts, if using them. Butter a 9x13-inch dish and pour mixture in. Let sit for 5 minutes then refrigerate for 1/2 hour. Cut in squares and wrap in plastic wrap.

Cookies & Candies

Boston Drops
Submitted by: Margaret Beran

Meal: Dessert   Servings: 24 cookies
Prep Time: 30 minutes   Cost: Inexpensive

Ingredients

1/2 cup shortening   1/2 teaspoon baking powder
2/3 cup sugar   1/2 teaspoon salt
2 eggs   1 teaspoon vanilla
1-1/2 cups flour   Nuts

Preparation

Mix together shortening, sugar and eggs, set aside. Sift together flour, baking powder and salt then add to the sugar mixture. Add the vanilla and mix well. Drop by teaspoons onto a cookiesheet and top with a nut. Bake in a preheated 375 degree oven for about 10 minutes.

Nut Filled Tortes

Submitted by: Margaret Beran

Meal: Dessert	Servings: 24 cookies
Prep Time: 1 hours, 30 minutes	Cost: Inexpensive

Ingredients

1/2 cup butter, plus 2 tablespoons
1 package cream cheese
1 cup flour
1 cup light brown sugar

1 egg
1 teaspoon vanilla
Dash of salt
3/4 cup walnuts, ground

Preparation

Cream 1/2 cup butter, cream cheese and flour, refrigerate until easy to handle. Mix together the brown sugar, egg, vanilla, 2 tablespoons butter, salt and walnuts. Put cheese mixture in small torte pans then top with the filling. Bake in a preheated 325 degree oven for 25 minutes.

Cookies & Candies

Starlight Mints
Submitted by: Margaret Beran

Meal: Dessert   Servings: 24 cookies
Prep Time: 2 hours, 30 minutes   Cost: Inexpensive

Ingredients

3 cups sifted flour
1 teaspoon baking soda
1/2 teaspoon salt
1 cup butter
1 cup sugar

1/2 cup firmly packed brown sugar
2 eggs
1 teaspoon vanilla
9 ounces solid mint chocolate wafers

Preparation

Mix together flour, baking soda and salt, set aside. Cream together butter, sugar and brown sugar. Add the eggs and the vanilla, beat well. Gradually add dry ingredients, mix well. Cover and refrigerate for 2 hours. Shape cookies into a ball with a mint between, flatten cookie, be sure the mint in completely enclosed. Bake in a preheated 375 degree oven on an ungreased cookie sheet 2 inches apart for 9 to 12 minutes.

Chocolate Peanut Butter Chip Cookies

Submitted by: Dr. Pearl McNall

Meal: Dessert   Servings: 10
Prep Time: 1 hour   Cost: Inexpensive

Ingredients

2 cups granulated sugar   1 cup all purpose flour
1 cup shortening   1 cup chopped nuts, walnuts or pecans
4 eggs   1 cup peanut butter chips

Preparation

Cream sugar and shortening together then add eggs one at a time. Beat in cocoa and flour. Add nuts and peanut butter chips. Spread into a greased and floured 9x13-inch pan. Bake in a preheated 325 degree oven for 40 minutes. Score while warm. Cool completely before removing from pan.

Annie Glenn's Baked Fruit

Submitted by: Senator John Glenn

Meal: Dessert
Prep Time: 1 hour, 15 minutes

Servings: 4
Cost: Inexpensive

Ingredients

1 pound (2 cups) cling peach halves
1 pound, 4 ounces (2-1/2 cups)
   pineapple slices
1 can pear halves

Several maraschino cherries, with stems
1/3 cup butter
3/4 cup light brown sugar, packed
4 teaspoons curry powder

Preparation

Drain fruit and dry well on a paper towel. Arrange in a 1-1/2 quart casserole dish. Melt butter then add brown sugar and curry powder. Spoon over fruit. Bake in a preheated 325 degree oven for about 1 hour, depending on the oven.

Cookies & Candies

Cathy's Can't Fail Fudge

Submitted by: Cathy Peters for all of God's children.

Meal: Dessert or Snack   Servings: 10
Prep Time: 1 hour   Cost: Inexpensive

Ingredients

2-1/2 cups sugar   1/2 teaspoon salt
1/4 cup butter   1 teaspoon vanilla extract
1 small can (3/4 cup) evaporated milk   1 (12-ounce) bag chocolate chips
1 (7-1/2-ounce) jar marshmallow fluff   1 cup nuts, optional

Preparation

Combine sugar, butter, evaporated milk, marshmallow and salt. Stir over low heat until blended. Bring to a boil over medium heat, be careful not to mistake air bubbles for boiling. Boil slowly for 5 minutes, stirring constantly. Use a timer, you don't want to over cook the fudge or it will be hard. Remove from heat. Stir in vanilla extract and chocolate chips until chocolate is melted, add nuts if using them. Turn into a buttered 9x9-inch pan. Cool before cutting.

Cookies & Candies

Lime Nuts

Submitted by: Evelyn Brock

Meal: Dessert or Snack   Servings: 6
Prep Time: 30 minutes   Cost: Inexpensive

Ingredients

1 cup sugar
1/2 cup water
1 tablespoon white corn syrup
1/8 teaspoon salt
Green food coloring

60 miniature marshmallows
1/2 teaspoon peppermint flavoring or
   essence of peppermint
1 pound shelled walnuts

Preparation

Cook sugar, water, corn syrup syrup and salt until it forms a soft ball. Add 2 drops green food coloring. Next add the marshmallows and the peppermint flavoring. Stir together and add the walnuts. Stir until walnuts are covered, drain on brown paper bag.

White Trash

Submitted by: Joshua Watt

Meal: Dessert
Prep Time: Overnight

Servings: 8
Cost: Inexpensive

Ingredients

1 box French vanilla pudding
12 ounces cream cheese, softened
1 pint milk

12 ounces cool whip
1 pound Oreo cookies, frozen then
   crushed

Preparation

Prepare pudding then refrigerate. Mix cream cheese then add milk, cool whip and the pudding. Beat until smooth, about 3 minutes. In a medium pan, put a layer of cookies then a layer of the pudding mixture above the cookies. Keep repeating the process until all the mixtures are used, ending with the cookie mixture. Chill overnight.

Cookies & Candies

Birds Nest Cobbler

Submitted by: JoAnn Swartz

Meal: Dessert

Prep Time: 1 hour

Servings: 6

Cost: Inexpensive

Ingredients

1 cup sugar
1 cup water
6 cups blueberries
3 tablespoons cornstarch

Nutmeg to taste
Dash lemon juice
2 sticks plus 2 tablespoons butter, melted
1 roll filo dough, cut into strips

Preparation

Combine sugar, water, blueberries, cornstarch, nutmeg, lemon juice and 2 tablespoons butter in a saucepan until well mixed. Divide dough strips in half and toss each half of the strips with a stick of butter. Layer half of the strips in a baking dish and cover with the berry mixture. Cover berry mixture with remaining dough strips. Bake in a preheated 350 degree oven for about 35 minutes or until dough is done. Firm, brown and crispy. Serve with warm cream.

Cookies & Candies

Cherry Tarts
Submitted by: Barbara Shearer

Meal: Dessert   Servings: 10
Prep Time: 1 hour   Cost: Inexpensive

Ingredients

1/2 cup graham cracker
3 tablespoons butter, melted
1 tablespoon sugar
1 egg, beaten

1 (8-ounce) package cream cheese
1/4 cup sugar
1/4 teaspoon vanilla
Canned cherries or other fruit

Preparation

Mix together graham cracker, butter and sugar. Press 1 tablespoon of mixture into the bottom of paper cups. Mix together egg, cream cheese, sugar and vanilla. Spoon mixture on top of graham crust. Bake in preheated 350 degree oven for 10 minutes. Cool thoroughly and top with fruit.

Cookies & Candies

Alcoholic Jell-O

Submitted by: Hank Hanneken

Meal: Dessert   Servings: 4
Prep Time: 3 hours   Cost: Inexpensive

Ingredients

1 package Jell-O, preferably red berry   Burgundy wine
Hot water

Preparation

Put very hot water equal to 1/2 the amount required on the directions in a mixing bowl. Stir in entire package Jell-O until fully dissolved. Add wine equal to the amount of cold water used, stir. Place in refrigerator until cooled and jelled. Eat and enjoy.

Suggestions

Any berry Jell-O and compatible wine can be used. Alcohol will be jelled with the Jell-O. Makes a wonderful desert or great ending to a meal. Feel free to experiment.

Cookies & Candies

Lady Locks

Submitted by: Pat Crawford for Ed Crawford, Jr.

Meal: Dessert   Yields: 12 dozen
Prep Time: Overnight   Cost: Inexpensive

Ingredients

4 egg yolks   6 cups flour
2-1/2 cups water   4 cups shortening
4 tablespoons sugar   Clothes pins wrapped in tin foil

Preparation

Beat egg yolks and water, set aside. Add sugar to flour and cut in 1/2 cup shortening. Add egg mixture and mix as for pie dough. Beat until smooth, add more flour if needed to get the right consistency. Make a round ball and refrigerate covered for 1 hour,or overnight. Divide the dough into 6 pieces. On a floured surface, roll out each piece and spread shortening on the dough. Keep the shortening close because all of it will be used during the rolling out stages. Don't spread it too thick, just spread it like you're buttering bread. Fold the pieces into squares. Top down a 1/3, bottom up a 1/3 and a 1/3 side to side to make a little package. Put on a plate, cover loosely and refrigerate for 1 hour. Repeat the roll out procedure 3 times. Each time the package gets a little bigger as you work the dough and spread the shortening. One hour after the final roll out and spreading of shortening, roll dough out, cut into strips 8-inches by 1-1/2-inches wide and 1/4-inch thick. Sometimes it is easier to cut the package in 1/2 before the final roll out. Wrap the dough around the foil covered clothes pins in an angular motion. Place on ungreased cookie sheets. Bake in a preheated 400 degree oven for 10 minutes. Watch for a light brown coloring, do not overbake. Cool completely before filling.

Filling Ingredients

2-1/2 cups milk   5 cups confectioners sugar
10 tablespoons flour   3 to 4 teaspoons vanilla
2-1/2 cups shortening   15 tablespoons marshmallow fluff
                                  (1 small jar)

Preparation

Cook the milk and flour until thick using a wire whisk to prevent burning, set aside and let cool. Cream together completely the shortening and the confectioners sugar. When confectioners sugar and shortening are mixed add the milk mixture and the vanilla. Beat for a while with electric mixer to get a real fluffy consistency. Add the marshmallow fluff and mix thoroughly. Use a pastry bag and a long tip to fill the pastries. Sprinkle with confectioners sugar.

Cookies & Candies

Dirt
Submitted by: Floyd Patterson

Meal: Dessert   Servings: 8 to 10
Prep Time: 30 minutes   Cost: Inexpensive

Ingredients

2 (8-ounce) packages cream cheese
2 cups powdered sugar
2 (3-1/2-ounce) boxes instant vanilla
   pudding
3 cups cold milk

1 (16-ounce) container whipped topping
1 (20-ounce) package Oreo cookies,
   crushed
1 package gummi worms (optional)
Chocolate chips and/or chunks (optional)

Preparation

Cream together the cream cheese and powdered sugar in a large mixing bowl. In a separate bowl mix the pudding and milk with a wire whisk. Blend the whipped topping into the pudding. In a sand pail, metal bucket, or flowerpot (be creative) alternate layers of crushed cookies and cream mixture. Start and end with crushed cookies. gummi worms and chocolate chips and/or chunks can be layered in for effect.

Suggestions

This is a fun dessert so have fun with it. Top it off with either an artificial flower or add an icing flower. Serve it with a sand shovel or garden trowel.

Cookies and Candies

Esbat Crescent Cakes

Submitted by: Sean Leasure in memory of Scott Cunningham.

Meal: Any
Prep Time: 2 hours

Servings: 24
Cost: Inexpensive

Ingredients

1 cup finely ground almonds
1-1/4 cups flour
1/2 cup confectioners sugar

2 drops almond extract
1/2 cup butter, softened
1 egg yolk

Preparation

Combine almonds, flour, sugar and extract until thoroughly mixed. With the hands, work in the butter and egg yolk until well blended. Chill dough. Pinch off pieces of dough about the size of walnuts and shape into crescents. Place on greased sheets and bake in a preheated 325 degree oven for about 20 minutes. Serve during Cakes and Ale, especially on Esbats.

Cooking Helps

EQUIVALENTS

3 teaspoons	1 tablespoon
4 tablespoons	1/4 cup
5-1/3 tablespoons	1/3 cup
8 tablespoons	1/2 cup
10-2/3 tablespoons	2/3 cup
12 tablespoons	3/4 cup
16 tablespoons	1 cup
2 cups	1 pint
4 cups	1 quart
4 quarts	1 gallon
16 ounces	1 pound
32 ounces	1 quart
1 ounce liquid	2 tablespoons
8 ounces liquid	1 cup

WEIGHTS AND MEASURES

Baking powder
1 cup = 5-1/2 ounces

Cheese
1 pound = 2-2/3 cups cubed

Cocoa
1 pound = 4 cups ground

Coffee
1 pound = 5 cups ground

Corn meal
1 pound = 3 cups

Cornstarch
1 pound = 3 cups

Cracker crumbs
23 soda crackers = 1 cup
15 graham crackers = 1 cup

Eggs
1 egg = 4 tablespoons liquid
4 to 5 whole = 1 cup
7 to 9 whites = 1 cup
12 to 14 yolks = 1 cup

Flour
1 pound all purpose = 4 cups
1 pound cake = 4-1/2 cups
1 pound graham = 3-1/2 cups

Lemons, juice
1 medium = 2 to 3 tablespoons
5 to 8 medium = 1 cup

Lemons, rind
1 lemon = 1 tablespoon grated

Oranges, juice
1 medium = 2 to 3 tablespoons
3 to 4 medium = 1 cup

Shortening, margarine or butter
1 pound = 2 cups

Sugar
1 pound brown = 2-1/2 cups
1 pound cube = 96 to 160 cubes
1 pound granulated = 2 cups
1 pound powdered = 3-1/2 cups

Section 13

Cooking Helps

Metric Conversions

	Standard	Metric	Multiplier
Length	inches	millimeters	25
	feet	centimeters	30
	yards	meters	0.9
	miles	kilometers	1.5
Area	square inches	square centimeters	6.5
	square feet	square meters	0.09
	square yards	square meters	0.8
	square miles	square kilometers	2.6
Mass	ounces	grams	28
	pounds	kilograms	0.45
Liquid Volume	ounces	milliliters	30
	pints	liters	0.47
	quarts	liters	0.95
	gallons	liters	3.8
Temperature	degrees Fahrenheit	degrees Celsius	5/9 (after subtracting 32)

Equipment

3 teaspoons	1 tablespoon	15 ml
4 tablespoons	1/4 cup	60 ml
5-1/3 tablespoons	1/3 cup	79 ml
8 tablespoons	1/2 cup	118 ml
16 tablespoons	1 cup	237 ml
1 fluid ounce	2 tablespoons	30 ml
8 fluid ounces	1 cup	237 ml
16 fluid ounces	2 cups or 1 pint	473 ml
32 fluid ounces	4 cups or 1 quart	946 ml

Dry Measure

0.035 ounces ... 1 gram
1 ounce ... 28.35 grams
1 pound ... 453.59 grams or 0.45 kilograms
2.21 pounds ... 1 kilogram

Liquid Measure

1 teaspoon ... 4.9 milliliters
1 tablespoon ... 14.8 milliliters
1/2 cup ... 118.3 milliliters
1 cup ... 237 milliliters
1.06 quarts ... 1 liter

Time Table for Cooking Meats

Roasting

Cut	Weight Range	Cooking Temp.	Internal Meat Temp.	Approximate Time
Beef				
Standing ribs	6-8 lbs.	325º F		
Rare			140º F	16-18 min. per lb.
Medium			160º F	20-22 min. per lb.
Well Done			170º F	25-30 min. per lb.
Rolled rib	5-7 lbs.	325º F		Add 10-12 min. per lb. to above time
Rump boneless	5-7 lbs.	325º F	170º F	30 min. per lb.
Veal				
Leg (center cut)	7-8 lbs.	325º F	170º F	25 min. per lb.
Loin	4½-5 lbs.	325º F	170º F	30-35 min. per lb.
Rack 4-6 ribs	2½-3 lbs.	325º F	170º F	30-35 min. per lb.
Shoulder bone-in	6-7 lbs.	325º F	170º F	25 min. per lb.
Shoulder boneless	5-6 lbs.	325º F	170º F	35-40 min. per lb.
Lamb				
Leg	6-7 lbs.	325ºF	175º-180º F	30-35 min. per lb.
Shoulder bone-in	5-7 lbs.	325º F	175º-180º F	30-35 min. per lb.
Shoulder boneless	4-6 lbs.	325º F	175º-180º F	40-45 min. per lb.
Fresh Pork				
Loin	4-5 lbs.	350º F	185º F	30-35 min. per lb.
Cushion Shoulder	4-6 lbs.	350º F	185º F	35-40 min. per lb.
Shoulder boneless	4-6 lbs.	350º F	185º F	40-45 min. per lb.
Shoulder butt	4-6 lbs.	350º F	185º F	45-50 min per lb.
Fresh ham	10-14 lbs.	350º F	185º F	30-35 min. per lb.
Spare ribs (1 side)	1½-2½ lbs	350º F	185º F	1-1½ hrs. per lb.
Smoked Pork				
Ham whole	10-12 lbs.	325º F	150º-155º F	18-20 min. per lb.
	14-16 lbs.	325º F	150º-155º F	16-18 min. per lb.
Ham half	6-8 lbs.	325º F	150º-155º F	25-27 min. per lb.
Ham 2-inch slice	2½-3 lbs.	325º F	170º F	1½ hrs. total
Picnic	5-8 lbs.	325º F	170º F	33-35 min. per lb.
Poultry				
Chickens stuffed weight	4-5 lbs.	325º F	185º F	35-40 min. per lb.
Chickens over 5 lbs		325º F	185º F	20-25 min. per lb.
Turkeys stuffed weight	6-10 lbs.	325º F	185º F	20-25 min. per lb.
Turkey	10-16 lbs.	325º F	185º F	18-20 min. per lb.
Turkey	18-25 lbs.	325º F	185º F	15-18 min. per lb.

Geese - same as turkey of similar weight.
Duck - same as heavy chicken of similar weight.

Time Table for Cooking Meats

Broiling

Cut	Thickness	Weight Range	Approximate Total Time (Minutes)		
			Rare	Medium	Well
Beef					
Rib Steak	1 inch	1-1½ lbs.	8-10	12-14	18-20
Club Steak	1 inch	1-1½ lbs.	8-10	12-14	18-20
Porterhouse	1 inch	1½-2 lbs.	10-12	14-16	20-25
	1½ inch	2½-3 lbs.	14-16	18-20	25-30
	2 inch	3-3½ lbs.	20-25	30-35	40-45
Sirloin	1 inch	2½-3½ lbs.	10-12	14-16	20-25
	1½ inch	3½-4½ lbs.	14-16	18-20	25-30
	2 inch	5-5½ lbs.	20-25	30-35	40-45
Ground Beef					
Patties	¾ inch	4 oz. each	8	12	15
Tenderloin	1 inch		8-10	12-14	18-20
Lamb					
Rib or Loin					
Chops (1 rib)	¾ inch	2-3 oz. each	—	—	14-15
Double Rib	1½ inch	4-5 oz. each	—	—	22-25
Shoulder					
Chops	¾ inch	3-4 oz. each	—	—	14-15
	1½ inch	5-6 oz. each	—	—	22-25
Lamb Patties	¾ inch	4 oz. each	—	—	14-15
Ham, Bacon & Sausage					
Ham Slices	½ inch	9-12 oz. each	—	—	10-12
	¾ inch	1-1¼ lbs.	—	—	13-14
	1 inch	1¼-1¾ lbs.	—	—	18-20
Bacon					4-5
Pork Sausage					
Links		12-16 to the lb.	—	—	12-15
Broiling chickens					
(drawn) halves		1-1½ lbs.	—	—	30-35

Time Table for Cooking Meats

Braising

Cut	Weight Range	Approximate Time
Beef Pot Roast, Chuck, Rump or Heel of Round	3-5 lbs.	Brown then simmer 3½-4 hours
Swiss Steak 1 inch thick	2 lbs.	Brown then simmer 1½-2 hours
Flank Steak	1½-2 lbs.	Brown then simmer 1½ hours
Beef Short Ribs	2-2½ lbs.	Brown then simmer 2-2½ hours
Rolled Lamb Shoulder Pot Roast	3-5 lbs.	Brown then simmer 2-2½ hours
Lamb Shoulder Chops	4-5 oz. each	Brown then simmer 35-40 min.
Lamb Neck Slices	½ lb. each	Brown then simmer 1-1½ hours
Lamb Shanks	1 lb. each	Brown then simmer 1½ hours
Pork Rib or Loin Chops	4-5 oz. each (¾-1 inch)	Brown then simmer 35-40 min.
Pork Shoulder Steaks	5-6 oz. each	Brown then simmer 35-40 min.
Veal Rolled Shoulder Pot Roast	4-5½ lbs.	Brown then simmer 2-2½ hours
Cutlets or Round	2 lbs.	Brown then simmer 45-50 min.
Loin or Rib Chops	3-5 oz. each	Brown then simmer 45-50 min.

Stewing

Cut	Weight Range	Approximate Time
Beef - 1-1½ inch cubes from neck, chuck, plate or heel of round	2 lbs.	2½-3 hours
Veal or Lamb 1-1½ inch cubes from shoulder or breast	2 lbs.	1½-2 hours
Chicken	3½-4 lbs.	2-2½ hours

Simmering in Water

Cut	Weight Range	Approximate Time
Fresh Beef Brisket or Plate	8 lbs.	4-5 hours total
Corned Beef Brisket half or whole	4-8 lbs.	4-6 hours total
Cross Cut Shanks of Beef	4 lbs.	3-4 hours total
Fresh or Smoked Beef Tongue	3-4 lbs.	3-4 hours total
Pork Hocks	¾ lbs.	3 hours total
Whole Ham	12-16 lbs.	18-20 min. per lb.
Ham Shanks	5-6 lbs.	25-30 min. per lb.
Smoked Pork Butt	2-3 lbs.	40 min per lb.
Picnic	7-8 lbs.	35-40 min. per lb.
Chicken	3½-4 lbs.	2-2½ hours total

Methods for Cooking Seafood

Fish	Broiled	Baked	Broiled Steamed	Fried Sauteed	Months in Season
Barracuda	2	1		3	Varies
Bluefish	2	1		3	All Year
Bonito	2	1		3	All Year
Bullheads		2	1	3	April-Oct.
Butterfish	2	3		1	April-Dec.
Carp	2	1		3	All Year
Catfish			2	1	All Year
Cod	1	2	3		All Year
Croaker	2	3		1	Feb.-Nov.
Eels		2	3	1	All Year
Flounder	2	3		1	All Year
Grouper		1			Nov.-April
Haddock	1	2	3		All Year
Halibut	1	2	3		All Year
Herring	1	3		2	All Year
Kingfish	1	2	3		Jan.-June
Lake Trout	3	1		2	April-Nov.
Mackerel	1	2	3		All Year
Mullet	1	2		3	June-Oct.
Perch	2	3		1	All Year
Pike	3	2		1	All Year
Pickerel	3	2		1	All Year
Pompano	1	2		3	All Year
Porgies	2	3		1	All Year
Red Snapper		1	2		All Year
Salmon	2	1	3		All Year
Sea Bass	1	3		2	All Year
Sea Trout	1	3		2	Nov.-May
Shad	2	1		3	Dec.-June
Sheepshead	3	2		1	All Year
Smelts	2	3		1	Sept.-May
Snappers	2	1	3		All Year
Sole	2	3		1	All Year
Spanish Mackerel	1	2		3	Nov.-April
Striped Bass			1		All Year
Sturgeon	2	1	3		April-Jan.
Sunfish	2			1	April-Oct.
Swordfish	1	2	3		Varies
Tautog	1	2		3	All Year
Trout	2	3		1	April-Nov.
Tuna	2	1	3		All Year
Weakfish	1	2		3	April-Nov.
Whiting			1		May-Dec.
Whitefish	2	1		3	April-Dec.

Methods ratings: 1 = Excellent   2 = Good   3=Fair

Seasoning Guide

Get acquainted with spices and herbs. Add in small amounts, 1/4 teaspoon for each 4 servings. Taste before adding more. Crush dried herbs or snip fresh herbs before using. If substituting fresh for dried herbs, use 3 times more fresh herbs. Freeze fresh herbs and enjoy them all winter. Wash, then blanch the herbs in boiling water for 10 seconds. Chill in ice water 1 minute; pat dry. Package in small moisture-vaporproof bags or foil. Seal, label, and freeze. Use while frosty.

Appetizers, Soups	Breads, Pasta	Eggs, Cheese
Cranberry Juice: Add cinnamon, allspice and/or cloves. Serve hot or chilled.	Biscuits: Add caraway seed, thyme or savory to flour. Serve with meat.	Deviled Eggs: Add celery seed, cumin, mustard, savory, chili powder or curry powder.
Fruit Cocktail: Try adding mint or rosemary.	Bread: Add caraway seed, cardamom or poppy seed.	Omelet: Add dash of marjoram or rosemary.
Stuffed Celery: Mix caraway seed with cream cheese; fill celery. Dash with paprika.	Coffee Cake: Mix crushed aniseed in batter. Sprinkle cinnamon-sugar mixture atop or add poppy seed filling.	Scrambled Eggs: Sprinkle lightly with basil, thyme, rosemary or marjoram. Add seasonings near the end of cooking.
Tomato Cocktail: Add 1/4 teaspoon dried basil, per cup.	Corn Bread: Add poultry seasoning or caraway seed to dry ingredients. Add 1/2 teaspoon rosemary to batter.	Souffle: Add 1/4 teaspoon marjoram to 4-egg souffle. To cheese souffle, add basil or savory.
Chicken Soup: Add a dash of rosemary, tarragon or nutmeg.	Croutons: Toss toast cubes in melted butter seasoned with basil, marjoram, or onion salt.	Cheese Casseroles: Add dash of sage or marjoram.
Clam Chowder: Add a dash of caraway seed, sage or thyme.	Doughnuts: Add mace or nutmeg to dry ingredients. After frying, roll in cinnamon sugar.	Cheese Fondue: Add dash of basil or nutmeg.
Consommé: Dash in basil, marjoram, savory or tarragon.	Dumplings: Add thyme or parsley to batter.	Cheese Rarebit: Add mace or mustard.
Fish Chowder: Add bay leaves, curry powder or dill.	Muffins: Blueberry - add dash of nutmeg to ingredients. Season plain muffins with caraway seed or cinnamon.	Cheese Sauce: Add mustard or a dash of marjoram or thyme.
Mushroom Soup: Season with curry, oregano or marjoram.	Noodles: Butter, then sprinkle with poppy seed.	Cheese Spread: Blend sage, caraway seed, thyme or celery seed into melted process cheese.
Onion Soup: Add marjoram.	Rolls: Add caraway seed, or sprinkle with sesame seed.	Cottage Cheese: Blend in chives or a dash of sage, caraway seed, dill, anise or cumin. Prepare several hours ahead.
Oyster Stew: Lightly add cayenne, mace or marjoram.	Spaghetti: Toss with butter, Parmesan and snipped chives.	
Potato Soup: Dash with mustard or basil. Top with snipped chives or parsley.	Waffles: Add poultry seasoning to batter, serve with creamed chicken. Add cardamom to honey; pour over waffles.	Cream Cheese: Blend in curry powder, marjoram, caraway seed or dill. Sprinkle paprika or cayenne atop. Use as celery filling or appetizer spread.
Split-Pea Soup: Add dash basil, chili powder or rosemary.		
Tomato Soup: Dash in basil, dill, oregano, sage or tarragon.		
Vegetable Soup: Try allspice, oregano, sage or thyme.		

Cheese Guide

Cheese	How it looks & tastes	How to serve
American, Cheddar	Favorite all-around cheeses. Flavor varies from mild to sharp. Color ranges from natural to yellow-orange; texture firm to crumbly.	In sandwiches, casseroles, souffles, and creamy sauces. With fruit pie or crisp crackers on a snack or dessert tray with fruit.
Blue, Gorgonzola, Roquefort	Compact, creamy cheeses veined with blue or blue-green mold. Sometimes crumbly. Mild to sharp salty flavor (Stilton is similar, but like a blue-veined Cheddar).	Crumble in salads, salad dressings, dips. Delicious iwth fresh pears or apples for dessert. Blend with butter for steak topper. Spread on crackers or crusty French bread.
Brick	Medium firm; creamy yellow color, tiny holes. Flavor very mild to medium sharp.	Good for appetizers, sandwiches, or desserts. Great with fresh peaches, cherries, or melons.
Brie	Similar to Camembert, but slightly firmer. Distinctive sharp flavor, pronounced odor.	Serve as dessert with fresh fruit. Be sure to eat the thin brown and white crust.
Camembert	Creamy yellow with thin gray-white crust. When ripe, it softens to the consistency of thick cream. Full, rich, mildly pungent.	Classic dessert cheese. Serve at room temperature with fresh peaches, pears, apples, or with toasted walnuts and crackers.
Cottage	Soft, mild, unripened cheese; large or small curd. May have cream added.	Used in salads, dips, main dishes. Popular with fresh and canned fruits.
Cream	Very mild-flavored soft cheese with buttery texture. Rich and smooth. Available whipped and in flavored spreads.	Adds richness and body to molded and frozen salads, cheesecake, dips, frostings, and sandwich spreads. Serve whipped with dessert.
Edam, Gouda	Round, red-coated cheeses; creamy yellow to yellow-orange inside. Firm and smooth. Mild nutlike flavor.	Bright hub for dessert or snack tray. Good in sandwiches or crunchy salads, or with crackers. Great with grapes and oranges.
Liederkranz, Limburger	Robust flavor and highly aromatic. Soft and smooth when ripe. Liederkranz is milder in flavor and golden yellow in color. Limburger is creamy white.	Spread on pumpernickel, rye, or crackers. Team with apples, pears and Tokay grapes.Serve as snack with salty pretzels and coffee.
Mozzarella, Scamorze	Unripened. Mild-flavored and slightly firm. Creamy white to pale yellow.	Cooking cheese. A "must" for pizza, lasagna; good in toasted sandwiches and hot snacks.
Muenster	Between Brick and Limburger. Mild to mellow flavor, creamy white. Medium hard, tiny holes.	Used in sandwiches or on snack or dessert tray. Good with fresh sweet cherries and melon wedges.
Parmesan, Romano	Sharp, piquant, very hard cheeses. Come in shakers grated. Parmesan is also available shredded, or grate your own.	Sprinkle on pizza, main dishes, breads, salads and soups. Shake over buttered popcorn.
Port du Salut	Semisoft, smooth and buttery. Mellow to robust flavor between Cheddar and Limburger.	Dessert cheese. Delicious with fresh fruit; great with apple pie. Good for snack tray.
Provolone	Usually smoked, mild to sharp flavor. Hard, compact and flaky. Pear or sausage shaped.	Use in Italian dishes, in sandwiches, or on snack and appetizer trays.
Swiss	Firm, pale yellow cheese with large round holes. Sweet nutlike flavor.	First choice for ham-cheese sandwiches and fondue. Good in salads, sauces, or as a snack.
Process cheeses	A blend of fresh and aged natural cheeses, pasteurized and packaged. Smooth and creamy; melts easily. May be flavored.	Ideal for cheese sauces, souffles, grilled cheese sandwiches, or in casseroles. Hand for the snack tray.

Cooking Glossary

Bake - To cook covered or uncovered in an oven or oven-type appliance.

Baste - To moisten foods during cooking with pan drippings or special sauce to add flavor and prevent drying.

Beat - To make mixture smooth by adding air with a brisk whipping or stirring motion using a spoon or electric mixer.

Blend - To thoroughly mix two or more ingredients until smooth and uniform.

Boil - To cook in liquid at boiling temperature (212 degrees Fahrenheit at sea lever) where bubbles rise to the surface and break. For a full rolling boil, bubbles form rapidly throughout the mixture.

Braise - To cook slowly with a small amount of liquid in tightly covered pan on top of range or in oven.

Broil - To cook by direct heat, usually in broiler or over coals.

Candied - To cook in sugar or syrup when applied to sweet potatoes and carrots. For fruit or fruit peel, cook in heavy syrup till transparent and well coated.

Chill - To place in refrigerator to reduce temperature.

Chop - To cut in pieces about the size of peas with knife, chopper, or blender.

Cool - To remove from heat and let stand at room temperature.

Cream - To beat with a spoon or electric mixer till mixture is soft and smooth. When applied to blending shortening and sugar, mixture is beaten till light and fluffy.

Cut In - To mix shortening with dry ingredients using pastry blender or knives.

Dice - To cut food in small cubes of uniform size and shape.

Dissolve - To disperse a dry substance in a liquid to form a solution.

Glaze - A mixture applied to food which hardens or becomes firm and adds flavor and a glossy appearance.

Grate - To rub on a grater that separates the food into very fine particles.

Marinate - To allow food to stand in a liquid to tenderize or to add flavor.

Mince - To cut or finely chop food into very small pieces.

Mix - To combine ingredients, usually by stirring, till evenly distributed.

Poach - To cook in hot liquid, being careful that food holds its shape while cooking.

Precook - To cook food partially or completely before final cooking or reheating.

Roast - To cook uncovered without water added, usually in an oven.

Sauté - To brown or cook in a small amount of hot shortening.

Scald - To bring to a temperature just below boiling point where tiny bubbles form at the edge of the pan.

Scallop - To bake food, usually in a casserole, with sauce or other liquid. Crumbs are often sprinkled on atop.

Steam - To cook in steam with or without pressure. A small amount of boiling water is used, more water being added during steaming process if necessary.

Stir - To mix ingredients with a circular motion until well blended or of uniform consistency.

Toss - To mix ingredients lightly.

Truss - To secure fowl or other meat with skewers to hold its shape during cooking.

Whip - To beat rapidly to incorporate air and produce expansion, as in heavy cream or egg whites.

Our Sponsors

Sponsors

We gratefully acknowledge the following for their generous contributions to this effort:

Jessica Arcand

Craig Bierko

Anthony and Sandra Cardenas

John F. Cerasini

Pat Crawford

Lou Danilovics

Rob D'Orazio and Roxane Laboratories, Inc.

Winnie Flynn

Peter Grunwald and Broadway Cares

Brian Hays

Erin Hill and Borders Books, South Hills

Elsie H. Hillman

Cheryl Hockman

Helen Jariabko in memory of her
nephew John J. Pingree

Sponsors

Bill Kaelin

William Kaminski and Cost Cutters

Dorothy Lakatos in memory of her
nephew John J. Pingree

Sally Lapiduss

La Roche College Alumni Association

Dr. Louis and June Le Bras

Elliott Levenson

Lynne Hylands-Lister and Borders Books, North Hills

Barb McCully

Krista Mechling

Sandra L. Mervosh and Venture Graphics

Anne Meyer and The Mercury Phoenix Trust

Anna Milko in memory of her
nephew John J. Pingree

Tony Neshoff

Tricia Nowalk and The Names Project

Sponsors

Demetra Patukas

Ellie Pingree in memory of her son John J. Pingree

Renée Petrichevich and The Pittsburgh Penguins

The Phillips Collection, Washington, D.C.

Harold and Nancy Phillips

Melvin and Beverly Pollock

Ada Rapp

George and Christine Romero

Colleen Russell

Cheryl Saunders in memory of Kerry Stoner

Grant E. Scott, III

Tom Sokolowski and The Andy Warhol Museum

Beth Steenbergen and Ortho Biotech

Jennifer Stone

Pat Visella and Borders Books, Monroeville

David Wiser

Sponsors

Ken Woodson

Pat and Dennis Zerega

BORDERS

BOOKS·MUSIC·CAFE

We're your style.™

North Hills Village
4801 McKnight Road
Pittsburgh, PA 15237
(412) 367-5820
M-F 10-9 SAT. 9-9 SUN. 11-6

Raff Printing, Inc.

P.O. Box 42365 • 2201 Mary Street
Pittsburgh, PA 15203
(412) 431-4044 • Fax (412) 488-0770
E-Mail: raffinc@aol.com

THE ANDY WARHOL MUSEUM

The Andy Warhol Museum is one of the Carnegie Museums of Pittsburgh.

Sponsors

TEMPORARY SERVICES, INC.

North Point Office Park
9800 McKnight Road, Suite 230
Pittsburgh, PA 15237

VOICE (412) 681-9050
FAX (412) 681-9058

Allegheny Bindery Corp.

The Tri-State's Most Complete Trade Bindery

3700 BIGELOW BLVD.
PITTSBURGH, PA 15213

GEORGE MERVOSH III

MERVOSH INSURANCE, INC.
All Lines of Insurance

Main Street • Russellton, PA 15076
(412) 265-1508 / Fax (412) 265-4520

Ordering Information

Won from the Heart

Order additional copies while they last!

Ordering Information

Fill out the form below to receive additional copies of
Won from the Heart

Name:			
Shipping Address:			
City:	State:	Zip:	Country:
Home Phone: ( )		Work Phone: ( )	
Number of Copies:		Subtotal @ $19.95 per copy: $	
Add $3 per copy shipping and handling.		Total enclosed: $ *(US Funds Only)*	

Payment Method *(Check One)*

___ Check   ___ Money Order   ___ Mastercard

___ Visa   ___ Discover   ___ American Express

Credit Card #:	Expiration:

Please make your remittance payable to:
Won from the Heart/SWC.

Mail with your check to:
Won from the Heart/SWC
PO Box 5619
Pittsburgh, PA 15207-0619

Tel: 412-421-2069   FAX: 412-421-2067
Email: swc@nauticom.net
WWW: http://www.thelynx.com/www/thelynx/swc/